FILM
AND THE
NARRATIVE
TRADITION

FILM
AND THE
NARRATIVE
TRADITION

John L. Fell

**UNIVERSITY
OF
OKLAHOMA
PRESS**

Library of Congress Cataloging in Publication Data
Fell, John L   1927–
    Film and the narrative tradition.
    Bibliography: p. 258
    1. Moving-pictures—United States—History.
I. Title.
PN1993.5.U6F4   1974   791.43'0973   73–7428
ISBN 0–8061–1127–5

Copyright 1974 by the University of Oklahoma Press, Publishing Division
of the University. Composed and printed at Norman, Oklahoma, U.S.A.,
by the University of Oklahoma Press. First edition.

This book is dedicated to
ELIZA, JOHNNY, JUSTINE, and SUZY,
Who have stood for quite a lot.

Preface

My own early enthusiasm for thinking and talking about motion pictures began with a primitive film society in Clinton, New York, after World War II. Blind luck coincided my teaching with the explosion of movie courses during the sixties, so that for years I have been in the enviable position of earning a living at what is pleasurable—thinking and talking about movies.

Film made a long trek from the Bijou to the quad, and there at the end of the trail stood Pauline Kael, advising us that if one doesn't think that flicks can be made dull in courses, he underestimates the power of higher education. Some of us have tried to leave a live art breathing, but at some point another kernel of misgiving attached itself to me. Anxieties commenced to attend the standard *idée fixe* of motion picture history as it has usually been represented. Perhaps this happened on reading for the umpteenth time that D. W. Griffith invented the flashback in *Enoch Arden*. If Mr. Griffith invented the flashback, what had Marcel Proust been working on all those years, isolated in his cork-lined room? And was not Joseph Conrad shifting sequence around some time before both of them?

Another element with which film teachers must deal is a child of their own creation: that sewn-together, emotion-ridden, rageful, and disorder-prone flesh-and-blood product of pedagogical laboratories which is the Film Student. Film students seem at times to maintain about as much interest in learning from books as might Boris Karloff when he lurched toward Lionel Atwill's arm just before pulling it off for a second time. On closer examination, though, students may often be seen to be defending themselves from the earlier hurt: textbooks that turned film into anything but what it was by giving it a sanitized, tedious, respectable history, pristine in its integrity. This is the academic pitch which has movies unbeholden to any other popular form, partly to get film out of the scholarly clutches of other (no more deserving) departments.

There's nothing wrong with a Film Department that is not, I suspect, wrong with all departments; that is, they are departments. It may even be necessary to isolate a cantankerous subject somewhat in order to approach it, but movies, like jazz musicians, work best in free interchanges with the culture. They always have.

In any case, that is the premise of this book, and that is where it came from: shoeboxes of old stereograph cards, yellowed posters, brittle pulps, art museums, and scratchy phonograph records. In following back the earliest impulses here, I light on three teachers at Hamilton College: Earl Wendel Count, who told me about the strange eye examination in *The Clansman*; the late Robert Barnes Rudd, who read aloud James Fenimore Cooper's paragraph about the buckhorn haft; and George Lyman Nesbitt, who taught me that all the things which we never believed came from the nineteenth century really did.

Other sources of aid and advice were sometimes even more transient, but nevertheless they are appreciated. They include: Irene Anderson, Bob Bell, Eileen Bowser, Sandy Buehler, Hugh Churchill, William Cole, Walter A. Coslet, Ralph A. Cummings, Robert C. Dale, Joe Diaz, Doug Gallez, Daniel C. Gerould, Jameson Goldner, Rose Hawley, Dave Hilberman, Art Hough, Mike Howard, Torsten Jungstedt, Hal Layer, Edward T. LeBlanc, Stan Lee, Ron Levaco, Bob Lewis, Sande Marston, Clarence Miller, William Schuyler, Gary Silver, Jim Storey, Stuart A. Teitler, and Bob Wagner.

My appreciations are also extended to the Audio-Visual Center and the Creative Arts Library at California State University at San Francisco, Sutro Library in San Francisco, the Special Collection at the San Francisco Public Library, the Rare Books Room at the New York Public Library, the Lincoln Center Library for the Performing Arts, the Library of Congress, the Film Library at the Museum of Modern Art, the Rose Hawley Historical Museum in Ludington, Michigan, the Institute for Sex Research, Inc. at Indiana University, and Svenska Filminstitutet.

And thanks to many, many students over a dozen years.

Finally, I'd like to note that a number of the older film references for which I had to dig are now, happily, available through *The New York Times* Arno Press reprint series.

JOHN L. FELL

San Francisco
January 15, 1974

Introduction

The surrealities of historical event are not always self-evident until we begin to look at names and dates together. In 1886, for example, while Buffalo Bill's Wild West Show (now incorporating cowgirls) was scheduled at the old Madison Square Garden, Geronimo, leading forty Apaches, went on a rampage. Seurat finished *Sunday Afternoon on Grande-Jatte*. Ned Buntline died, and a Philadelphia printer, Ives, perfected a halftone screen. A quarter of a century later, in 1911, Irving Berlin published *Alexander's Ragtime Band*. David Belasco completed a fiction version of *The Girl of the Golden West* for A. L. Burt. D. W. Griffith made *The Lonedale Operator* for Biograph. Picasso finished a Cubist painting named *Accordionist* for himself.

In general, these dates mark the boundaries of our study, and we shall try to give some sense of relationship to the events noted. However, much that is interesting to us will fall before 1886, although likely within Victoria's reign, which began in 1837.

About halfway between Geronimo and Picasso the Queen passed away, but for the sake of economy her name has here been given to the entire era. The year of Victoria's death (1901) the first signals were sent across the Atlantic, and two years later the Wright brothers made their first successful flight. It was a time of rapid transition, fostered in part by inventions. The changes, the new electronic and mechanical marvels, and the great population shifts to the United States and across its frontiers—all seem to have both enlisted and echoed innovation in the arts. This is the setting for the book. Its plot, while it may at times disappear like one of H. G. Wells's inventions, is that particular kind of narrative form whose expository devices had eventuated by 1911 into the visual conventions of popular moviemaking, largely as we know it yet today. However, what is more interesting to our purpose here is the very nonuniqueness of the movies' techniques. They are reflected in media as seemingly different from one another as the nineteenth-century novel, early comics, magazine illustration, the Cubists and Impressionists, the most pop of popular literature, and entertainments of the theater, fairground, and parlor. Together they evidence a common narrative direction which has until now been largely neglected because the separate strands of the tradition have been considered in isolation, if they were thought about at all.

This study, then, collects a number of experiences from industry, art, and commerce, and tries to point up a culmination of the storytelling impulses when these techniques finally find their secure home in nickelodeons. In this respect the book is perhaps radical because it denies disciplinary conventions for the sake of less apparent formal ones.

The point of our investigation is rarely "who did what first," any more than it is "who influenced whom." Rather, its intent has been to spell out some elements of a conventional narrative code which was really public domain. For that matter, artists and writers are not great respecters of copyright conventions anyway, although this is not always apparent. Composers know that chord sequences are more useful in the marketplace than are song lyrics.

The strategy of posing narrative form as a central issue in a book whose ultimate concern lies with motion pictures poses certain problems in argumentation. One can speak of prose narrative, and the sequential panels of a comic strip have "story lines," although other "visual things" may seem to be going on as well. Theater is easily narrative, but when we come to graphic arts the parallels are sometimes more difficult of access (less so to younger film enthusiasts, whose sensibilities are not geared to literature or to drama).

One workable tactic is to press home similarities of composition and of palette which are evident in both media. Additionally, however, there exists the entire representational scheme of painting, which must include the concerns of illustration and anecdote—in short, the narrative tradition.

Raymond Durgnat, a sometimes exemplary filmwriter, touched on "what the painterly purist may dismiss as anecdotal interest or literary values."

> . . . literature has no particular primacy or monopoly on the exploitation of ideas and emotion; verbal description of, say, a distressed man running is no more final than a picture of a distressed man running. To say that the general public wants literary values from art is really a misleading way of saying that it wants something like resonant experience. And while any artist is perfectly within his rights in saying that for him resonant experience is of no interest at all, it is still true that much art, from religious paintings to Rembrandt's flayed ox, is impoverished by such limitations. Surely the game of art is best played by those rules that maximize its richness and range of interest rather than by minimizing them.[1]

It was this very "richness and range of interest" which always encouraged film to crib from any of the arts and many of the technologies. The movies, free to prance in youthful high spirits on the playgrounds of time and space, always had it both ways and only needed to appropriate from everybody else's games and then to evolve a self-consistent set of ground rules.

Also, the sense of art as illustration reached a kind of pitch during this period. The influences of the pre-Raphaelites, abetted by Ruskin's enthusiasms, still operated. William Morris' Kelmscott Press was in full swing. A sculptor like John Rogers (1829–1904) found widespread popular acceptance when he perfected a technique to produce inexpensive plastic replicas of his anecdotal genre scenes.

The enthusiasms of Vachel Lindsay epitomize something of the common ground of art and story. His aptly titled *The Art of the Moving Picture* was not published until 1915, but Lindsay's early art-student experience in Chicago and New York is pervasively evident on almost every page (the qualification comes because Robert Henri might not have shared his student's gushes over Blanche Sweet and Mae Marsh). In the index, William Blake rubs shoulders with *The Birth of a Nation*, and Thomas Dixon,

[1] Durgnat, "Fake, Fiddle, and the Photographic Arts," *The British Journal of Aesthetics*, V, No. 3 (July, 1965), 270–88.

Jr. with Donatello: "It would be a noble thing if American experts in the Japanese principles of decoration, of the school of Arthur W. Dow, should tell stories of old Japan with the assistance of such men as Sessue Hayakawa";[2] "The photoplay of the American Indian should in most instances be planned as bronze in action. The tribes should not move so rapidly that the panther-like elasticity is lost in the riding, running, and scalping. On the other hand, the aborigines should be far from the temperateness of marble";[3] etc.

With the popularization of still photography that followed George Eastman's marketing of roll film, Kodak art as illustration permeated the culture even further and turned attentions onto more varied and more local subjects. In one of the Little Colonel series, *The Little Colonel's Knight Comes Riding* (the kind of summer cottage reading the reader will be persistently reminded of in forthcoming chapters), the characters plan outings into the countryside to find illustrative settings and literary situations to photograph. Originally they propose a *Garden Fancies* series, after Browning, but Tennyson is quite as useful when, like Maud, "there's a bit of terrace for you to come tripping down." Finally, the pictures which are executed come from an invented couplet:

> "Alex, you take Lloyd down into the garden again beside the phlox, and turn so that I'll get your profile. It is so like your uncle's. I'll call that one 'Hand in hand when our life was May.' Then I'll take Mrs. Shelby and the doctor in exactly the same position as a companion piece, and call that 'Hand in hand when our hair is gray.' "[4]

The shots are even organized for continuity. (A film editor would call it matching screen position). Boys' books had something similar. The Outdoor Chums (a rod, gun, and camera club) enjoyed rural adventures in which comrade Will Milton, "a camera crank of the first water", recorded the highpoints of their escapades on film. As we shall see soon, male juvenilia is more committed to action than it is to decor. Will Milton snaps

2 Lindsay, *The Art of the Moving Picture*, 64–65.
3 *Ibid.*, 114.
4 Johnston, *The Little Colonel's Knight Comes Riding*, 146.

the shooting of a mad dog, an ominous ghost, and a theft,[5] all encapsulating the highpoints of the narrative.

Stories, drawings, and photos journeyed hand-in-hand into the next century, exploring new ways to "see material." We are so surrounded by it all now that we can not always keep our sights straight. In an earlier world circumscribed by Bill Cody and *Alexander's Ragtime Band,* there may be more possibility of making out some of the stages of the trip.

Some general outline of the book's argument may be in order before beginning. First an effort is made to establish a broad setting for the period: population characteristics and movements, developments in technology, merchandising, tendencies toward standardization. From there the preoccupation moves progressively from theater, print, optical amusements and "shows," and graphics (comics, engraving, lithography, photography, painting) to film. In each section I try to echo the same concerns among the media: the rendering of movement, space, time, and consciousness. In the last two chapters an attempt is made to give something of the character of the early films and auditoria and then to consolidate notions from preceding sections, paralleling them with like forms and substances in the movies.

I believe that in the motion pictures there surfaced an entire tradition of narrative technique which had been developing unsystematically for a hundred years. It appears sporadically not only among the entertainments thus far mentioned, but in ephemera as diverse as stereograph sets, peep shows, song slides, and postal cards.

Midway in the century still photography had begun to penetrate the general consciousness. From this point a true sharing among the media accelerates, an interaction which continues until audiences distinguish themselves from one another, or else evaporate.

As movies grew they coalesced these fragments of expository technique into a reasonable coherence. Other forms were then required to reorganize their natures in response to new demands

---

5 Allen, *The Outdoor Chums in the Forest, or Laying the Ghost of Oak Ridge.*

for uniqueness. Those which survived often profited in terms of sophisticated audiences, for early film absorbed the great, unselective mass, of whom it asked little more than nickels and dimes in return.

Two themes recur throughout: melodrama and mechanics. Melodrama had special significance for theater and print and figures most prominently in Part I. Here I think it first consolidated an armor of general forms as well as what power it still maintains.

The mechanical genius of the era defined, more than we realize, many of our entertainments, particularly as any given medium required a special approach to common narrative problems. Mechanics and invention figure strongly in Part II, which is devoted to preponderantly visual forms. After that, in Part III, the new films begin to try to get it all together.

Contents

Illustrations

Part One
Verbal Arts

The guiding myth, then, inspiring the invention of cinema, is the accomplishment of that which dominated in a more or less vague fashion all the techniques of the mechanical reproduction of reality in the nineteenth century, from photography to the phonograph.—ANDRE BAZIN

[Most movies of the twentieth century can be identified with] the relatively debased catch-all genre of bourgeois melodrama. To say you enjoy movies is thus comparable to saying you enjoy bourgeois melodrama, and how can you possibly have such bad taste, you who have savored the great treasures of antiquity?—ANDREW SARRIS

The world has changed immeasurably in the seventy years since the birth of cinema; for one thing "world" now includes the microcosm of the atom and the macrocosm of the universe in one spectrum. Still, popular films speak a language developed by Griffith, Lumière, Méliès, derived from traditions of vaudeville and literature.—GENE YOUNGBLOOD

Cinema did not only develop technically out of the magic lantern, the Daguerreotype, the phenakistoscope and similar devices—its history of Realism—but also out of strip cartoons, Wild West Shows, automata, pulp novels, barn-storming melodramas, magic—its history of the narrative and the marvelous. Lumière and Méliès are not like Cain and Abel; there is no need for one to eliminate the other. It is quite misleading to validate one dimension of the cinema unilaterally at the expense of all the others. There is no pure cinema, grounded on a single essence, hermetically sealed from contamination.—PETER WOLLEN

It is only on the basis of the closest contact with the culture of literature, theatre, painting and music, only in the most serious examination of the newest scientific disclosures in reflexes and psychology and related sciences, that the study of cinema specifics can be coordinated in some constructive and workable system of instruction and perception.—S. M. EISENSTEIN

1

Mise en Scène

The railroads and old party bosses
  Together did sweetly agree;
And they thought there would be little trouble
  In working a hayseed like me.
                              —Political song

It was a shakedown, a time of consolidation. Although there remained a few Indian matters to clear up, the frontier was closed (Frederick Jackson Turner announced the end of that era at the 1893 meeting of the American Historical Society). Washington, Idaho, Montana, Wyoming, and the Dakotas were admitted to the Union between 1889 and 1900; Utah had to straighten out its marriages first. The Oklahoma Territory was opened for settlement. Buffalo disappeared, and cowboys became ranchhands working inside fences. The mines were now owned by the big operators.

The 1890 census showed 4,047 millionaires. John Jacob Astor said, "A man who has a million dollars is as well off as if he were rich." Thorstein Veblen published his *Theory of the Leisure Class* in 1899.

Among the nonmillionaires of the rural areas, behavior in the cities often seemed to corroborate what they had learned from the touring melodramas. John D. Rockefeller doubled the price of axle grease and kerosene. Even the eastern *Harper's* magazine of 1894 characterized Wall Street as a "dark, mysterious, crafty, wicked, rapacious and tyrannical power."

Sectional suspicions were organizing too, replacing the agonies of twenty-five years earlier. Populism was in formation, although,

3

reinforced by the 1886 Haymarket Riot in Chicago, farmers still harbored suspicions of the union movement.

The 1880 census had counted fifty million heads. Ten years later it was sixty-three, of whom seven million were blacks and five million immigrants. The new Americans settled, penniless, in eastern cities, or else in the big mill towns of Pennsylvania and Ohio or in Chicago. Many of their children never got to school at all. Adding machines and typewriters brought more women into offices and factories. In 1896, New York City laundresses struck in support of the sewing-machine workers, and a popular play was *Bertha the Sewing Machine Girl*.

Yet the general tenor of the country was one of optimistic, expansive confidence, at least from those voices that were heard. Teddy Roosevelt's rhetorical advocation of "The Strenuous Life" was well received.

As far as it could keep up with the new wizards, industry, too, was consolidating its gains. Henry Ford designed his first assembly line in 1893. Marconi transmitted wireless messages in 1895. Samuel P. Langley sent an unmanned, steam-powered airplane across the Potomac River in May, 1896. In 1909, Blériot flew the English Channel. New York built its first skyscraper, the Flatiron Building, in 1902, and a subway two years earlier. Boston had trolleys and subways in 1898.

Alexander Graham Bell's 1876 patent for the transmission of articulate sounds over wires had resulted in a growing network of phone systems. In the summer of 1890, at the Grand Hotel in Saratoga, eight hundred people listened by wire to a concert from the new Madison Square Garden, along with "remotes" from other locations where dance music was played and a recitation delivered—*The Charge of the Light Brigade*. Rural parochialisms diminished with the rise of telephone poles.

The first practical electric light bulbs, developed in 1879 by Edison and, earlier, Sir Joseph Wilson Swan, had now begun to illuminate entire cities, and in the process to lengthen hours for reading.

The new typewriters, originating from an 1868 machine, were most favored by business, but they were increasingly taken up

4

by professional writers, who were often paid by the line or some other bulk measure. Lewis E. Waterman's 1884 invention of the fountain pen also helped to encourage a writer to ply his trade on location, at odd moments of the day and night.

Typesetting became increasingly simpler with the invention of the linotype machine of Ottmar Mergenthaler, and Tolbert Lanston's 1885 Monotype, which justified the lines automatically. Combined with assembly-line mechanics (like gathering, casemaking, rounding, and backing) the new technology mechanized production almost completely. High-speed rotary presses in the nineties were able to produce both the modern magazine and newspaper (although weeklies still outcirculated the dailies). Photoengraving turned out dependable replicas of an artist's or a photographer's work without recourse to intermediary tools. After the turn of the century halftone printing had automated the printshop line engraver into obsolescence.

McGuffey Readers (one hundred million by 1900) were the bestseller of the century. The U.S. census of 1880 marked illiteracy at 17 percent. At the end of the decade nonreaders were down to 13 percent, and by 1910 92 percent of the population could make out some words. Earlier subscription libraries gave way to free, municipal (or school) supported ones, often housed by Andrew Carnegie. There were fifty-four hundred at the turn of the century; among these, seventeen hundred housed more than five thousand books.

The average level of school attendance was about fourth grade, and whether everyone who could read did so was an open question. Apparently most did. Around range campfires twenty-five-dollar-a-month cowhands might do no more than study canned-food labels, but a New York publisher like Erastus Beadle would soon be able to furnish them with a *Deadwood Dick* or *Mustang Sam*, perhaps written by some young man who had never gotten west of New York's Hell's Kitchen.

Railroads now spanned the country and dropped sparks from elevated tracks on city dwellers. Population growth, urban concentrations, better transportation—all helped a new breed to hustle careers from other citizens' pennies. The modern man was a dispenser of popular merchandise, distributed on a grand basis at minimal investment. Mark Twain was one. He became increasingly concerned with reaching "the masses" through Chautauqua and other speaking tours, and burned his fingers on C. L. Webster and Company, his own venture into the popular press.

Although the pragmatism of the marketplace was uncovering a growing breadth of reading habits, the established authors profited too. Strengthened with new copyright agreements and now sometimes dominated by banking interests, the big publishers raised their antes. Magazine serialization seemed only to increase book sales, and *Harper's Monthly* offered Henry James five thousand dollars for the rights to *The Ambassadors*. At the other end, writers might receive seventy-five to one-hundred dollars from Edward Stratemeyer for a complete novel written at breakneck speed and published under a hack-house pseudonym. The son of the author of Uncle Wiggley recalled his father's stories of typing underneath a blanket so as not to waken him in the night. The nickel and dime novels paid writers even less, and fattened their publishers. *Beadle's Pocket Library* made its owner a millionaire.

New rural free delivery combined with photogravure to develop ten- and fifteen-cent magazines in competition with the staid (and more expensive) *Harper's, Atlantic,* and *Century. McClure's, Cosmopolitan, Collier's, Ladies' Home Journal,* and a revitalized *Saturday Evening Post* could now afford illustrations which had been prohibitively expensive as woodcuts. By the turn of the century they were paying top dollar for authors; fifteen years earlier an author could often get his best money from religious magazines. Now half the country went to church, but this did not seem to make much of an impression on their reading.

Editors, too, began to serve different functions. They were no longer mere intermediaries, screening writers for the public. Now they sought out "trends," proposed subjects, and even outlined plots (as did Edward Stratemeyer). If he was good enough, an independent writer could ignore these strictures and still be published, but serial rights and newspaper syndication sometimes corroded his integrity.

As lines were drawn between city and country the biggest urban centers began to develop cultural domination in new and unsuspected ways. Standardization and syndication were an inevitable response to the realities of the current economic world. Transportation, communication, and new marketing techniques could promote products nationally, and advertising took more and more pages. This was the time of "Ivory Soap—It Floats," "Eastman Kodak—You Push the Button, We Do the Rest," and "Schlitz—The Beer That Made Wilwaukee Famous" (Figure 1). Cereals

FIG. 1. New technology in typesetting, high-speed rotary presses, and improved techniques in photoengraving, coupled with increasing urbanization and new marketing techniques, caused an increase in advertising, as shown in this 1886 satirical drawing from *Judge*. (Reproduced from Marshall B. Davidson, *Life in America*.)

7

could be packaged too, and the food cans whose labels the cow-boys puzzled over.

Corporations like the American Publishing Company commissioned young men to canvass and solicit house-to-house, a technique they shared with Montgomery Ward drummers and the manufacturers of stereograph slides. (See Appendix I for a parallel development in the music publishing business.) In 1899, Ward built a huge warehouse in Chicago on the corner of Madison and Michigan, but by then they were battling for the market with Sears, Roebuck & Company, whose munificently illustrated catalogues used the mail system more effectively than young men with sample cases could ever manage.

The American News Company, a distribution firm, grew to monstrous proportions and even began to dictate content to the publishers it "serviced." Distributors could advance money to fly-by-night publishers for additional titles to push.

Concentrations of power strangled competition. A culturally lively but modest sized city like San Francisco, which earlier had been able to maintain a brisk regional publishing business, now succumbed to eastern muscle.

Standardization dominated. Set pieces for theater staging were manufactured in the east to be distributed across the country. Road-show troupes and music hall programs were packaged in New York for programing on the circuits. Joseph Pulitzer and William Randolph Hearst built their syndicated empires out of stereotype mats, a process of making duplicate printing plates from a form of type or photoengraving blocks by pouring molten metal onto a matrix made in plaster of Paris or papier-mâché. The rich got richer—and the poor got the Yellow Kid. One by-product was the Sunday Supplement, for many the only periodical that was ever read or, increasingly, *looked at.*

The syndication of fiction in newspapers was an eighties development, soon to be followed by the comics, commentators, and advice columns. William Dean Howells found syndication the best-paying market for the second rate.[1] He felt that the newspaper could not support better writing because it was read by men

---

[1] Charvat, "Literature as Business," *Literary History of the United States*, 965.

8

and boys rather than women. This viewpoint underlines America's matriarchal system of culture, but it also says something about the state of that culture's merchandising. Entertainment and enrichmen were packaged for age, sex, taste, background, and pocketbook. The ones who did not care to read could look at pictures. Yet, as we shall see, packaged ingredients were not altogether different, whatever the labels said.

What generalizations can be made from this barrage of facts and functionaries? Clearly, the United States, for the first time in history, was open to cultural exploitation on a scale without parallel in Europe. While wealth and industry centralized in the cities systems of standardized production, marketing, and entertainment learned to indulge for profit the suspicions and aspirations of a vast public. The telegraph was a harbinger. Invention shrank continents of space, sometimes ellipsizing the communicative act into an exhilarating sense of sender-receiver simultaneity.

While literacy predominated across the country, its common level remained minimal. Fourth-grade training was a ready market for simple, concrete kinds of prose description, which often barely clothed high fantasy in the costumes of realism. Yet print, however visual its vocabularies and syntax, also adapted to new graphic conventions. These were the products of photography and of applied technologies that successfully wedded press and picture.

1886   First appearance of Nick Carter.
      Kidnapped and *Dr. Jekyll and Mr. Hyde* (Stevenson);
        The Mayor of Casterbridge (Hardy).
      Abbe and Schott develop new lens achromatics.
      Buffalo Bill's Wild West Show appears at Madison Square
        Garden.
      Frederic Ives patents the crossline halftone screen.
      Samuel Gompers establishes the A.F. of L.
1887   *She* (Haggard).
1888   *Les Lauriers Sont Coupés* (Dujardin).
      Bandit's Roost (Riis).
1889   Alexandre Gustav Eiffel designs tower for Paris Exposition.

1890 Saratoga party listens to telephone concert.
1891 *Peter Ibbetson* (Du Maurier).
1892 *At the Moulin-Rouge* (Toulouse-Lautrec).
After the Ball (Harris).
1893 Henry Ford designs the assembly line.
Chicago Exposition "to commemorate the progress of the nation in art, industry and agriculture."
Frederic Jackson Turner announces the closing of the frontier.
1894 Outcault's first color comic strip published in the New York *World*.
1895 Marconi transmits a wireless message.
Robert W. Paul patents a film theater.
1896 New York laundresses strike.
Langley sends a plane across the Potomac.
The Island of Dr. Moreau (Wells).
1897 *The Nigger of the Narcissus* (Conrad); *Dracula* (Stoker); *The Soul of Lilith* (Corelli).
1898 Boston has subways.
The War of the Worlds (Wells).
1899 *Between Rounds* (Eakins).
The Theory of the Leisure Class (Veblen).
1900 *Sister Carrie* (Dreiser).
1901 *The Four Feathers* (Mason); *The Octopus* (Norris).
The first telegraph signals are sent across the Atlantic.
1902 The Flatiron building is constructed in New York.
Mary Pickford appears in *The Fateful Wedding*.
Bergson lectures on time.
1903 *Tonio Kröger* (Mann).
The Wright brothers fly.
Little Nemo in Slumberland (McCay).
The Great Train Robbery (Porter).
1904 Alexander Black presents *Miss Jerry*.
1905 *The Clansman* (Dixon, Jr.).
Only a Message from Home, Sweet Home (Fleming and Florant).
1906 *The Man of Property* (Galsworthy).

Psychology: Briefer Course (James).

1907 *Stag at Sharkey's* (Bellows).

1908 D. W. Griffith joins Biograph.
Henry Ford designs the Model T.

1909 Griffith freezes action in *A Corner in Wheat*.
Edward Titchener lectures on images of thought.
Meet Me Tonight in Dreamland (Wilson and Friedman).
Little Nemo appears as an animated cartoon.
Blériot flies the English Channel.

1910 Rotogravure presses are placed in commercial use.

1911 *Death in Venice* (Mann); *Pilgrimage* (Richardson).
Alexander's Ragtime Band (Berlin).
The Futurists exhibit in Rome.
Accordionist (Picasso).
The Lonedale Operator (Griffith).

2

Dissolves by Gaslight

Drama is the necessary product of the age in which it lives, and of which it is the moral, social, and physical expression. The contemporaneous drama possesses an archaeological value. It is the only faithful record of its age. In it the features, expressions, manners, thoughts and passions of its period are reflected and retained.

—DION BOUCICAULT (1877)

By 1911 a narrative structure for film had more or less established itself. The devices of any television thriller today are little different in essence from those one- and two-reelers which came from the old Biograph studio just off New York's Union Square.

For their stories early films largely cannibalized the innards of the last century's theatrical melodrama. The process seems almost pat evidence for Marshall McLuhan's proposition that a new medium devours as content the medium it seeks to replace.

However, similarities of expository form between movies and melodrama are striking too. Clearly, both often responded to the same shaping forces, melodrama colored and defined (and sometimes anticipated with its own tools) the later film techniques. Then melodrama transmigrated into the movies and fiction; in theater it died or went underground. As a profitable venture it had disappeared by World War I. New styles of acting and writing evolved. Theater had captured a more sophisticated audience. Its earlier one, the urban, artisan spectators, drifted into the music halls and storefront nickelodeons.

One serious study has defined relationships and similarities between nineteenth-century theater and twentieth-century film: A.

12

Nicholas Vardac's *Stage to Screen.*[1] Vardac's thoroughly documented work concludes that motion pictures were the more successful medium in reconciling those trends of realism and romanticism which prevailed in the period. Further, photography captured with little effort the qualities of spectacle, fantasy, naturalism, and mime that had required unbelievably complicated and unwieldy stage machinery and designs. Vardac is particularly rich in his analysis of stage construction and those transitional techniques which were developed to smooth the carryovers between stage scenes. His book is essential to an understanding of the period.

Here, however, we shall delimit ourselves to melodrama and try to isolate this single aspect of popular culture, whose little-noted counterparts today are quite as active and as interwoven in the social fabric as was the earlier theatrical form. Moreover, the *functions* of formal elements are to be stressed. It is a matter of historical interest that D. W. Griffith used, for example, theatrical lighting in his early films. But of deeper aesthetic moment is the fact that what Griffith's lighting accomplished it did better in film, so that movies commandeered an approach which had theretofore worked its greatest successes on the stage. (The usual argument of motion-picture histories traces storytelling techniques from the one-shot accomplishments of Edison and the Lumière brothers through Méliès and Edwin S. Porter to Griffith. Although Griffith's indebtedness to Dickens was both acknowledged by himself[2] and discussed by S. M. Eisenstein in a noteworthy essay,[3] the general tenor of movie historians has been self-protectingly provincial—understandably so if one considers the competitive, strenuous efforts of filmmakers, critics, and theorists to define their craft during its great period of expansion as unique and therefore unbeholden.)

In spelling out theatrical devices and conventions which had direct counterparts in early films, it becomes clear that many such relations were causal. Boucicault to Belasco to Griffith is an ob-

[1] Vardac, *Stage to Screen: Theatrical Method From Garrick to Griffith.*

[2] Jacobs, *The Rise of the American Film*, 103.

[3] Eisenstein, "Dickens, Griffith, and the Film Today," *Film Form.* See also Eisenstein, "Form and Content: Practice," *The Film Sense*, 165–66.

13

vious example. However, a matter of greater concern here is the need to identify parallel solutions to shared problems.

Melodrama was the product of an industrial society—the urban working-class—and the topical excitements of its period—crime, military adventure, wilderness explorations. It developed out of morality plays and sentimental plays as well as from the Gothic novels of Walpole, Mrs. Radcliffe (herself influenced by Schiller's *Die Raüber*), and Monk Lewis. French melodrama flourished after the Revolution. The English picked it up (a euphemism for what was often out-and-out theft from Pixérécourt) in the early nineteenth century. Because speech and mime were accomplished by or interspersed with music, the form enjoyed lattitudes under the 1737 Licensing Act which were less available to dramas per se.

By 1830, English rural populations were moving to the cities, and class-based antagonisms on the stage readjusted their context to worker–factory-owner conditions. Audience participation was strong. The people who attended this theater, and later its filmed equivalent, shared a desire to see dramatized allegories of human experience. Presentations were simplified to trivial ethical dimensions. Where any efforts toward characterization took place, they were externalized into visible evidence.

Speech, behavior, and settings were coded for instant recognition. Justice prevailed—an inevitable consequence of the struggle and torment. Thus melodrama guised fantasy in the costume of naturalism. As a theatrical form melodrama developed into a conventionalized entertainment whose qualities were determined both by the sensibilities and the perceptions of its audience. It presented a world of problems and characters made fraudulently comprehensible, then costumed with palatable thrills, climaxed in reassuring resolutions. The narrative form developed to guarantee unflagging interest by omitting the "dead spots" of other drama, enlisting identifications with the performers and refining resources of suspense.

In the *Oxford Companion to the Theatre*, Disher proposes that melodrama was finally outmoded by two developments: the success of plays by women novelists and the development of copyright laws which discouraged the free "adaptations" which had made inexpensive scripts so accessible. By the end of the century, certainly, last-minute stage rescues had fallen off. They survived mostly among the road companies and in theaters which catered to working-class spectators. Through much of the century genteel audiences had tended more toward the novel and poetry; in so doing they drew conceptual talents away from the stage. But by the last decades a city like New York was able to support several new theaters built to attract the middle-class.

After midcentury melodrama was also diminished by the rise of the music hall, where any appeals to strong feelings or plays upon common anxieties were nonexistent. In a compromise at the expense of the older form the increasingly popular vaudeville houses condensed melodramas into thirty-minute segments on their program. When motion pictures appeared in the nineties in the same setting, often at the bottom of the bill to clear the house, they displaced their live counterparts.

In the same decade there was one mercantile effort to revive the older form—the Ten-Twenty-Thirty Melodrama, a theatrical equivalent of attempts by other popular-culture salesmen to profit from the leisure and increased salaries of metropolitan workers. (The same impulse surfaced in the evolution of the nationally circulated magazine and in the newspapers of Pulitzer and Hearst. A new symbiosis—intellectual hack and artisan consumer—is evidenced in such an observation as the following by a Harvard-educated melodramatist who started his career in 1902:

> One of the first tricks I learned was that my plays must be written for an audience who, owing to the huge, uncarpeted, noisy theatres, couldn't always hear the words, and who, a large percentage of them having only recently landed in America, couldn't have understood them in any case. I therefore wrote for the eye rather than the ear and played out each emotion in action, depending on dialogue only for the noble sentiments so dear to the audiences of that class.[4]

The concept of "writing for the eye" was not altogether a product of language barriers. Because of the Licensing Act, Gothic dramas were presented early in the century as dumbshows,

---

4 Owen Davis, "I'd Do it Again," quoted in Rahill, *The World of Melodrama*, 278.

15

mimed to music. Later they survived in the melodrama's non-dialogued action scenes, and this element translated easily into the silent film. Indeed, mimed parts continued almost intact in such roles as the Frankenstein monster (early adapted to the stage from Mary Shelley's novel). Vampires, too, were popular in early melodrama: Planche's *The Vampire* (1820), George Blink's *The Vampire Bride* (1834), and Boucicault's *The Vampire* (1852), which he reworked as *The Phantom* (1862).

Where explanations were in order during mimed performances placards were displayed, not unlike the intercutting of titles in silent films. A common practice was to counterpose ripostes by heroes and villains against the mimed action of later, spoken melodrama, in the manner of Batman and the Joker.

> HAWKSHAW. Now, Jem Dalton! It's my turn!
> DALTON. Hawkshaw!
> *They struggle.*
>
> —*The Ticket-of-Leave Man*
> (Act IV Scene 3)

Undoubtedly, the matter of visual climaxes was in part a response to theater posters and other sorts of nineteenth-century illustration, themselves the product of modern lithographing techniques. The new printing process fostered showers of gaudy, colored posters. Melodrama was especially rich in moments of lurid incident and ennobling or pathetic sentiment. "Once he had a title, he'd discuss scenes that would make good lithographs—things like the burning of Brooklyn Bridge or the blowing up of the Capitol. Even before I'd begin to write a play, Al Woods would have the lithographs illustrating it ready for the billboards, sometimes twenty or thirty thousand dollars worth."[5]

This sense of scene-as-illustration underlines melodrama's affiliation with popular graphics. In the first half of the nineteenth century George Dibdin Pitt wrote several plays whose structure provided sequential pictures of a personality or career in the matter of cartoon series. In fact, one play, *The Drunkard's Children*, grew out of a series of plates by Cruikshank. Similarly, a

---

5 Vardac, p. 43, traces the development of *The Colleen Bawn* from steel engravings.

version of the life of Napoleon devoted itself to such "moments" as crossing the Alps, the escape from Elba, the last campaign, and the general meditating on a setting sun at Saint Helena—an editorial cartoon if there ever was one! (Catalogues of early film distributors title and describe each motion-picture scene in quite the same vein.)[6] The device of "historical reconstruction," which resulted in hundreds of early short films—sometimes masquerading as newsreels—reappears in *The Birth of a Nation*: Lincoln signing a proclamation, Lee's surrender at Appomattox, and the assassination.

During the nineteenth century the broader melodrama plots resolved into identifiable subspecies. Each reappeared in motion pictures. Film often revived the same theatrical properties. Melodramas could be military, horror, nautical, crime, or evidence for the perils of city life. Some plays which were later filmed also exemplify the detective mystery (*Sherlock Holmes*), the frontier (*Billy the Kid, The Westerner*), slavery (*Uncle Tom's Cabin, The Clansman* which became *The Birth of a Nation*), historical spectacle (*Ben Hur*), romance (*Camille*), romantic adventure (*The Prisoner of Zenda, The Corsican Brothers, The Count of Monte Cristo*), and religion (*The Sign of the Cross*).

One popular form was the animal drama. In Frederic Reynold's *The Caravan; or The Driver and his Dog* (1803), a dog named Carlo saves a girl from the sea. Carlo's movie doppelgänger showed up first in *Rescued by Rover* (1905). In midcentury, at the Bower Saloon in Lambeth, one dog shared Hamlet's conversation with the ghost, watched Claudius at the play, supervised the duel with Laertes, and killed the king on his master's voice.[7] Late in the century animal melodramas were part of the New York revival. In *Deadwood Dick's Last Shot*, derived from a dime-novel hero, a horse raised an American flag to signal the attack which saves the hero, who is about to be burned at the stake. Within a few years Tom Mix's Tony became an equally resourceful steed.

Many plot devices in early films were directly appropriated from earlier plays. Rescue by telegraph (*The Lonedale Operator*,

6 Jacobs, 38–41, 43–46.
7 Booth, *English Melodrama*, 86–87.

1911) appears in *The Long Strike* (1866) by Boucicault. The climax to *The Birth of a Nation* (1915) is the relief of a besieged party whose women are about to be shot and clubbed rather than face a fate far worse than the plot. It appeared in *The Girl I Left Behind Me* (1893), a frontier play by Belasco and Franklin Fyles, drama critic of the New York *Sun*. Indians substituted for crazed black militia in the former play, and the Ku Klux Klan replaced the U.S. Cavalry.

The essence of much melodrama was speed and mounting tension, qualities that required rapid transitions between scenes as well as special juxtapositions and skills in movement and change on stage. Echoing related preoccupations with time and space in other narrative forms, the nineteenth-century theater explored transitional devices which clearly anticipate the techniques of the motion picture. Many of the new effects derived from technical innovations in lighting and projection as well as changes in theater architecture. Previous to the 1880's a curtain was rarely introduced between scenes, but only as a frame to each act; scenes were changed in view of the audience. Melodrama seems to have indulged two impulses: to introduce the scene curtain in order to make drastic changes in its increasingly realistic decor,[8] and to create a sense of movement in space as a transitional technique which maintained temporal continuity rather than interpreting the action. This accounts for such a "trucking camera" shot (Figure 2) as the following:

> The interior of a prison: large window R., an old fireplace, R.C., small window, C., door, L. Through window R. is seen exterior and courtyard. The scene moves—pivots on a point at the back. The prison moves off, and shows the exterior of tower, with *Conn* clinging to the walls, and *Robert* creeping through the orifice. The walls of the yard appear to occupy three-fourths of the stage.
> —*The Shaughraun* (Drury Lane, 1875) by
> DION BOUCICAULT (Act II Scene 5)[9]

[8] As sets grew larger and machinery more cumbersome and complicated, intervals for scene changes increased. Booth quotes a note on *The World* (Drury Lane, 1880) whose effects included a boat adrift on a great sea. "In consequence of the elaborate scenic effects it will be necessary to have an interval of five or six minutes between heaviest sets." Act intervals began to take from a half hour to an hour. Plays started to run as long as five hours.

18

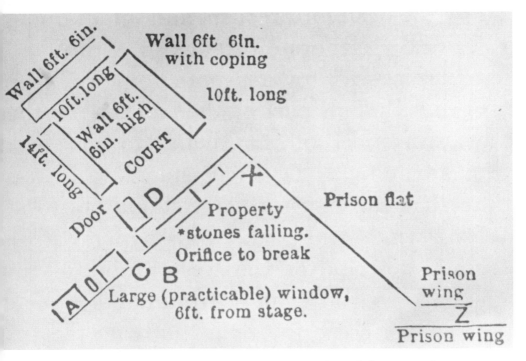

Wall 6ft 6in. with coping

10ft. long

Wall 6ft 6in.

Wall 6ft. 6in.

10ft. long

14ft. long

Wall 6ft. 6in. high

COURT

Door

D

Property *stones falling. Orifice to break

Prison flat

A O C B

Large (practicable) window, 6ft. from stage.

Prison wing

Z

Prison wing

FIG. 2. Camera techniques were anticipated in early melodramas, such as the "trucking shot" in *The Shaughraun* (1875), where the stage set pivots to reveal an exterior scene. (From Allardyce Nicoll, *A History of English Drama, 1600–1900.*)

Similarly, one finds this involved visual descent in another Boucicault play; it sounds very like a camera tilt, and stage machinery simulated that very effect (Figure 3).

The scene changes in the exterior of the same tower; the outside of the cell is seen, and the window by which he has just escaped. *Shaun* is seen clinging to the face of the wall; he climbs the ivy. The tower sinks as he climbs; the guard room windows lighted within are seen descending, and above them a rampart and sentry on guard. . . . As *Shaun* climbs past the window the ivy above his head gives way and a large mass falls carrying him with it; the leaves and matted branches cover him. His descent is checked by some roots on the ivy which hold fast. An alarm . . . he eludes the sentry and disappears round the corner of the tower, still ascending. The scene still

9 Quoted in Nicoll, *A History of English Drama 1600–1900* V, 45.

19

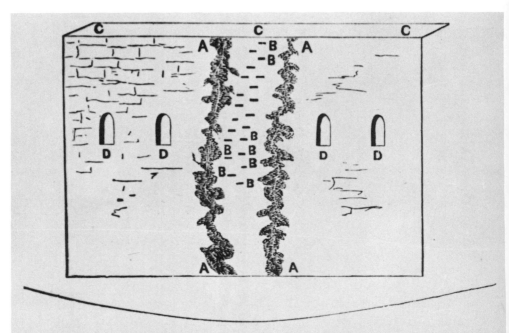

Flat (A), in 3rd grooves to descend. A, A, A, A, outlines of a mass of ivy to cover practicable steps, marked B. B.; SHAUN is discovered halfway up, therefore no steps on lower half of flat; darken the shadows around the steps to hide them. Wall of old gray stone, mossy, etc. The top joins the platform, c. (two feet wide), which laps on the bottom of flat (B) and helps to bring it down in continuous descent. All the face to the audience is in shadow, the light being up at back. D, D, D, D, are arched windows.

FIG. 3. Another example of "stage to screen," this from *Arrah-na-Pogue* (1864), where the scenery literally "sinks" as the hero climbs upward—a technique later known as the "camera tilt." (From Allardyce Nicoll, *A History of English Drama, 1600–1900*.)

descends, showing the several stages of the keep, until it sinks to the platform, in which *Arrah* is discovered, seated and leaning over the abyss, still singing the song. Beyond, there is seen the lake and the tops of the castle.

—*Arrah-na-Pogue*[10]

[10] Quoted in Booth, *op. cit.*, 167–70. A similar staging of the same play is described by Vardac, 26.

20

The panorama was also used as a method to simulate movement of a shoreline as seen from a moving ship.[11]

Perhaps the most striking of all the mobile, camera-affecting stagings occurs in the Prologue to *The Girl of the Golden West*. Belasco rolls a painted backdrop in a lengthy "pan" down from a peak in the Sierras, from mountain slope to a cabin, down a footpath to a miner's camp, then "trucks" into the exterior of the Polka Saloon. Here the sounds of a banjo, singing, and gambling are introduced. The stage then fades to black. With the fade-in the set is the saloon's interior, and action commences. Belasco's stage directions refer to what he calls "first picture" and "second picture" ". . . the scene represents a little world by itself, drawn in a few crude strokes, to explain more than the author could tell in a thousand pages." In 1911 a novel was published, credited to Belasco and based on the play. It neither begins nor ends with the stage settings.[12]

The same impulse toward fast transitions in space, visible to the audience or not (a "pan" or "cut") is found in Steele MacKaye's invention of the "sliding stage" and the "double elevator stage," wherein one scene could be raised or lowered into view.

The other main structural problem confronted by melodrama was that of simultaneity. The stories turned so often on coincidental appearances of characters at unexpected moments and on rescues in the face of imminent danger that staging had to facilitate two or more playing areas at the same time. Monk Lewis' *Venoni* (Drury Lane, 1808), used two cells separated by a partition. In Fitzball's *Jonathan Bradford* (Surrey, 1833) four apartments are organized on two floors: two bedrooms above, the windows opening on a tile floor. Below, a back parlor and a bar are separated by a hallway, giving onto the stage through a front door. The play's action progresses from one apartment to another, or sometimes occurs simultaneously. Another instance of mul-

---

11 The idea of a panoramic scene in the theater is antedated by the public Panoramas and Dioramas. See Chap. 5.

12 Vardac quotes another version of the same play which emphasizes the tight-scheduled lighting cues used to establish the time as sunset in order to coincide with the inception of activity in the saloon.

tiple staging takes place in *Lady Audley's Secret* (Royal Victoria, 1864). Act II Scene 3 is introduced as follows:

> A divided scene of two rooms; in R. a table, chairs and flight of steps, supposed to lead to a hayloft, in C. flat; a door piece, R., and key in it; in L., room, table, chair, and window in flat showing moonlight perspective.

The action moves from one room to the next while parties in adjacent quarters either sleep or listen. Thus the exposition depends on an audience vantage which has an omniscience unknown to the players—a device of both film and the nineteenth-century novel.

Another advantage of multiple staging was the ease with which action could be shifted in space without the interruptions of scene changes. Vardac notes an involved double-set staging for *A Race for Life* (1883), followed in a later act by a double set and revolving lighthouse.[13]

Sensation scenes, of course, often required that two storylines, separately situated but simultaneous, meet at the climax. The archetypal rescue is from a railroad track, and it may have appeared first in 1867 in Augustin Daly's *Under the Gaslight* (Figure 4).[14]

Boucicault appropriated it for his 1868 production of *After Dark*. In both cases a character has to break out of an enclosure to untie the ropes. Daly staged track and ticket office on one set. Boucicault's procedure is more elaborate. In Scene 1 the victim is captured. Scene 2 finds the rescuer, Old Tom, in his enclosure (a dark cellar; he burrows through a wall to reach the London underground). In Scene 3, Tom breaks through and makes the rescue. The staging is such that the most likely technique for its execution would appear to be that of successively lighting the cellar and then the railroad track, with the broken wall as a connecting element. It would be rewarding to locate further evidence on the performance at the Princess's Theatre.

Griffith's narrative solution to the sensation scene embodied

13 Vardac, *op. cit.*, 20–24.
14 Vardac quotes a contemporary review that may document an earlier train-on-the-stage in *London by Night* (1814), 50.

FIG. 4. A poster depicting the archetypal rescue scene from Augustin Daly's *Under the Gaslight*. (From Michael Booth, *Hiss the Villain*.)

what has come to be known as parallel editing, a strategy of inter-cutting from one locale to the other at increasing tempo until the two storylines are joined. The film's equivalent to multiple staging first appeared in double-exposed or optically printed "split screens." Kirk Bond remarks on an early version of this in Cecil B. DeMille's 1915 *Carmen*, mentioning "a shot that has at the top of the screen a small rectangle looking out of the tent to show action in the smuggler's camp. The effect is literally that of an experimental film of today with its small frame within the large frame."[15]

In the realm of fantasy, where special staging is less needful of being "explained" by reality, the use of a split screen by Méliès (*The Damnation of Faust*, 1903) is described by Kemp Niver. The employment of optical projection and mattes to achieve a

15 Bond, "Eastman House Journal," *Film Culture*, No. 47, (Summer, 1969), 45.

23

similar effect is found in another Méliès production a year later, *Au Clair de la Lune*.[16]

Sensation scenes in the last half of the century grew so ambitious (with smashing locomotives, military battles, sinking ships) that their execution often became the point of the performance. Outdoor spectacles date as far back as *A Time of Mystery* (1802). *The Siege of Gibralter* (Sadler's Wells, 1804) has man-of-wars and floating batteries in a tank with eight thousand cubic feet of real water. Moncrieff introduced a diorama in *Zoroaster* (1824). Fitzball's *Paul Clifford* (1835) had a stage coach and six real horses.

The translation of the sensation scene into motion pictures is self-apparent.[17] What has been less remarked is the melodrama as a training ground for the nineteenth-century novelist. Dickens, for example, staged *The Miller and His Men* as a schoolboy, exploding the robbers' den with firecrackers.[18] Jacques Barzun speaks of the "esthetic melodrama" of "modern prose fiction, from Richardson to Balzac and Lawrence" and later remarks on the deep influence of Daly and Boucicault on Henry James.[19]

The "modernized revivals" of melodrama at the turn of the century were training grounds for several young Biograph stars in the Griffith troupe. This movement resuscitated the stock company and the salaried "staff author," although by now performances were limited largely to local theaters rather than to the road show.[20] Authors wrote to the talents of their players, and each player devoted his energies to one or two stereotyped roles; the parallel to the later Hollywood star system is clear. Mary Pickford starred in the second company (this one on the road) of *The Fatal Wedding* by Theodore Kremer in 1902 and in Hal Reid's *The Gypsy Girl* (1905).[21] Lillian Gish, at the age of five,

16 Niver, *Motion Pictures from the Library of Congress Paper Print Collection 1894–1912*, 178, 340.

17 As well as thoroughly documented in Vardac.

18 Johnson, *The Dickens Theatrical Reader*, 9.

19 Barzun, "Henry James the Melodramatist," *The Energies of Art*, 237.

20 Early film equivalents to the stock companies were the traveling exhibitors who played fairs and small towns with motion pictures plus live entertainment. See Sharp, *The Picture Palace*, 38–48.

21 The father of Wallace Reid, Hal was a prolific author, also responsible for *The Little Red Schoolhouse* in which both Pickford and Lillian Gish appeared.

debuted in *Her First False Step* by Lillian Mortimer, an authoress-actress who specialized in plays about working girls victimized by sophisticated wealth. Dorothy Gish played in *East Lynne*. In *Convict Stripes*, Lillian Gish was saved from dynamite by a hero who swung across the stage on a rope. Perhaps it is significant that the first picture in which the Gish sisters worked for Griffith was *The Unseen Enemy* (1912). Dorothy and Lillian try to telephone the police while burglars shoot at them through a stovepipe hole.

Griffith combined penchants for both popular melodrama and the "new drama" of Henry Arthur Jones and Pinero which was replacing it. When he pursued nonmelodramatic subjects, Griffith is said to have been criticized by the Biograph producers. Additionally, Griffith brought to the motion picture the abilities of a theatrical stage manager, a role which had been developing since the 1880's, both as a coordinating agent dealing with the minutest particulars of the overall production and as supervisor to the performances of the actors.[22]

Griffith is also respected for his efforts to encourage the new screen actors to minimize exaggerated expressions and gestures associated with the stage. But this impulse was not unique to film; it can also be seen in the efforts of David Belasco during his Broadway period. Belasco tried to diminish acting extravagances and to seek effect through minimal means with a quieter, colloquial style.[23]

As stage presentations began to regain the monied audiences which had forsaken them, and as the constituency of drama be-

---

[22] Early stage-manager types were Boucicault, W. S. Gilbert, and Tom Robertson, a playwright and actor who tried to de-emphasize star performances and require ensemble work through detailed directions. Gilbert praised him for showing "how to give life and variety and nature to the scene by breaking it up with all sorts of little incidents and delicate by-play." Sidney Dark and Rowland Grey, *W. S. Gilbert: His Life and Letters* (1923), 59. Quoted in Nicoll, 32. For Griffith, "breaking it up with all sorts of little incidents" meant, in part, analyzing a single sequence into a series of shots.

[23] Rahill, 266–68. The close scrutiny of the camera had its earlier equivalent in postgas illumination of the stage. New lighting devices threw the performers into a sort of visibility which hadn't existed under gas, oil, and candlelight. Rahill credits Brander Matthews and Daniel Frohman with proposing that lighting accounted for the disappearance of theatrical "asides," except of course in revivals.

came increasingly a homogeneous middle-class, theaters grew in size and in the elaborateness of their decor. The disappearance of the apron, which had pressed into the auditorium since Elizabethan times, established the idea of a "picture frame" stage that in turn became another argument for naturalism. Pits were replaced with reserved stalls of cushioned seats, or else they were pushed back under the dress circle. The effect was to give a clearer vantage to audiences more attentive to the performance.[24] A better view (there were more box seats as well) for more patrons also argued for greater emphasis on visual detail and for more considered, less stylized uses of expression.

With the disappearance of the apron and its stage doors, a frame was introduced around the stage. This created an effect strikingly like that of the motion-picture theater screen.

> A rich and elaborate gold border, about two feet broad, after the pattern of a picture frame, is continued all around the proscenium, and carried even below the actors' feet. . . . There can be no doubt the sense of illusion is increased and for the reason just given: the actors seem to be cut off from the domain of prose; there is no borderland or platform in front; and, stranger still, the whole has the air of a picture projected on a surface.[25]

Similarly, the early film screens were fancy bordered; for example, the gold-framed screen at Koster & Bial's Music Hall on Herald Square, where Edison's first public performance took place on April 23, 1896 (Figure 5). The same tendencies toward size and elaborateness in stage architecture reappeared with the movie palaces of the 1920's, when Hollywood began to lust after its own middle-class clientele.

In the course of the nineteenth century melodrama sets increasingly used elaborate carpentry and painting as more effort was made to integrate their function with the plot. Backdrops, for example, were sometimes partly painted with transparent dye to look like the surrounding areas from the front. When lights were

---

24 See illustration of the *New Booth's Theater*, opened in New York in 1869. Hughes, *A History of the American Theatre 1700–1950*, 194.

25 The description is of the new Haymarket Theatre from Perry Fitzgerald, *The World Behind the Screen* (1881), 20–21. Quoted in Nicoll, 29.

FIG. 5. Edison's first public performance took place on April 23, 1896, at Koster & Bial's Music Hall on Herald Square in New York. Note the gold-framed screen, reminiscent of the elaborate facades of the theater's proscenium arch. (From the *New York Herald*, May 3, 1896.)

turned on behind, the painted front would either fade out or be replaced by what had been designed on the back of the sheet, an effect especially useful for fires and sunsets.

However, the last quarter of the century found audiences increasingly dissatisfied with cut cloths and painted flats. The new direction, accelerated by photography's abilities to report the epidermis of reality, was toward box sets with three solid walls and a ceiling—something not introduced into movie carpentry until *Citizen Kane* (1941).[26]

The execution of painted exteriors was heavily influenced by the naturalism of nineteenth-century salon painting. As with the Dioramas, lighting was commonly used to simulate changes of time and weather, and Griffith carried the same techniques into the movies. Compare the following report on an amateur melodrama at the home of Charles Dickens with Mrs. Griffith's memory of her husband's lighting effects:

> As the light fades with the advancing evening a grey tone comes over the landscape with the most natural effect. . . . The warm red hues of the west pale into the grey and spectral moonshine (an effect marvelously achieved . . .).[27]

> He figured on cutting a little rectangular place in the back wall of Pippa's room, about three feet by one, and arranging a sliding board to fit the aperture much like the cover of a box sliding in and out of groove. The board was to be gradually lowered and beams of light from a powerful klieg shining through would thus appear as the first rays of the rising sun striking the wall of the room. Other lights stationed outside Pippa's window would give the effect of soft morning light. Then the lights full up, the mercury tubes asizzling, the room fully lighted, the back wall would have become regular back wall again, with no little hole in it.[28]

26 Edison films like *The Great Train Robbery* (1903) revert to earlier melodramatic decor in their interiors; *cf.*, the painted pot-bellied stove in the square-dance scene or the combination of painted mountains, toy steamboats, and real water in *Uncle Tom's Cabin* (1903). For illustrations, see Richard Griffith and Arthur Mayer, *The Movies.* New York, Simon and Schuster, 1957, 11.

27 *The Leader*, Jan. 10, 1857, 44–45. Cited in Brannan, *Under the Management of Charles Dickens*, 76–77.

28 Arvidson, *When the Movies Were Young*, 128.

Mrs. Griffith then quotes a review which says in part: "As for Pippa without words, the first films show the sunlight waking Pippa for her holiday with light and shade effects like those obtained by the Seccessionist Photographers."[29]

Clearly, these lighting techniques also echo the painters' capacities to direct a viewer's attention and to manipulate tempo by the visual evidence of time change. In these respects a projected image is not only simpler to control than a stage set, it is easier to create. Further, the omnipotent director can the more facilely indulge his audience's (false) sense of omniscience.

By the 1820's candles had been replaced by gas. After mid-century auditorium chandeliers and wall brackets were no longer kept burning during a performance, but dimmed. Gas not only gave brighter light, but could be controlled on cue from a single source. This allowed light to be written into the script as an element functional to the story. Such effects as the following from *Sweeney Todd the Demon Barber of Fleet Street* could not have occurred in earlier theater.

> The fierce glow of a furnace. . . . (Act II Scene 4)
> The beams of the moon play with a bluish tinge on [*Mark's*] face, which is deadly pale; his hair is dishevelled and his clothes soaked with blood. Sweeney starts as if he looked upon an apparition. *Picture.* (Act III, Scene 1)
> A gas light burns at the gauze window, and the form of *Mark Ingestrie* appears for an instant. (Act III Scene 4)

Additionally, gas might be used for spectacular effects; for example, "red fire," an apparently safe simulation of a large-scale conflagration. In the ending to one version of *Sweeney Todd* large amounts of red fire in the wings seemed to suggest that all the performers had gone up in smoke.

The technique of fading into or out from a darkened stage was a consequence of the unilateral control of gas lighting. With careful planning it became possible to "dissolve" from one scene to the next. Vardac speaks of scenes dissolving into one another in the DeWitt version of *Arrah-na-Pogue* (1864).[30] He describes a

29 *The New York Times*, Oct. 10, 1909.
30 Vardac, *op. cit.*, 27.

slow dissolve done without lights in an 1887 *David Copperfield*.[31] As early as 1874 one New York reviewer was sick of it and objecting to "a display of dissolving views."[32]

Contemporary with gas, but longer lived, lime or calcium light provided a brilliant white, especially useful in simulating twilight, moonlight, rippling water, clouds, etc. Because limelight had a small area of intense brightness it could be focused with lenses (see Appendix IV) and used to spotlight and also to follow actors.[33]

Modern theatrical lighting developed from Edison's invention of the incandescent-filament lamp in 1879. While it was low in efficiency and its spectrum leaned to the reds, electric light was safe and could be reliably dimmed from full light to out. Edison personally installed the overhead lighting in the Madison Square Theatre, New York City, in 1879 when Steele MacKaye gained control of the auditorium and remodeled it in accordance with new concepts of technical equipment.[34]

Belasco, especially, recognized the potential of electric lighting, introducing a portable light bridge above the proscenium, a portable switchboard, and a staff of electricians expanded from the usual two or three to twenty-four.[35]

A combination of controlled light sources, lenses, and stage machinery encouraged the development of ectoplasmic elements in the plots. Given the new resources, playwrights introduced to the melodrama a battery of visual effects which doubtless suggest many of film's later accomplishments. Figures could be "dissolved" into a scene by way of elaborate combinations of glass, mirrors, light, and cloth.[36] Traps in the floor—known backstage

---

31 *Ibid.*, 32.

32 *Ibid.*, 34.

33 Limelight was portable to the extent that cylinders were strapped to the backs of operators who would move about above the stage, directing their illumination as demanded. See Fuchs, *Stage Lighting*, 43.

34 Various electrical spectaculars were staged in the theaters in the 1890's, including the Spectatorium, New York City, 1893, and E. L. Bruce's Aerial Graphoscope at Kensington, 1896. Projected effects (like clouds) were attempted by Professor Herkomer at about the same time. See Nicoll, 47.

35 Rahill, *op. cit.*, 167.

36 See "Pepper's Ghost" in *Oxford Companion to the Theatre*, 726. See also illustrations of exhibitions at the Boulevard du Temple in Sharp, 15.

by such fanciful terms as the Vamp Trap, the Star Trap, the Corsican Trap, and the Ghost Glide—eased spectral entrances and exits.[37]

Vision scenes seem to have developed out of magic-lantern projections and other devices of rear projection in the second half of the century. Vision scenes usually indicated premonitions, hallucinations, or dreams, and were represented at the rear of the stage behind gauze or else "thrown" above and behind the actors. An early example occurs in the Dickens-Collins collaboration *The Frozen Deep* (1857), in which a tired traveler sees in his campfire at the North Pole a glimpse of the girl he left behind.[38]

In *The Bells* by Leopold Lewis (1871) an undiscovered murderer (Mathias) is sleeping at an Alsatian village inn, whereupon the curtain behind a backdrop of muslin rises to disclose a trial set with an effect rather like that of an abrupt film cut. The action proceeds with Mathias' dream, during which a hypnotist leads the guilty man to incriminate himself. The rear curtain then descends, Mathias is awakened, and the story is resolved.[39] Here the vision scene serves, too, as a transitional device. Fifty-odd years later the Lewis play reappears in a film version (*The Bells*, 1926) starring Lionel Barrymore as the innkeeper and Boris Karloff playing the hypnotist in a style and costume designed by Barrymore and straight out of *Dr. Caligari*. By this time dissolves have replaced the "projected" aspect of the vision scene so that the dreaming Mathias is never visible simultaneous with his trial. However, double exposures are repeatedly used to evidence both Barrymore's obsession with bells and his hallucinated image of the murdered Jew.

Besides indulging supernatural characters in the plot (angels, ghosts), vision scenes externalized thoughts, fears, wishes, and impulses (Figure 6). In these respects, as well as in the mechanics of their actual execution, the vision scene reappears in early film.

---

[37] A famous one was the barber chair of Sweeney Todd, who would seat his customers and then pitch them into an assassin's pit below. Sometimes the victims got out, bloody and dazed, but more often they were served to customers of a nearby bakeshop as part of the meat pies.

[38] Dickens liked to use apparitions in his public readings of *The Haunted Man*.

[39] Act IV Scene 4.

31

FIG. 6. A scene from Edwin'S. Porter's *The Life of an American Fireman* (1903) illustrating an early use in film of the Vision Scene. (Still, struck from the Edison Film.)

The magician-filmmaker Méliès brought such stage devices directly to the studio. Edwin S. Porter's *Uncle Tom's Cabin* (1903) shows an angel taking Little Eva to heaven and Eva beckoning to Uncle Tom to make the same trip. Finally, projected onto a space above and screen right of Tom's body, a symbolic tableau of Lincoln and some slaves enthusiastically promises freedom for the oppressed (Figure 7).

Another practice of the melodramatist was to prolong moments of uncommon excitement or of special visual significance by "freezing" moments of action. The customary stage direction is *Picture, Living Picture*, or *Tableau*. Often it anticipates a curtain,

32

FIG. 7. Scenes from Edwin S. Porter's *Uncle Tom's Cabin* (1903). Above, Little Eva beckons Uncle Tom to join her in heaven; below, Lincoln promises freedom to all slaves—further examples of the film's use of the Vision Scene. Note also the "stage" lighting coming through the window above Tom's body. (Stills, struck from the Edison Film.)

but the *Picture* may equally well mark a moment within a scene.

> With a violent effort of strength, the old man suddenly turns upon *Wolf* and tears open his vest, beneath which he appears armed. *Wolf*, at the same instant, dashes *Kelmar* from him, who is caught by the *Count*—the *Count* draws his sword—*Wolf* draws pistols in each hand from his belt, and his hat falls off at the same instant—tableau—appropriate music. (*The Miller and His Men*, Act II Scene 4)

> Music—*Sambo* and *Quimbo* seize *Tom* and drag him upstage. *Legree* seizes *Meeline* and throws her round to R.H.—she falls on her knees with hands lifted in supplication.—*Legree* raises his whip, as if to strike *Tom*—Picture—Closed in. (*Uncle Tom's Cabin*, dramatized by George L. Aiken)[40]

As a posed still the "freeze frame" occurs in films as early as Griffith's 1909 *A Corner in Wheat*. Griffith used it to great effect in the war-dead shots of *The Birth of a Nation*. Vertov integrated the technique of optically arrested motion with consummate skill in *Man With a Movie Camera* (1929). Since *The Four Hundred Blows,* it has been increasingly common in contemporary films.

By its very definition melodrama used music in tandem with stage action from its inception. Indeed, one likely proposal is that the form originated in the eighteenth-century practice of commissioning composers to write incidental music to accompany spoken scenes with passages that would underline the emotion, rather as screen musical scores later came to do. As with the silent motion picture, the size of the orchestration increased with the elegance of the setting. In working-class theaters instrumentation was minimal, though always present.[41] There are contrary stage directions as to whether musicians should be placed in front of or behind the stage. It seems likely that this matter was resolved at the discretion of the author or stage manager.[42]

Music cues accompany the stage directions of most published melodramas. From the earliest period the character of these cues

---

[40] From the stage manager's promptbook, p. 47. Quoted in Leverton, *The Production of Late Nineteenth Century American Drama*, 96. Many other examples of pictures are located in Leverton, *op. cit.*, 95–104.

[41] Booth, *op. cit.*, 37–38.

[42] Leverton, *op. cit.*, 109.

has a quality very like the indexing vocabularies of a film-music library. In *A Tale of Mystery*, an 1802 adaptation of *Coelina* by Thomas Holcraft, the descriptions include *alarming, confused, music to express chattering contention, pain and disorder, doubt and terror, pain and alarm, and hurrying.*[43]

The music is customarily interspersed with the action or else it tries to establish a general mood behind the spoken play. However, there are occasions when its rhythm and intent are clearly synchronized to stage movement, much in the paralleling design common to film animation.

> The combatants, each armed with a short, blunt, basket-hilted sword, timed every blow with the orchestra. Sometimes, each note had its corresponding clash, at others, the contestants had to rest their "minim rest" and engage only upon the beat of the bar.[44]

The evidence of striking similarities between theatrical and filmed melodrama in terms of techniques, structure, and the aesthetic common to both is to be expected; indeed, it is inevitable. Many theater people on the fringes of the New York scene drifted into film in the early years of this century purely as an expedient. Often they must have brought the experiences and traditions of melodrama in the baggage of their theatrical skills.

Beyond this, narrative film and nineteenth-century theater share certain preoccupations and tastes whose ramifications sneaked into many other cultural areas. Writing about Marx as a stylist, Stanley Edgar Hyman follows a cue from Bernard Shaw in suggesting that the dramatic form of *Capital* is Victorian melodrama.[45] By the same token it could be proposed that *The Birth of a Nation* pressed the Civil War and the Reconstruction period into melodrama, or that Eisenstein accomplished much the same thing in *The Battleship Potemkin*.

The motion picture was the logical extension of theater's inclination to place real objects on its stage. More important than the location of the performance—as we have seen, theaters and

---

43 Rahill, *op. cit.*, 121.

44 *Maid of Genoa* (1820), reviewed by H. Barton Baker, *The Old Melodrama*, 335. Cited in Booth, 68.

45 Hyman, *The Tangled Bank*, 146.

moviehouses become very much alike in any case—was the reading audiences gave to this "reality," which in practice clothed the most bizarre sort of fantasy. The deformed evil of Frankenstein's monster, pursued by a lynch mob, the sinking of a battleship with all hands rallied 'round the flag, a poor girl victimized by wealth and cynicism—these are images which press upon our perceptions and bequeath to our privacy special demands on feeling. Melodrama allows us to carry emotions to their extremes. (The duple rhythm, lyrics, and blues changes of rock music may be doing quite the same thing for young people today.)

Yet at the same time the relevance of any piece of popular culture (rock, comics, posters, melodrama) is a trapped, doomed victim of rapid stylistic transience. What appears on the surface to be "real" has always been reconstituted into an extremely artificial collection of abbreviated forms and shorthand messages skillfully combined to do their job on our emotions. Their efficacy is short lived, and outdated ephemera turns quickly into something else again. American films of the fifties, for example, now strike us like cultural artifacts—the Orphan Annie mugs of the Eisenhower years. James Bond soon becomes Hawkshaw the detective. Outdated ephemera is ridiculous.[46]

[46] For a list of representative melodramas and their sources see Appendix II.

3

It Is Not a Good Book, My Son

"My son," said a thoughtful father with a fair bald head and a kind blue eye, "I observe with feeling of deep regret that you have been reading *Bow Legged Jack; or The Road Agent's Retreat.* It is not a good book, my son, and a continued perusal of such literature may wean you from the path which leads to success and honorary position. It would break my poor heart, John Henry, to have you become a road agent or pirate or a burgler for the mere pittance that such callings bring to those who pursue them, when there are such grand opportunities for your energy and talent in this great country. Lay that book aside and be patient, my son, and in time you may be able to steal the entire capital of a great bank."

—*Philadelphia Press*, ca. 1880

Since the time of Samuel Richardson (whose *Pamela* was commissioned by a pair of London booksellers), many authors have written frankly for a great market of readers unmolded by refinements of prose tradition. Stephen Marcus' fascinating study of Victorian pornography[1] spelled out certain salient features in one largely unexamined genre; blended into the candid period prose are characterizations (and plots) which could have come only from Dickens. The stories also contain specificities of class relationships that are far less common among the niceties of "popular" fiction.

Such fields of subliterature have been most often served by writers uncelebrated in English courses. Usually composing at great speed, these men turned out innumerable stories for modest fees, commissioned by publishers who thought in terms of a pre-sold market, or at least an audience for whom the quality of writ-

1 Marcus, *The Other Victorians.*

37

ing was not a factor which might affect purchase. (For a short summary of this field see Appendix III.)

As we shall see, subliterature shares several elements with early movies: a guaranteed audience, simplistic stories and characterizations, middle-class morality, genres, the costumes of melodrama, and plots like exoskeletons. What appears most striking is that amid all this trivia there developed a particular kind of mimed action-description that impressively anticipates the strengths of analogous movie forms: Westerns, detectives, and adventure yarns.

A boyishness permeates most of this material,[2] yet it should not mislead us into any notion that all these works were written specifically for adolescents. Education raised standards of literacy largely by teaching the young, but parents, too, stumbled over primers and then turned to reading substance which maintained their interest by reinforcing their fantasies. Publishers' efforts to identify and exploit such fields become more visible by the turn of the century, when "back-of-the-book" advertisements itemized series stories and *kinds* of books which *kinds* of publishers were circulating. At this stage juvenilia becomes self-apparent.

Of course some books are born juvenile (*Frank Merriwell*), some achieve juvenilia (*The Three Musketeers*), and some have juvenilia thrust upon them (*Huckleberry Finn*). The young people's market, especially in growing cities, was clearly affected by developing interests and enthusiasms of a new industrial, urban age. Ensuing cultural changes help to explain "trends" of subliterature, like frontier scouts to cowboys to cowboy detectives to city detectives; or balloons to airplanes to interplanetary travel. In *The War in the Air* (1908), H. G. Wells motivates the aero-

---

[2] I cannot work out any design that would make girls' books relevant to my thesis. There were lady authors of dime novels. (Louisa May Alcott, for instance, wrote them for *Loring's Tales of the Day*.) However, these are little different in form from the male writers. The later counterparts to the *Rover Boys* and *Frank Merriwell* (like Laura E. Richards' many series [*Honor Bright, Hildegarde-Margaret*], the *Little Colonel* books of Annie Fellows Johnston, the *Meadow-Brook Girls*, the *High School Girls*, the *Madge Morton* series, the *College Girls, Grace Harlow*) either parallel the boys' adventures or else they are atmosphere sketches. Try Miss Richard's *Captain January*. Sometimes they follow the experiences of young ladies entering new phases of life. I confess I have not read them all, but something like Mrs. L. T. Meade's *A Sweet Girl Graduate* (1910) emphasizes information and social maneuvers.

nautical enthusiasm of his hero by explaining how it was "driven home" by the cinematograph, his "imagination stimulated" by a six-penny edition of the classic *Clipper of the Clouds* by George Griffith. He learned of actual flights "by means of the magazine page of the half-penny newspapers or by cinematograph records."

There are many as yet undefined relationships between what we call literature and subliterature. Just as the detective story grew out of Poe and Doyle, and the western from James Fenimore Cooper,[3] lesser-known titles become germinal to later forms (each of which, of course, has its movie equivalent). A Frenchman, Louis S. Mercier, wrote what is perhaps the earliest utopian novel of the future, published in English in 1772: *Memoirs of the Year Two Thousand Five Hundred*. Like the ideas of Flammarion in *Lumen*, Mercier's conceptions of technological change affected many later writers. Flammarion could be said to be a predecessor of C. S. Lewis and Mercier of Arthur C. Clarke.

Within genres (for example, fantasy), there are subgenres (spiritualism, occultism, lost worlds, xenophobic paranoia, science fiction), and subsubgenres (religious science fiction, technological science fiction, political science fiction, which often blends with lost-world fantasy), etc.[4]

Distinctions between kinds and levels of writing were sometimes blurred by audience enthusiasms. Lincoln and Seward read dime novels. The president said that *Maum Guinea and Her Plantation Children* by Mrs. Netta V. Victor was "as absorbing as *Uncle Tom's Cabin*." Among literary critics, however, the dime novels and pulps remained less than artful, if only because they purveyed predigested daydreams. But this is what commercial films have always done, and these have their partisans too. We

---

[3] Compare the introduction to Cooper's *The Prairie* with the first page of *Deadwood Dick the Prince of the Road, or The Black Rider of the Black Hills* (Beadle's Half Dime Library I, 1, 1877. Reproduced in Johannsen, *The House of Beadle and Adams*, I, 252.)

[4] Fantasy fiction needs a published history. For references see Everett F. Bleiler, *The Checklist of Fantastic Literature*, Chicago, Shasta, 1948; Bradford N. Day, *The Supplemental Checklist of Fantastic Literature*, Denver, B. Day, 1966; Lyle H. Wright, *American Fiction 1876–1900*, San Marino, Calif., The Huntingdon Library, 1966. The interested reader is referred to catalogues of Kaleidoscope Books, P.O. Box 699, El Cerrito, Calif. 94530.

may yet discover an *auteur* theory of pulp. Too, many authors, especially those who graduated from the literary basement to higher paid "slicks" (more clay in the paper), have often argued that the cheaper medium only betrays skeletons of design which the middle-class consumer magazines learned to clothe.

The relation of story to its circumstances of production can be highlighted in two ways. First, major publishers publicly emphasized very specific "standards." The following instructions were distributed by Erastus Beadle to hopeful authors:

> So much is said, and justly, against a considerable number of papers and libraries now on the market, that we beg leave to repeat the following announcement and long standing instructions to all contributors:
>
> Authors who write for our consideration will bear in mind that
>
> We prohibit all things offensive to good taste in expression and incident—
>
> We prohibit subjects of characters that carry an immoral *taint*—
>
> We prohibit what cannot be read with satisfaction by every right-minded person—old and young alike—
>
> We require your best work—
>
> We require unquestioned originality—
>
> We require pronounced strength of plot and high dramatic interest of story—
>
> We require grace and precision of narrative, and correctness in composition.
>
> Authors must be familiar with characters and places which they introduce and not attempt to write in fields of which they have no intimate knowledge.

Except for its call to originality (!), such an ukase reads surprisingly like the premises of the Motion Picture Production Code as composed in the 1920's: (1) No picture shall be produced which will lower the moral standards of those who see it. Hence the sympathy of the audience shall never be thrown to the side of crime, wrong-doing, evil, or sin; (2) Correct standards of life, subject only to the requirements of drama and entertainment, shall be presented; (3) Law, natural or human, shall not be ridiculed, nor shall sympathy be created for its violation.

In both instances the producers appear to have made some effort to adapt their merchandise to the presumed standards not necessarily of the country, but of their audience. (Of course, many potboilers did not fall within such strict moral claims. Prostitutes did not have to die of unspeakable diseases or to plunge suicidal daggers. When story series became standardized good advertising and common sense often required major villains to live and fight another day. For example, a five-book series by Guy Boothby featured a diabolical master of occult science named Dr. Nikola.)

Another consequence of such rules underlines a second point: these requirements demanded simple characterizations, high dramatic interest, action growing out of place, and precise, strong plotting. This is the very soul of melodrama, if melodrama can be said to have a soul.

Plotting was paramount. Publishers often "suggested" lines to follow (as they did for comic strips and later for movies). When an episodic story was running well an author might be asked to stretch it beyond the originally proposed number of installments. If it commenced to fail an unanticipated rescue might save the readership (Figure 8).

The adaptation of plot to production line was epitomized by Edward M. Stratemeyer, author of a hundred and fifty juveniles who started the Stratemeyer Syndicate in 1906. This amounted to a pulp factory in which its founder supplied plots to writers who performed anonymously to order and length. This method regurgitated much of the *Bobbsey Twins*, *The Motor Girls*, *The Outdoor Girls*, *Tom Swift*, *The Motor Boys*, *Baseball Joe*, *The Rover Boys*, *Six Little Bunkers*, *Bunny Brown*, and many, many dime novels.

Since Stratemeyer owned the original copyrights he would often reuse the same plots after a decent interim, changing only names, locale, and the epidermis (so that a horse, say, would become an airplane). With such a continuity of authorship many names (Laura Lee Hope, Arthur M. Winfield, Roy Rockwood) have boasted a longevity that defies medical science, although some have bequeathed their heritage to blood descendants. Thus the current *Tom Swift* series is written by Victor Appleton II.

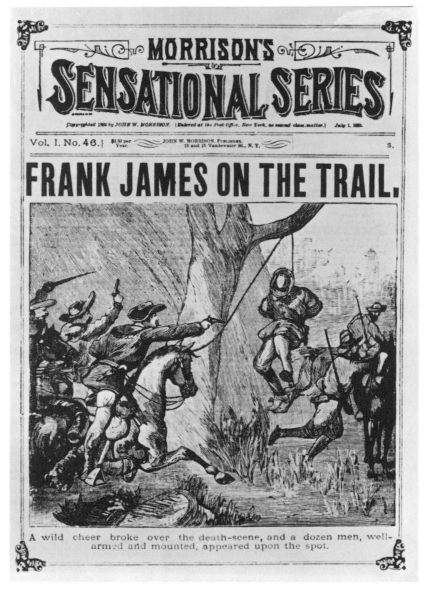

MORRISON'S

SENSATIONAL SERIES

Copyrighted 1882 by *JOHN W. MORRISON.* [Entered at the Post Office, New York, as second class matter.]   July 1, 1882.

Vol. I. No. 46. | $2.50 per Year. ——— JOHN W. MORRISON, Publisher, 13 and 15 Vandewater St., N. Y. ———   S.

FRANK JAMES ON THE TRAIL.

A wild cheer broke over the death-scene, and a dozen men, well-armed and mounted, appeared upon the spot.

FIG. 8. A precursor of the Saturday afternoon serial was the dime novel. Illustrated above is a typical example, this one dating from 1882.

Among the ensuing masses of head-over-heels prose most of the devices of fictive description, continuity, and point-of-view reappear, now writ clumsily large. Violent actions were performed so quickly they escaped language. Dickens cliff-hangers stumbled between chapters. Parallel-plotted stories joggled gracelessly from point to point.

The more striking, then, is one particular characteristic of sub-literature, a quality which reappears too frequently to be explained away either as stemming from accident or out of a singular talent. This phenomenon—a sort of mimed movement which transcends frenzied, muddled violence—appears noticeably among the stories of Nick Carter, Detective.[5]

Carter was exceptionally strong, an excellent fighter who wrestled and fenced brilliantly. He neither drank nor smoked; he had no vices at all. With women he was truthful and gallant. His mastery of disguises rivaled (and perhaps derived from) Hawkshaw in Tom Tyler's melodrama, *The Ticket-of-Leave Man*.

Russell Coryell, son of one of Nick Carter's many authors, described his father's method of work. "The climax of each story was worked out backward, situation by situation to the beginning. Situation was always more important to him in detective stories than character. . . . As a result, his characters never took the bit in their mouth and altered his stories for him. He made them do what he had planned they should."[6]

The consequences of such a *modus* appear early in the series in such a germinal work as *Nick Carter, Detective* (1891). Here the hero is following two suspicious "swarthy, ill-conditioned fellows." Walking past them to an avenue two hundred feet ahead, Nick stops in a hallway and changes his disguise. The men separate, the one called "the captain" jumping on a streetcar and taking a stand on the rear platform with his back to the interior, as though fearing he might be followed.

A car was coming up the avenue. It had to pass between Nick and the car that the captain had boarded.

[5] This exception to the general mudpuddle of action-description first appeared as a name in the Street and Smith dime novels of the 1870's. He emerged in full grandeur, however, on September 18, 1866, with the publication of *The Old Detective's Pupil; or the Mysterious Crime of Madison Square* in the *Street and Smith Weekly*. Originally Carter was written by John Coryell, a cousin of Ormond Smith, who was one of the partners. In 1889 the series was picked up by Frederick Marmaduke Van Renssaleer Dey, who wrote a twenty-five-thousand-word story a week. The series ran until the 1920's, ghosted by many authors, including Frederick William Davis and Eugene T. Sawyer. More recently Nick has returned in paperbacks and as a movie for TV.

[6] *Nick Carter, Detective*, xv.

For a moment, Nick would be screened from view from the platform of the down-town car.

He utilized the moment to the best advantage.

He leaped nimbly into the street and succeeded in getting two doors away before the cars had passed each other.

When they had passed, he was standing idly before the door of a "gin mill" leisurely picking his teeth as though he had just come out.

Presently he walked down the street, rather rapidly, to be sure, but not fast enough to excite the suspicion that he was following anyone.

Soon a second car overtook him, and he got upon the front platform.

The two cars were less than a block apart, and the detective could see his man clearly.

At Fourteenth street the captain turned and abruptly entered the car on which he was riding and passed out upon the front platform.

Here the spasmodic flashing of a match presently denoted that he was lighting a cigar.

Then, with a quick run, Nick left his car and overtook the one in which the captain was a passenger, and going inside, seated himself at the forward end.

"This is more comfortable," he thought. "It is much less work to watch him from here."

Block after block was passed, but the captain showed no sign of leaving the car, nor did he, until it reached the end of the route at the Astor House.

The he stepped off and boarded a south-bound Broadway car, upon which he remained until it reached South Ferry.

There the captain took the Hamilton Ferry boat, landed in Brooklyn, and started away down the street along the water-front.

Nick followed for a mile or more, when suddenly the captain turned and went out upon a pier.

"He will stop and look around when he gets out there," thought Nick, "so I will wait here."

He dodged into a deep shadow close to the water's edge, just where a boat was tied by a rope to a cleat upon the dock.

"The Very Thing!" thought Nick.

In an instant, he had untied the rope and seized one of the oars; the next, he was sculling the little craft rapidly and silently along the shadow of the pier.

Suddenly, the man whom he was following paused. Then, turning, he came to the edge of the pier and looked over, full at Nick.

To be sure, the writing is prosaic and sometimes clumsy, but—excepting a pair of "thought Nick's" and one inexcusable concern on Carter's part for his own comfort—the entire passage describes a continuous mimed sequence, truncating the passage of time as necessary. It is executed in terms of visible detail: dock cleats and gin-mill doors and the shadow of the pier. With a minimum of trouble it would translate into a motion-picture script, and details are quite as explicit as pictures where necessary ("the spasmodic flashing of a match"; "[he] succeeded in getting two doors away before the cars had passed each other"). Of course the passage is neither momentous nor "significant," but it is the genesis of that "niggling, reaming" style which Manny Farber described with such effect in a famous essay in which he contrasted the "water buffalo" directors of choreographed violence with the movie "action men," Chandler and Hammett, whose best sequences were built on the pulps.[7]

Comparisons between Nick Carter and Dashiell Hammett (who began his stories in a pulp entitled *Black Mask*) are fruitful and extend beyond a similarity of name between Carter and Nora Charles's husband. Nick Carter combines the suavity of Nick Charles with the toughness of the Continental Op. Except for the element of disguise (which soon departs the field), the stories are often remarkably similar, and even certain crimes have counterparts. For example, as with Brigid O'Shaughnessy in *The Maltese Falcon*, Dey (presumably the author) has a villainess employ confederates to mislead the police. These people betray her, and she hires Carter to help regain her "property." Nick discovers the meaning of the "dingus" (Sam Spade's term) and finally turns his client in (*Nick Carter's Mysterious Case, or the Road House Tragedy*, 1896). Carrying it all back a step farther, *The Murder in Forty-seventh Street, or Nick Carter, Detective* (1891) uses a plot spinoff from *The Mystery of the Speckled Band*, or (back again) *The Murders in the Rue Morgue* (Figure 9).

The Carter stories often show a particular interest in the geog-

[7] Manny Farber, "Underground Films," *Commentary*, November, 1947.

NICK HURLED HIM AT THE RUFFIANS

YOU BO. EH? WELL LOOK AT THIS!

FIG. 9. Perhaps the most famous of the pulp fiction heroes was Nick Carter, Detective, whose descendants included such masterful movie luminaries as Sam Spade (Humphrey Bogart) and Nick Charles (William Powell). The illustration above is from *Nick Carter, Detective*, published by Macmillan in 1963.

raphy of a given situation, as if to make every possible effort to insure a reader's necessary three-dimensional familiarity with the terrain so that he understands the murder locale as characters wander about its grounds. In *Nick Carter's Mysterious Case, or The Road House Tragedy* the author is so concerned that he diagrams the points of reference:

C ┌─────────────────┐ D
  │   │
B └─────────────────┘ A

and then refers to Corner C, Corner D, and so forth.

Space (as it is described by terrain) figures with remarkable frequency among these stories. It seems almost to follow from Erastus Beadle's requirement that authors "must be familiar . . .

46

with places that they introduce and not attempt to write in fields of which they have no intimate knowledge." However, we know that many writers were altogether ignorant of the settings for their fiction. A more likely explanation for emphases on movement in space may arise from the combination of reader interest with (by elimination) the few options left a pulp author.

An early instance of topography and action appears in James L. Bowen's *The Mohegan Maiden, or the Stranger of the Settlement; A Story of King Phillip's War* (Dime Novel No. 117, February 12, 1867). Fleeing from Indians, a young man drops down a tree trunk into a gulley.

> . . . the pine grew from a shelf on the face of the almost perpendicular wall, springing out of the wall at a point where a growth of bushes indicated the existence of a foothold for soil. A stone loosened in his efforts at exploration went crashing down, sending up echoes from the gulf underneath, to warn him that the base of the cliff was yet far beneath him. It did more, for a shout followed from below which was followed by a responsive shout from above:— the Narragansetts were still there; and as the faintest streaks of dawn now began to shimmer in the air overhead, the hunted man realized that it was full time for him to find a spot of retreat in the face of the wall. . . .
>
> Continuing the search carefully along the thin shelf, he found it to narrow and end abruptly, but a few feet along the wall, arrested by a huge buttress of a rock. Several indentations, however, were found along the path, which offered ample shelter from observation, . . .

In this passage, as with Nick Carter's shadowing, the dimensionality of the protagonist's situation seems to operate in a fashion unique to such stories. Introspection among pulp heroes is nonexistent. However, they are constantly required to make professional decisions about what to do next. The wisdom of such judgments (and it is often a life-or-death matter) is likely to rest on considerations of timing, distance, and obstacles. For example, the present story continues with the attempt by a savage to lower himself down to the ledge by a suspended thong.

> Crouched down close in his little cave, he was somewhat sur-

47

prised to perceive a fissure in the wall at his back, which darkness hitherto had hidden. It was large enough to admit his body, but should he use it? If penned up there the indian would have easy work in dispatching him, so he crouched still lower; and the swaying body of the Narraganset now half appeared before the hidden chamber.

The hero (whose name appears to be Archibald) seizes the scout's knife and kills him with it.

Now armed with a keen knife, he had no fears of any hand-to-hand encounter, and turned back through the fissure to behold a powerful savage already standing before it, having slid down from above with the agility of a cat. The Narragansett had caught sight of his antagonist first, and, with a wild war whoop, bounded into the narrow entrance of the cavern. Archibald could not fall back before the sudden onslaught, pressed closely by the savage, whose stalwart form so filled the passage as to darken the chamber. This gave the white the momentary advantage of taking a position for defense . . .

And so on. This sort of narrative prose lent itself to equivalencies in the silent (or the non-lip-synced) film because everything was quite visible. If "thought" transpired, its character became immediately evident by the most pragmatic measures. No Leon Edel simultaneous experience or Siegfried Kracauer Material and Mental Continuum. The pulp hero used his head with singular determination in existential response. In one of Guy Boothby's Dr. Nikola books (*A Bid for Fortune*, 1895) an imprisoned man must reconstruct the location of his cell by identifying and locating the sources of sound around him.

. . . a cock in a neighboring yard on my right crowed lustily, a dog on my left barked, and a moment later I heard the faint sound of some one coming along the street. The pedestrian, whoever he might be, was approaching from the right hand, and what was still more important, my trained ear informed me that he was lame of one leg, and walked with crutches.

Closer and closer he came. But to my surprise he did not pass the window; indeed, I noticed that when he came level with it the sound was completely lost to me. This told me two things; one, that the window, which, as I have already said, was boarded up, did not look into the main thoroughfare; the other, that the street itself ran along on the far side of the very wall to which my chain was attached.

In some respects sound was a coordinate of space, and action writers were aware of this. Mimed actions are often punctuated with sound effects. In *Nick Carter's Enemy; or Bringing a Murderer to the Gallows* (1902) one entire chapter ("A One-Sided Battle") is devoted to a shootout between the detective and his quarry as the two glide silently about the Hudson, the evening silence marked only by rifle bursts.

Zane Grey, who numbered Robert Louis Stevenson and Cooper among his favorite authors, uses sound interestingly in a "repeat" incident in *Spirit of the Border*. In Chapter 24 a rifleman tries to pick off targets in a distant camp. His shots are "Crack!" The same action is redone in Chapter 25, this time from the point of view of the campers, who hear the gun reports as "Spang!"

All of these narrative passages, tied as they are to the outside world as it may be seen or heard and to simple, consistent motives,[8] seem to be functions of one great, ineluctable plot. The requirements of the master plot were simple. First, hook the audience into concern for the well-being of the protagonist, then provide plenty of action and peaks of suspense. Set up the end in the beginning. Roger Garis[9] recalls his father's constant emphasis on "laying pipes"—inserting early in any story a requisite plant in a paragraph that could be reintroduced as necessary to resolve later matters. This was another way of accomplishing what Russell Coryell remembered his own father managing by "working out the story backwards." It was Poe's technique for managing Dupin's deductions in *The Murders in the Rue Morgue*.

Under such conditions of concise organization the reins set on characters' behaviors are apparent. The people live in an enclosed, predictable world: the universe of melodrama which has been the mainstream of the entertainment film. Such a world lacks the open-

8 A Frank Merriwell villain cries, "It's too late for me to turn back now. I started wrong at school, and I have been going wrong ever since. It's natural for me; I can't help it." Bert L. Standish, *Frank Merriwell Down South* (1903).

9 Roger Garis, *My Father Was Uncle Wiggley*.

endedness of "modern" fiction and its movie derivatives, as well as Kracauer's "found stories." All of those demand unpredictability.

Spontaneities of behavior and outgrowths of character complexities call for time and thoughtful preparations. A writer paid by the line could not type clean, first-draft copy for the printer if he was engaged with any hero likely to get out of control. (The mechanics of large-scale commercial film production made similar demands on tight scripts.) Conversely, the "ragged edges" and "things that have no bearing" which E. M. Forster worried over in *Aspects of the Novel* clearly take several drafts to produce, just as "improvising" film directors who make production decisions on location require special circumstances (or far less money) with which to work.

The Victorian period saw many carryovers from the dime novel into other forms. Ned Buntline, for example, dramatized his Buffalo Bill material at Niblo's Garden in New York in 1872 with a popular melodrama actor impersonating the western hero. Later, in the eighties, when Cody's Wild West Show was on tour, its promoter hired another dime novelist, Prentiss Ingraham, to write publicity. Cody himself appeared in at least one film.[10]

Augustin Daly's *Under the Gaslight* was written up for the *Fireside Companion*, a "family paper" of George Munro. Boucicault's *Led Astray* was published as a novel by "John Thompson, Comedian" in *Family Story Paper*. Boucicault collaborated with Charles Reade in the writing of *Foul Play* (London, 1868; *Fireside Library*, 101, June 30, 1881).

As the motion picture began to assemble itself into a competitive form able to do battle with the printed page, it sometimes cannibalized the dime novel. In France a popular Nick Carter series appeared in 1908 under Victorin Jasset, commencing a film genre for which movies seemed to have special affinity.[11] Fantômas, beloved of the Surrealists, arrived here in book form

---

10 Sell and Weybright, *Buffalo Bill and the Wild West*.

11 Compare Kracauer's enthusiasm for sleuthing as a "cinematic motif." Kracauer, *Theory of Film*, Chap. 15.

around 1910.[12] Louis Feuillade's popular series began three years later.

In 1907 the *Atlantic Monthly* published a defense of the dime novel by Charles M. Harvey which ends with an equation of melodrama to the ethos of the times:

> Was everything that the dime necromancers told us melodrama? Much of it unquestionably was. But an age which has seen a nation rise from Balboa's isthmus at the wave of a Prospero Wand from Washington; which has recently looked on while a people in the Carribean committed suicide; which is watching Nome's argonauts up under the Pole star, rival the glories of the Comstock under the reign of Mackay, Flood and O'Brien; and which held its breath in November, 1906, while Roosevelt and Crocker, like Castor and Pollux, rushed to rescue the nation from a New York editor who had built up an army in a night, has no right to object to melodrama in fiction.[13]

History as melodrama. It is, of course, not an uncommon notion today. Melodrama itself has always purported to be history (that is, *real*) yet remained a victim of built-in cultural obsolescences which pose special problems in a society that seems to need constant replenishments of vicarious thrills. If we can come to laugh so quickly at what we favored only months before (last year's television series), then certain strains are bound to be imposed on the resilience and the longevity of our feelings. For one thing we are continually called upon to rediscover that we were foolish when we were younger, and our children are reminded of it too. Furthermore, we have to stay in touch with the new popular culture (directed at our kids) because the old will not hold up. We cannot grow old (in the Elizabeth Barrett sense) with our own melodrama because it cannot grow old with us. The flats keep dating on the sets of our cultural scene.

The melodrama of history escapes this insufficiency: today's newspaper is always "relevant." Broadcasters market news as drama, and movie hucksters scheme like their forefathers to mer-

12 Marcel Allain and Pierre Souvestre, *Fantômas* (New York; Brentano's, 1910).
13 Harvey, "The Dime Novel in American Life," *Atlantic Monthly*, C, July, 1907.

chandise drama as news. Today we are seeing a developing tension between the requirements of film and television entertainment and their capacities to sustain plot contrivances that are not out of Edward Stratemeyer; horses may be metamorphosized into rockets, but the idea of a terrestrial range war is unacceptable to us in a way that was not true for Teddy Roosevelt.

A narrative scheme which plots individual actions so that they relate causally to great, even transcending, events must be almost as old as religious ritual, and it permeates the poetic epic. Yet as heroic proportions shrank from Oedipal to human dimension, credibility risks have come to enter fictional patterns where singular acts have to produce society-restoring consequence. The atomic-ridden world cannot be rescued by answering the riddle of the sphinx. Consequently, connections between the two story elements—the macro and micro versions of a writer's cosmos—must be constructed with extreme care. And historically, melodrama has not been a very sophisticated popular form.

Under such circumstances one critical strategy has been to identify melodrama with a bourgeois ideological unity that preceded the breaking up of literary consciousness (around 1850) into individual tragic awarenesses of the world.[14] By such measures melodrama exists as a vestigial survival of an earlier time, only as alive now as are shared middle-class values: a calcified style existing independent of individual authorship.

Jean-Luc Godard assumes something of this posture when he identifies western entertainment film (and much Communist too) as melodrama in one permutation or another.[15] Where such a generalization breaks down is in the notion of melodrama as a monolithic form that has neither affected other expository styles nor itself been subject to change.

Indeed, melodrama has maintained certain structural features through its several incarnations. (The present study testifies to some of them.) At the same time other kinds of writing and performance are hardly exempt from many of these same qualities.

14 Roland Barthes, without referring to melodrama, puts this general argument cogently in *Writing Degree Zero*.
15 *Cf. Vent d'Est.*

Further, the very surface and spatial elements uppermost in its tradition themselves amount to requisite constituents of naturalism. The evidence must be tangible.

From this perspective it is the *later* developments in narrative form which are bourgeois as they focus attention on states of individual consciousness. (Is it possible that the amalgamations of action and introspection in a film like Resnais's *La Guerre Est Finie* may nurture a more auspicious development in movie narrative than *Vent d'Est* and *Pravda?*) Neither can the closed universe of Nick Carter be altogether set aside, for Cocteau's worlds were equally contained. So are myths, and so, for that matter, are most of Godard's characters in any period.

Melodrama is not so easily dismissed, at least as long as it calls up allegorical/psychological dispositions yet operative deep in the consciousness of western man. When this happens melodrama is *perceived* as nonstereotyped conflicts that must somehow be resolved through confrontation. We see such resolution as the last consequence of a moral energy which is expressed in a universe where incidents determine and control characters. The world of representational filmmaking, like that of Erastus P. Beadle, may, in the long run, be just such a place.

4

Space, Time, and Victorian Prose

The notion of finding movies in old documents, fiction or otherwise, is hardly original. Eisenstein studied hieroglyphs, Japanese painting, dance, Dickens, and Maupassant. In *Through the Vanishing Point,* McLuhan and Parker speak of "shots" in the opening lines of *Dover Beach.* A recent study identifies visual sequences in *Beowolf.*[1] Indeed, the rather literary term *cinematic,* first conceived to distinguish movies from other forms, seems to be popping up across campuses in English literature classrooms. Not immune from the politics of body counts, professors are discovering that motion pictures may effectively serve to "highlight" one or another aspect of novels, plays, and poems.[2]

Victorian writing is especially interesting for its filmlike predispositions. It concludes at the moment of the movies' entrance and of the new medium's popular thrust into the ghettos, clothed in garbs of narrative form that were adapted from popular precedents—like an old costume for a roadshow melodrama that has been resewn for a new production.

We gain a workable sort of perspective by allowing the idea of storytelling technique to transcend disciplinary boundaries, especially if we try to view it as one among several evidences of mounting dispositions: concerns with fragmenting exposition in terms of time sequence, with particularizing the images and their compositions, with the interjection of "movement," and with the externalization of memory into tangible, "visible" experience.

---

1 See Eisenstein, *Film Form*; McLuhan and Parker, *Through the Vanishing Point*; Renoir, "Point of View and Design for Terror in Beowolf," in Fry, ed., *The Beowolf Poet.*

2 In my university there are additional film courses in psychology, education, art history, television, world literature, French, and creative writing.

The reader is reminded that such appearances occur quite un-systematically among writings which vary greatly in quality. Further, a technique of scrutinizing the past through the camera eye poses its own particular set of pitfalls, especially when much of the subject matter has the transience of popular entertainment.[3] On the other hand, this material fossilizes almost on sight, which may hold it in place for our purposes—a sort of last, Victorian self-exposure.

Action, however slight, is what film is about. Traditionally, prose has occupied itself with speech, reflection, and imagistic description. The last element, in point of fact, was quintessential to the nineteenth-century novel, and readers would open a new book in confident anticipation of the particular descriptive skills of a familiar author.

There was good reason for the relative absence of any note-worthy attention to movement, and especially to the kinds of move-ments so endowed with significance to the exposition that we think of them as action. Significance simply took other forms. What mattered was either what people said to each other or what hap-pened to them in a general way, beyond the visual evidence of the event itself. Thus when we do come across transitive verbs and that sense of the present attenuated far enough by syntax to allow its necessary descriptive execution, the discovery has almost a jarring note in a book like Cooper's *The Prairie*.

> Feeling for his knife, he took the blade between a finger and a thumb, and cast it with admirable coolness at his advancing foe. The keen weapon whirled a few times in the air, and its point meet-ing the naked breast of the impetuous Sioux, the blade was buried to the buck-horn haft.

A pair of such sentences is rare in Cooper, and—for the time—nonexistent elsewhere. What is striking is not the blade held between finger and thumb or its destination. It is the "whirled a

---

3 "Say, Mag, I'm stuck on yer shape. It's outa sight" (*Maggie, A Girl of the Streets*, Ch. 6); "The ordinary detective goes to pot-houses to arrest thieves; we go to artistic tea-parties to detect pessimists" (*The Man Who Was Thursday*); "My mother did not forbid it, but said it would be better not to on the whole, and that Tom Eakins was somewhat hipped on nudes" (response of a society girl on being asked to pose).

few times in the air" (what animators call the *in-betweens*) and then the last "buck-horn haft": visual punctuation to the violence.

Cooper, too, is a harbinger of the turn-of-the-century authors whose melodramas and romances often centered about a protagonist existing beyond the customary cultural contexts, where significance is attached to minimal "movements." But these new men of action were usually fuzzed by a prose that was inadequate to their behavior and often drew on the excuse of a temporary dislocation of the senses in order to cover. An example is drawn from Richard Harding Davis' *Soldiers of Fortune.*

> It was impossible to tell in the uproar which followed how many or how few had parties to the plot. The mob, shrieking and shouting and leaping in the air, swarmed across the parade ground, and from a dozen different points men rose above the heads of the people and harangued them in violent speeches.

More commonly, such passages share the "before and after" quality of certain lantern-slide entertainments like the Phenakistoscope that simulated movement by projecting in quick succession the start of a dramatic event and then its conclusion. In *Rupert of Hentzau*, Anthony Hope has his hero bested in a quick brawl:

> I hardly know what followed: there came—all in a confused blur of instant sequence—an oath from Rupert, a rush from me, a scuffle as though someone sought to hold him back; then he was on me; I felt a great thud on my forehead, and I felt nothing more.

(As emotion mounts, Hope can become even less adventurous; he stages the climactic sword fight between Rupert and Rudolf Rasendyll behind a closed door.)

Obviously, the talent of any given author will define in some measure what he writes about and how well he may respond to the demands of his material. On the other hand, just where and how emotion attaches itself to movement seems to be both a function of the kinds of meanings an author is after and the ways in which observed behavior can accommodate these needs.

In contrast, motion pictures impose our perceptions onto tangible, rather than once-removed, "realities"; they endow *every-*

56

thing with meaning, bypassing the value orderings which are implicit in language. But such a talent can be almost overwhelming. Dramaturgy must accept or reject material to particularize experience. At some stage words have usually been part of any film production whose material was predefined,[4] but we can distinguish some narrative difference between prose and pictures by comparing the use of words for either purpose. Consider, for example, the following scripted scene (which was never used) from *L'Avventura*:

> The raft continues on its way toward shore. A shorter distance away, Claudia is floating on her back—basking in the sun with her eyes closed, almost motionless. Her arms are outstretched and only the very slightest movement of her fingers in the water is sufficient to keep her afloat. Suddenly, her hand comes in contact with something viscous . . . which seems to be a fish that has shot up to the surface of the water. At first, she merely withdraws her hand without bothering to see what it is, but since it persists in following her, she opens her eyes and notices something moving right next to her. Frightened, she lets out a tiny yelp. At that moment, directly behind the fish, Raimondo's rubber fins appear above the water, and she realizes that it is Raimondo. He removes his mask and breaks into a hearty laugh as Claudia playfully splashes some water into his face.[5]

Writing aside, it is difficult to "see" such a passage transposed into a novel. The presentness does not sound like fiction, which continues to use past tenses to describe the moment. More important, the attentions to mimed detail, the "very slightest movement of her fingers in the water," would assume other dimensions in a written story, where a writer's selectivity must endow those elements he does pick with special moment.

Film detail and its execution are even more marked if we examine a description after the fact, a postproduction script prepared for book publication by describing the projected image.

4 I am begging the question of off-the-cuff writer-directors like Griffith. Predefining movie narrative need hardly diminish its effects. Note Hitchcock. Interestingly, Hitchcock is particularly attracted to expressionist angles, visual symbols, continuity bridges, sets, clever lighting, and pacing—all techniques to direct (or misdirect) the attentive concerns of his audience. He is a first-class melodramatist.

5 Antonioni, *L'Avventura*, 151.

Paul is watching. Madeleine laughs and Elizabeth glances at him mischievously. Madeleine takes a pair of glasses out of her purse and hands it to Elizabeth. Paul rises and steps back over his seat, crossing behind Elizabeth and Madeleine.

Elizabeth blows on her glasses before starting to clean them with her gloves, which she drops. Paul shakes his fist at Catherine and caresses Madeleine's hair as he passes left behind them out of sight. Catherine, now visible, is reading a magazine. The song is now alternating with a man's voice. Madeleine fixes her hair, using both hands. The camera moves slightly to reveal Paul sitting on the other side of Catherine and pauses on the empty seat between Catherine and Madeleine. Paul's knees are up against the seat in front of him.[6]

This is more than the novel can stand, but nevertheless its direction was undertaken by Victorian writers with increasing frequency; their aim was to break movement down into minimally describable components and to order those units in such a way as to provide a certain continuous sweep to the sequence. Such writing appears most frequently among the adventure stories, where the occurrence of oddly-dated language helps to highlight an author's effort at the general effect.

A great fellow bounded upon the platform, and Leo struck him dead with one blow of his powerful arm, sending the knife right through him. I did the same by another, but Job missed his stroke, and I saw a brawny Amahagger grip him by the middle and whirl him off the rock. The knife, not being secured by a thong, fell from Job's hand at that moment, and, by a most happy accident for him, lit upon its handle on the rock, just as the body of the Amahagger, who was undermost, struck upon its point and was transfixed thereon.

That was a moment in H. Rider Haggard's *She*. In *White Fang*, Jack London centrally poses the problems of prose mime for himself. White Fang is a wolfdog whose story is told in descriptions of his actions and London's conception of the dog's feelings. In a climactic battle between White Fang and a bulldog in Dawson City,

He caught Cherokee with head turned away as he whirled more

6 Godard, *Masculine Feminine*, 129.

slowly. His shoulder was exposed. White Fang drove in upon it; but his own shoulder was high above, while he struck with such force that his momentum carried him on across the other's body. For the first time in his fighting history, men saw White Fang lose his footing. His body turned a half-somersault in the air, in the effort to bring his feet to the earth. As it was, he struck heavily on his side. The next instant he was on his feet, but in that instant Cherokee's teeth closed on his throat.

Here, two years after *The Great Train Robbery*, we have accomplished not only the *in-betweens*—the half-somersault and catlike twist—but, more important, a three-dimensional frame of reference. White Fang misses the jump because of his height and exposes himself to Cherokee by losing time in landing on his side. The picture is filling in.

Stereographs, song slides, and popular chromolithographs placed great store in the important (and "picturesque") moment. Nineteenth-century melodrama was equally partial to heightening its effects by "freezing the frame"—literally, stopping the action for a momentary tableau of special effect. (Similarly, action is immobilized in Kabuki theater, and nineteenth-century composers and choreographers sometimes organize their movement about moments of static emphasis.)

In the same vein the period's authors would sometimes interrupt, and sometimes conclude, their chapters with posed compositions. The device is common in Dickens, whose enthusiasms for theatrical melodrama and its techniques were immense. An example is drawn from the ending of Chapter 15 in *Oliver Twist*:

> The gas-lamps were lighted; Mrs. Bedwin was waiting anxiously at the open door; the servant had run up the street twenty times to see if there were any trace of Oliver; and still the two gentlemen sat, perseveringly in the dark parlour, with the watch between them.

In *Bleak House* (ending to Chapter 48), Dickens is quite public about his painting function.

> [A Roman statue] is pointing at a table, with a bottle (nearly full of wine) and a glass upon it, and two candles that were blown out suddenly, soon after being lighted. He is pointing at an empty chair,

and at a stain upon the ground before it that might be almost covered with a hand. These objects lie directly within his range. An excited imagination might suppose that there was something in them so terrific as to drive the rest of the composition, not only the attendent big-legged boys, but the clouds and flowers and pillars too—in short the very body and soul of Allegory, and all the brains it has—stark mad.

Elsewhere in the previously cited Richard Harding Davis novel, the hero and his eventual bride first show their affection by shaking hands in front of some workers "smiling in appreciation of the tableau." The Picture Scene is also used to underline repressed feeling in the moment of mute pose. In *The Scarlet Pimpernel*, Armand St. Just meets his sister Marguerite on the shores at Kent. Watching, he reflects on her life, marriage, and unhappiness:

> Marguerite was gazing out towards the sunset. Armand could not see her face, but presently it seemed to him that something which glittered for a moment in the golden evening light, fell from her eyes upon her dainty fichu of lace.

Although *The Clansman* was a major source for *The Birth of a Nation*, its plot differs at various turns. One of these is a Picture Scene of such intensity that—abetted by the idea of photography —it becomes interiorized. A daughter of the Old South and her mother are both raped. To preserve their secret the ladies jump from Lover's Leap. Later, the girl's body is examined by a doctor in Book 4 Chapter 1:

> "We shall see," said the doctor, adjusting his instrument. "I believe that a microscope of sufficient power will reveal on the retina of these dead eyes the image of this devil as if etched there by fire. . . ."
> "What do you see?" asked the younger man, bending nervously.
> "The bestial figure of a negro—his huge black hand plainly defined—the upper part of the face is dim, as if obscured by a gray mist of dawn,—but the massive jaws and lips are clear—merciful God!—yes! It's Gus!"

Needless to say, the evidence is enough to hang Gus.

At one point in *Lessons With Eisenstein* the director's class is considering a proper vantage from which to film the murder scene from *Crime and Punishment*, to be executed in a single camera set-up as an exercise. An angle "slightly above" the action is agreed upon. " 'You've done well, anyway,' says Sergei Mikhailovich, 'in that none of you has suggested a flat frontal viewpoint. Picture to yourself such a scene shot from straight head-on—the action would be depicted without any author's relation to it of any kind.' "[7]

The matter of what shall be seen, then, involves the "place" from which it is witnessed as well as an order to its disclosure. A common film practice, used as long as directors wished to maintain stable orientations for the audience (less true today), has been to provide a general frame of reference (Establishing Shot) and then to approach details within the known scheme. Mary McCarthy has commented on this practice in the novel, emphasizing the author's commitment to a necessary period of commune with Nature before introducing his characters.[8] In *The Prairie*, Cooper begins with a general discussion of the Louisiana Purchase and the motives of emigrants from the east. Then he picks up a distant wagon train, singles out its leader and some passengers, and concludes with a meeting on the plain between Natty Bummpo and the travelers. Similarly, in *Kidnapped* (Chapter 2), Stevenson establishes an overview of the countryside and then cuts in to increasingly magnified details.

> On the afternoon of the second day, coming to the top of a hill, I saw all the country fall away before me down to the sea; and in the midst of this descent, on a long ridge, the city of Edinburgh smoking like a kiln. There was a flag upon the castle, and ships moving or lying anchored in the firth; both of which for as far away as they were, I could distinguish clearly.

The matter of the prose detail, the close-up, has been given thoughtful consideration elsewhere. Gerald Noxon cites Huysmans in *La Bas* to show how naturalism indulged very explicit successions of details. Noxon emphasizes the sophistication with camera angles to be found in *Madame Bovary* and proposes a

[7] Nizhny, *Lessons With Eisenstein*, 98.
[8] McCarthy, "Reflections: One Touch of Nature," *The New Yorker* (January 24, 1970), 45.

basis for this new skill in Flaubert's trip with Maxime Du Camp to photograph artifacts in Alexandria (1849–51).[9]

The detail and color changes were common practice among commercial novelists of the 1890's. An example is randomly drawn from F. Marion Crawford's *Children of the King* (Chapter 1):

> Then the big sails will hang like curtains from the long slanting yards, the slack sheets will dip down to the water, the rudder will knock softly against the stern-post as the gentle swell subsides. Then all is of a golden orange colour, then red as wine, then purple as grapes, then violent, then grey, then altogether shadowy as the stars come out—unless it chances that the moon is not yet full, and edges everything with silver on your left hand while the sunset dyes fade slowly to darkness upon your right.

By the end of our period the devices of the close-up have become altogether functional to the short story. In *A Municipal Report* (1910), O. Henry employs details ("a dollar bill pasted with a strip of blue tissue paper"; "a yellow horn overcoat button with frayed ends of coarse twine") quite as Alfred Hitchcock uses his Maguffin, a tangible piece of evidence on which the audience will pin its interests and anxieties.

A. Conan Doyle, in a sense, developed the entire personality of Sherlock Holmes from the abilities of his detective to single out details and to infer their significance: "My eyes tell me that on the inside of your left shoe, just where the firelight strikes it, the leather is scored by six almost parallel cuts." In a detective story the close-ups become the "clues." ("Across this bare space there was scrawled in blood-red letters a single word—RACHE.") *The Filigree Ball*, a 1903 mystery novel, finds its solution in print so tiny and disguised (in the lines of an engraving) that it must be enlarged with a magnifying glass.[10]

What is seen depends, of course, on who is seeing it. Galsworthy

---

[9] Noxon, "The Anatomy of the Close-up," *Journal of the Society of Cinematologists* (1961) I, 1–24. If further evidence be needed Noxon's emphasis on archaeological photography is substantiated by period photographs of building details, inscriptions, and manuscripts. See also Trutat, *La Photographie Appliquée à l'Archaéologie.*

[10] Green, *The Filigree Ball: Being a full and true account of the solution of the mystery concerning the Jeffrey-Moore Affair.*

is an early author to compose scenes with varying points of view on the part of his characters. Additionally, he places them in space so that their physical relation to one another and to the settings furthers the story. A family scene is thus described in *The Man of Property* (Part I Chapter 1):

> At the window his father, James, was still scrutinizing the marks on the piece of china. . . . Aunt Ann looked up from her velvet chair. . . . Putting the bowl pettishly down on the piano, he let his eyes wander to the group by the door.

His characters are from a like social stratum, and Galsworthy's vantage is almost always eyelevel, usually a medium shot.

> Aunt Ann turned her old eyes from one to the other. . . . In turn, the three brothers looked at Ann. She was getting shaky. . . . "Want of exercise," muttered James, his eyes on the china. . . . Swithin fixed him with a stare. . . . June shook hands one by one with her three great-uncles, and turned to Aunt Ann. . . . The girl passed on, and Aunt Ann looked after her slim little figure. The old lady's round, steel-grey eyes . . . followed her wistfully amongst the bustling crowd.

Perhaps because their central focus is on the conflict of attitudes ("views"), the stories of the bourgeoisie seem especially to indulge angles of view. Both *Tonio Kröger* and *Death in Venice*, for example, appear in the final analysis to be *about* how things are seen. In the earlier *Buddenbrooks* (1901), Mann, a master of *mise en scène*, diligently places his family in the context of their objects: sofa ("straight, white enameled, . . . with yellow cushions and a golden lion's head at the top"), Sevres inkstand ("in the shape of a black and white hunting dog"), tapestries ("sky-blue background against which, between slender columns, white figures of gods and goddesses"), candelabra ("a tall gilt candlestick with eight flaming candles, besides those in the silver sconces on the table").

In a Preface to the 1897 edition of *The Nigger of the Narcissus*, Joseph Conrad defined his craft with a phrase that reappears, curiously, out of the mouth of D. W. Griffith in many film histories:

> My task which I am trying to achieve is, by the power of the written word to make you hear, to make you feel—it is, before all, to make you *see*. That—and no more, and it is everything.

In theory Conrad's strategy is to isolate and "freeze" his material for our scrutiny.

> To snatch in a moment of courage, from the remorseless rush of time, a passing phase of life, is only the beginning of the task. The task approached in tenderness and faith is to hold up, unquestioningly, without choice and without fear, the rescued fragment before all eyes in the light of a sincere mood.

In practice Conrad draws assorted details in the context of a narrative line which, like a good movie editor, he controls in terms of sequence, duration, and tempo. The result is often to establish lines of movement within an overall composition.

> The door clattered open; a broad stream of light darted out on wondering faces; a warm whiff of vitiated air passed. The two mates towered head and shoulders above the spare, grey-haired man who stood revealed between them, in shabby clothes, stiff and angular, like a small carved figure, and with a thin, composed face. The cook got up from his knees. Jimmy sat high in the bunk, clasping his drawn-up leg. The tassel of the blue night-cap almost imperceptibly trembled over his knees.[11]

As early as 1902, Henri Bergson had considered the mechanics of the motion picture as a descriptive referent to his own conception of time: the notion of significant "still" shots which together make up our sense of movement and of duration.

> Form is only a snapshot view of a transition.[12]
> [The] mechanism of our ordinary knowledge is of a cinematographical kind.[13]

> The cinematographical method is therefore the only practical method, since it consists in making the general character of knowledge form itself on that of action, . . . action is discontinuous, like every pulsation of life; discontinuous, therefore, is knowledge.[14]

11 Conrad, *The Nigger of the Narcissus.* Garden City; Doubleday, 134.

12 Bergson, *Creative Evolution.* New York; Modern Library, 328. This section originates in a series of lectures on the history of the idea of time, dating from 1902–3.

13 *Ibid.,* 332.

14 *Ibid.,* 333.

64

The last statement seems to be a kind of epistemological reversion to Zeno of Elea, expressed in terms of film technology. The idea that movement is most effectively "created" through the ordering of a succession of static pictures finds re-expression among early film theoreticians in a Preface to the German edition of Pudovkin's *Film Technique*. Pudovkin places his emphasis on our perception of (apparent) motion:

> I claim that every object, taken from a given viewpoint and shown on the screen to spectators is a *dead object*, even though it has moved before the camera. The proper movement of an object before the camera is yet no movement on the screen, it is no more than raw material for the future building up, by editing, of the movement that is conveyed by the assemblage of the various strips of film. Only if the object be placed together among a number of separate objects, only if it be presented as part of a synthesis of different separate visual images, is it endowed with filmic life.[15]

Such an approach was not unknown to Ellen Glasgow in 1905:

> Will's eyes travelled helplessly around the room, seeking in vain some inspiration from the objects his gaze encountered. The tin safe, the basket of feathers, the pile of walnuts on the hearth, each arrested his wandering attention for an instant, and he beheld all the details with amazing vividness.[16]

The nineteenth-century sense of movement-as-exposition was manifest in the "camera zooming" kind of aerial shot which some-times introduced a story. In the previously mentioned *Reflections*, Mary McCarthy actually speaks of the "camera sweeping down to focus"[17] on Don Abbondio in the first chapter of Manzoni's *I Promessi Sposi* (1828).

Frank O'Connor is even more explicit about the camera zoom. "Long before the cinema [Hardy] had invented a technique that anticipates it, as in the wonderful chapter of *The Mayor of Caster-bridge* where the two women see the town for the first time. Hardy begins in the air above the town as it lies in the evening light; fades to a horizon view of it, far away and flat upon the plain; and then

15 Pudovkin, *Film Technique*.
16 Glasgow, *The Deliverance*, 519.
17 McCarthy, *op. cit.*

tracks slowly toward the tree-lined rampart that surrounds it and down the main street, pausing now and again to give a close-up view of bow windows, shutters, or inn signs."[18] What O'Connor does not note is that the long movement is carefully rationalized in Chapter 4 of Hardy's 1886 novel. Two ladies are viewing the town from the summit of a hill a mile distant. Their perspective is then "picked up": "To birds of the more soaring kind Caster-bridge must have appeared in this fine evening as a . . ." etc.

As technology came to expand the possibilities for previously unsuspected ways of seeing, overhead shots were able to take a more explicit turn. In H. G. Wells's *The War in the Air* (1908), Bert Smallways descends toward a German village in a balloon.

> As he trailed, Bert saw ahead of him one of the most attractive little towns in the world—a cluster of steep gables surmounted by a high church tower and diversified with trees, walled, and with a fine large gateway opening out upon a tree-lined high road. All the wires and cables of the countryside converged upon it like guests to entertainment. It had a most home-like and comfortable quality, and it was made gayer by peasant folk, in big, pair-wheeled carts and afoot, who were coming and going, besides an occasional mono-rail car; and at the car-junction, under the trees outside the town, was a busy little fair of booths. It seemed a warm, human, well-footed, and altogether delightful place to Bert. He came low over the tree-tops, with his grapnel ready to throw and so anchor him.

Lacking birds or balloons, the Victorian novelist was sometimes hard pressed to maintain the integrity of his camera movements. For example, in Arnold Bennett's *The Glimpse* (Book 2, Chap. 16), the protagonist dies and his soul departs the corpse. But Bennett, like (say) Howard Hawks, is a social observer who stays at a conversational level with his characters even in mortality. Thus the spirit never rises beyond eyelevel as it backs away: "I was prevented by the intervening foot of the bed from seeing more than the upper half of what lay on it, and by the dimensions of the doorway from seeing anything in the bedroom except the bed."

18 O'Connor, *The Mirror in the Roadway*, 245–46. Joseph Warren Beach also considers the affinity of *The Mayor of Casterbridge* to film technique, but his concern centers on mimed action and "exciting scenes." See Beach, *The Technique of Thomas Hardy*, 143–57.

We have always had a go at moving camera shots, albeit gravity controlled, just by walking. Lewis Carroll wrote a traveling shot into his introduction of Humpty Dumpty:

> The egg seems to get further away the more I walk towards it. . . .
>
> So she went on, wondering more and more . . . at every step, as everything turned into a tree the moment she came up to it, and she quite expected the egg to do the same.
>
> . . . However, the egg only got larger and larger, and more and more human; when she had come within a few yards of it, she saw that it had eyes and a nose and a mouth; and when she had come close to it, she saw clearly that it was HUMPTY DUMPTY HIM-SELF.

Movement, then, like camera angles, was to be perceived either by the author, independent of his creations, or by the characters. The whole matter of a development of singular points of view became an issue central to the next development of the novel.

Let us compare two stair ascents. In *The Four Feathers*, A. E. W. Mason describes his hero as a shy boy proceeding to bed up the staircase. The scene is viewed by an elderly friend, who is essentially the author's reporting device.

> And this is what he saw: Harry Feversham, holding in the centre of the hall a lighted candle high above his head, and looking up toward the portraits of the Fevershams as they mounted the walls and were lost in the darkness of the roof. A muffled sound of voices came from the other side of the door panels, but the hall itself was silent. Harry stood remarkably still, and the only thing which moved at all was the yellow flame of the candle as it flickered apparently in some faint draught. The light wavered across the portraits, glowing here upon a red coat, glittering there upon a corselet of steel. For there was not one man's portrait upon the walls which did not glisten with the colours of a uniform, and there were the portraits of many men. . . . Father and son, in lace collars and bucket boots, in Ramillies wigs and steel breastplates, in velvet coats, with powder on their hair, in shakos and swallow-tails, in high stocks and frogged coats, they looked down upon this last Feversham, summoning him to the like service.

The pictures are vivid in the flickering candlelight; the details are explicit and organized toward a particular effect. The call of the portraits to Harry Feversham is clear. What is absent is Harry's response. Indeed, the novel centers about that very ambiguity which is introduced here in the first chapter. (Alexander Korda's movie, in restructuring the scene to show the boy staring at the portraits, shifts the entire point of Mason's story.)

Consider next a stair climb by the first-person protagonist whose perceptions altogether make up an 1888 novel by Édouard Dujardin, *Les Lauriers Sont Coupés*:

> The stairs; the first steps. Supposing he has left early; he some-times does; but I have got to tell him the story of my day. The first landing; wide, bright staircase; windows. He's a fine fellow, friend of mine; I have told him all about my love-affair. Another pleasant evening coming on. Anyway he can't make fun of me after this. I'm going to have a splendid time. Now why is the stair carpet turned up at the corner here? A grey patch on the line of upward red, and on the red strip looping up from step to step. Second story; the door on the left. *Office.* I only hope he hasn't gone; no chance of running him to earth if he has. Oh well, in that case I'd go for a stroll down the boulevard. No time to lose; in![19]

Here the details of ascent, whatever the calls of the carpet on our attention, have been so subordinated to a narrator's interior monologue that fiction (temporarily) seems to escape the province of film. Dujardin's anticipation of James Joyce and Virginia Woolf mark off a sharp distinction from the earlier prose style against whose methods, in the words of Leonard Woolf, Virginia "re-volted—pre-eminently the fiction of Galsworthy, Wells and Ben-nett—and created the first versions of her own form and methods which ultimately and logically developed into those of *The Waves* and *Between the Acts.*"[20]

There are certainly two ways to consider the relation of the modern novel to film techniques. On the one hand, a consequence of the Dorothy Richardson–Joyce–Woolf innovations was the de-

[19] Édouard Dujardin, *We'll To the Woods No More*, 6–7.
[20] Woolf, *Downhill All the Way*, 58–59. Woolf says his wife initiated her technique with the short stories written between 1917 and 1921. Although Joyce published the first parts of *Ulysses* in 1914, Woolf claims that Virginia first read it in manuscript in April, 1918. Dorothy Richardson started *Pilgrimage* in 1911.

ployment of words and syntax previously used to report and to describe and now dedicated to less visual and journalistic purpose. It could be argued that film had to develop similar techniques and to free itself equally from the occupation of visually accurate reportage before it could "catch up." Thus entire and consistent stylizations, as found in the nonnarrative experimental films of the 1920's, set a precedent for such controls of composition, editing, exposure, and narration as Resnais reintroduced to the story film in *Last Year at Marienbad*.

On the other hand, what the stream-of-consciousness device does preeminently is altogether to interiorize exposition so that reader and writer have undertaken to share the events of the novel *as it happens* in the most direct experiential confrontations; in other words, to make the book like a good movie.

In *The Mirror in the Roadway*, Frank O'Connor proposes that as the nineteenth century saw an increasing isolation of the novelist (as "artist") from the mainstream of middle-class society, this change was marked in devices of exposition and style (like the camera zoom) which personalized his perception of the story. We err if we require a necessary intensity and depth of experience to eminate only from the subjectivity of a character's perceptions or from the author *qua* character (the expressionist traditions in film). The notorious movie *Lady in the Lake*, in which the camera "is" Phillip Marlowe, does not equate with the modern novel. *All* films that "work" are like the modern novel. For with movies, to use Leon Edel's description of modern prose, the experience is "simultaneous rather than consecutive"[21]—simultaneous in the representation of interior and exterior reality. Of course, in either case the experience is both, but it is simultaneous first.

An inclination on the part of experimental filmmakers and their spokesmen is to identify the very notion of "story," certainly popular story, so fully with Aristotelian unities that it becomes irrelevant to the modern sensibility. Thus Stan Brakhage equates story films with popular salon painting of the last century, and P. Adams Sitney proposed that "Dramatic time, with its nineteenth-century

21 Dujardin, Introduction by Leon Edel.

illusion of 'real time,' can no longer sustain radical art."[22] The extremes of imaginative execution among experimental filmmakers may, indeed, have shut them off from story as it falls within our province here (although I suspect that they are largely playing with snippets of the old narrative line), but on examination the nineteenth-century novel proves far more varied in its manipulations of time than might have been supposed. Another historian of the avant-garde, Parker Tyler, is more open to this possibility. "What we know as narrative time in fiction (film or otherwise) is strictly formal, selective, and summative; it is representation by the memoranda of signs."[23]

The idea of linking one episode with another in a long prose work is obviously as old as the form. Until the nineteenth century the common practice was to divide material, rather as separate acts were assembled on the stage.

As we have seen, theater saw radical changes in continuity techniques during the 1800's, changes which both required and were affected by the developments of stage machineries, by lighting techniques, and by severe alterations in building architecture. Something of the same thing happened to narrative prose with the appearance of popular periodicals and newsprint. Novels published as continued stories required the authors to investigate fanciful kinds of connections between episodes. In Chapter 17 of *Oliver Twist*, Dickens was quite open about the new style:

> As sudden shiftings of the scene, and rapid changes of time and place, are not only sanctioned in books by long usage, but are by many considered as the great art of authorship, an author's skill in his craft being, by such critics, chiefly established with relation to the dilemmas in which he leaves his characters at the end of every chapter; this brief introduction to the present one may perhaps be deemed unnecessary.

The chapter has been used most commonly to punctuate a break in a sequence of continuous time (as fades and dissolves telegraphed it to the audience of a commercial film through the fifties).

22 Sitney, "Ideas Within the Avant-Garde," *Film Library Quarterly*, III, 1 (Winter, 1969–70), 7.
23 Tyler, *Sex, Psyche Etcetera in the Film*, 15.

A simple practice was to set up the next chapter in front, as Edith Wharton connects Chapters 5 and 6 in *The House of Mirth*.

> . . . "Won't you devote your late afternoon to it? You know I must be off tomorrow morning. We'll take a walk, and you can thank me at your leisure."

> The afternoon was perfect. A deeper stillness possessed the air . . .

The time-gap may be as long as years (as in *Tonio Kröger*), but an elliptical cut is equally workable if the material requires only that unnecessary movements be discarded, like getting a movie actor into the elevator on one floor and then off at another without bothering with the ride. Chesterton does it with a cab between Chapters 1 and 2 in *The Man Who Was Thursday*.

> The cab whisked itself away again, and in it these two fantastics quitted their fantastic town.

> The cab pulled up before a particularly dreary and greasy beer-shop.

Or the transition could make a very short time link just to reorder the author's approach. Again from *The House of Mirth*, Chapters 1 and 2:

> . . . heedless of his protestations, she sprang into the rescuing vehicle, and called out a breathless order to the driver.

> In the hansom she leaned back with a sigh.

Cut rapidly enough and you have a montage. Dickens holds his effect together with the recurrent image of Dr. Manette in *A Tale of Two Cities*:

> It was the popular theme for jests; it was the best cure for headache, it infallibly prevented the hair from turning grey, it imparted a peculiar delicacy to the complexion, it was the National Razor that shaved close: who kissed La Guillotine, looked through the window and sneezed into the sack. It was the sign of the regeneration of the human race. It superseded the Cross. Models of it were worn on breasts from which the Cross was discarded, and it was bowed down and believed in where the cross was denied.

> It sheared off heads so many, that it, and the ground it most polluted, were a rotten red. It was taken to pieces, like a toy-puzzle for

71

a young Devil, and was put together again when the occasion wanted it. It hushed the eloquent, struck down the powerful, abolished the beautiful and good. Twenty-two friends of high public mark, twenty-one living and one dead, it had lopped the heads off in one morning, in as many minutes. The name of the strong man of Old Scripture had descended to the chief functionary who worked it; but, so armed, he was stronger than his name-sake, and blinder, and tore away the gates of God's own Temple every day.

Among these terrors, and the brood belonging to them, the Doctor walked with a steady hand; confident in his power, cautiously persistent in his end, never doubting that he would have Lucie's husband at last. Yet the current of the time swept by, so strong and deep, and carried the time away so fiercely, that Charles had lain in prison one year and three months when the Doctor was thus steady and confident. So much more wicked and distracted had the Revolution grown in that December month, that the rivers of the South were encumbered with the bodies of the violently drowned by night, and prisoners were shot in lines and squares under the southern wintry sun. Still, the Doctor walked among the terrors with a steady head. No man better known than he, in Paris at that day; no man in a stranger situation. Silent, humane, indispensable in hospital and prison, using his art equally among assassins and victims, he was a man apart. In the exercise of his skill, the appearance and the story of the Bastile captive removed him from all other men. He was not suspected or brought in question, any more than if he had indeed been recalled to life some eighteen years before or were a spirit moving among mortals.

The transition may also operate to change an angle of view, as in Chapters 1 and 2 of *Kidnapped*:

> ... Just as I came on the green drove road running wide through the heather, I took my last look at Kirk Essendean, the trees about the manse, and the big rowans in the kirkyard where my father and mother lay.
>
> On the afternoon of the second day, coming to the top of a hill, I saw all the country fall away before me down to the sea.

The reverse angle is a common switch, useful in introducing material which has been obscured by the previous angle of view. This occurs in Chapters 6 and 7 of *The Scarlet Pimpernel*:

... as she sailed out of the room. ... Only Sir Andrew Foulkes ... noted the curious look of intense longing ... with which ... Sir Percy followed the retreating figure of his wife.

Once outside the noisy coffee-room, alone in the dimly-lighted passage, Marguerite Blakeney seemed to breathe more freely. She heaved a deep sigh, like one who had long been oppressed with the heavy weight of constant self-control, and she allowed a few tears to fall unheeded down her cheeks.

An increasing preoccupation of the period was with simultaneity, the sense of various story elements separate in locale yet equally relevant to the narrative. Perhaps the most familiar early instance is out of Thackeray's *Vanity Fair*: "Darkness came down on the field and city; and Amelia was praying for George, who was lying on his face, dead, with a bullet through his heart."

H. G. Wells tended to stagger somewhat in his scene shifts, as in Book 2 Chapter 1 of *The War of the Worlds*, where he was prone to call attention to the process ("Look Ma! Both hands!"):

In the first book I have wandered so much from my own adventures to tell you of the experiences of my brother that all through the last two chapters I and the curate have been lurking in the empty house at Halliford whither we fled to escape the Black Smoke. There I will resume.

Within a given chapter transitions in space could be attended to with general variations on "Meanwhile, back at the ranch." George Washington Cable does this in Chapter 40 of *The Grandissimes*:

Frowenfield rather spoke to himself than answered: "If I had know that, I should have—." He checked himself and left the place.

While the apothecary was gathering these experiences, the free spirit of Raoul Innerarity was chafing in the shop like an eagle in a hen-coop.

A more elaborate technique sought to smooth the switchover by matching something common to each location, like an image:

On a Monday noon a small company of horsemen strung out along the trail from Sunk Creek to gather cattle over the alloted sweep of range. ...

> Upon a Monday noon likewise (for things will happen so) some tearful people in petticoats waved handkerchiefs at a train that was just leaving Bennington, Vermont.

The above is from Chapter 9 of Owen Wister's *The Virginian*. In *The Four Feathers* (Chapter 25), the device comes more easily when there is a single figure and a common function:

> At the time when Calder, disappointed at his failure to obtain news of Feversham from the one man who possessed it, stepped into a carriage of the train at Assouan, Lieutenant Sutch was driving along a high white road of Hampshire across a common of heather and gorse.

The cut might be marked with asterisks, which had something of the effect of interior chapter breaks. Again from *The Four Feathers*, Chapter 7:

> And so, turning on his side, he slept dreamlessly while the hosts of the stars trampled across the heavens above his head.
>
> *   *   *   *   *
>
> Now, at this moment Abou Fatma of the Kabibish tribe was sleeping under a boulder on the Khor Gwob. He fell asleep as the sun rose.

The sound bridge was another workable technique to move from place to place. Dickens, again, used it, even dissolving the effect connecting Chapters 6 and 7 of *Bleak House*.

> So I said to myself, "Esther, Esther, Esther. Duty, my dear!" and gave my little basket of housekeeping keys such a shake, that they sounded like little bells, and rang me hopefully to bed.

> While Esther sleeps, and while Esther wakes, it is still wet weather down at the place in Lincolnshire. The rain is ever falling, drip, drip, drip, by day and night, upon the broad, flagged terrace pavement.

Wells, too, uses sound effects in *The Invisible Man* to carry his story from one location to another and from Chapter 17 to Chapter 18. Again, he doesn't quite catch up with himself.

> "I'll show him," shouted the man with the black beard, and suddenly a steel barrel shone over the policeman's shoulder, and five

bullets had followed one another into the twilight whence the missile had come. As he fired, the man with the beard moved his hand in a horizontal curve, so that his shots radiated out into the narrow yard like spokes from a wheel.

A silence followed. "Five cartridges," said the man with the black beard. "That's best of all. Four aces and the joker. Get a lantern, someone, and come and feel about for his body."

Dr. Kemp had continued writing in his study until the shots roused him. Crack, crack, crack, they came one after the other.

"Hello!" said Dr. Kemp, putting his pen into his mouth again and listening. "Who's letting off revolvers in Burdock? What are the asses at now?"

A further step in this kind of spatial editing was to integrate the different story points for the sake of contrast and tensions. An early effort is apparent in Chapter 14 of *The House of Mirth*, whose first section ends, "And in the unwonted overflow of his feelings, [Seldon] left a cousinly kiss upon her cheek." Section two then proceeds, "At Mrs. Fisher's, through the cigar-smoke of the studio, a dozen voices greeted Seldon." From here the author cuts back to her first location: "Alone with her cousin's kisses, Gerty stared upon her thoughts. He had kissed her before—but not with another woman on his lips."

This technique is further refined in one of the final sequences of *The Octopus* (1901). Book 2 Chapter 8 describes the aimless wanderings of a destitute farm woman, starving to death with her small daughter in San Francisco, and Norris intercuts these scenes against a luxurious dinner in a nearby mansion. Each "shot" is detailed in progressively shorter length until, finally, the farm mother dies and the dinner is completed, each in single paragraphs. Edwin S. Porter was to use the same technique in *The Ex-Convict* (1904) and *The Kleptomaniac* (1905), both films which protested the social structure. In a bevy of last-minute rescues, Griffith refined the scheme, including the progressively shortened scenes.

In less elaborated form *Sister Carrie* (1900) concludes with a similarly pointed contrast, achieved again by the idea of simultaneity. Carrie peers out the window of her apartment at the Waldorf. Charles Droet, her first lover, departs his own hotel for a date with a chorus girl. Mrs. Hurstwood is seen in a Pullman car, pleased with her wealthy new son-in-law. Hurstwood enters a room in a Bowery flop house, there to gas himself.

A more complicated maneuver for the writer was to handle several simultaneous events as they occurred in one location. Wells, again, calls attention to the problem by admitting it. (In Chapter 12 the invisible man has been intimidating a doctor and vicar whom he surprised running through his personal papers in the parlor.)

> It is inevitable that at this point the narrative should break off again, for a certain very painful reason that will presently be apparent. And while these things were going on in the parlour, and while Mr. Huxter was watching Mr. Marvel smoking his pipe against the gate, not a dozen yards away were Mr. Hall and Teddy Henfrey discussing in a state of cloudy puzzlement the one Iping topic.
>
> Suddenly there came a violent thud against the door of the parlour, a sharp cry, and then—silence.

Some years earlier the control both of space and of simultaneous sounds was masterfully executed in the fair scene of *Madame Bovary* (1857), when a Best Manure award is bestowed at the moment Rodolphe takes Emma's hand. A dignitary's long speech is intercut with the couple's tawdry flirtation. Interestingly, Edel finds this scene a "distinct foreshadowing of cinema."[24]

Harry Levin is even more explicit. "The embryonic material for his novel comprised some 3600 pages of manuscript. The demiurgic function of reducing that mass to its present form might be compared to the cutting of a film; and rather than speak of Flaubert's 'Composition' in the pictorial sense, we might refer, in kinetic terms, to montage."[25]

It may be remembered that Leon Edel spoke of the steam-of-consciousness experience as simultaneous. Substituting the variable of subjective experience (with its free access to time past) for that of presently experienced space, we come upon another range

24 Dujardin, Introduction, xvi.
25 Levin, *The Gates of Horn*, 261.

of transitions which are curiously filmlike. Thus in *Tonio Kröger* (1903), the narrator watches from a distance as his two old loves dance a quadrille. While the orchestra leader calls the French steps, Mann uses a recurring phrase to trigger his flashback: *"Moulinet des Dames!"* The writer remembers how he disgraced himself before the girl years ago while they danced the moulinet.

A flashback may equally well be worked by calling on the image appropriate to both times. The madeleine is notorious, but novelists far more ordinary than Proust had the same impulse years before.

> In another minute, with a great clatter of hoofs, we sprang clear of the hamlet, and were well on the road to Melle, with Poitiers some thirteen leagues before us. . . .
>
> I remember three years before this time, on the occasion of the famous retreat from Angers . . . I well remember on that occasion riding, alone and, pistol in hand, through more than thirty miles of the enemy's country without drawing rein.

The above quotation comes from Chapter 5 of Stanley Weyman's *A Gentleman of France* (1893). More elaborately, the collaborations between Ford Madox Ford and Joseph Conrad pointed their attentions very directly to this line of inquiry, for if all time was equally accessible, and if a "straight-ahead" chronology wasn't requisite,

> It became very early evident to us that what was the matter with the Novel, and the British Novel in particular, was that it went straight forward, whereas in your gradual making acquaintanceship with your fellows you never do go straight forward. . . . To get . . . a man in fiction you could not begin at his beginning and work his life chronologically to the end. You must first get him with a strong impression, and then work backwards and forwards over his past. . . .
>
> Life does not say to you: in 1914 my nextdoor neighbor, Mr. Slack, erected a greenhouse and painted it with Cox's green aluminum paint. . . . If you think about the matter you will remember in various unordered pictures, how one day Mr. Slack appeared in his garden and contemplated the wall to his house.[26]

The idea of putting together these various unordered pictures,

[26] Ford, *Joseph Conrad: A Personal Remembrance*, 192–93.

moving backward and forward, is readily apparent if we date the events in each chapter of a novel like *Lord Jim*.[27] Although one may find it practically easier to rearrange pages than picture and sound tracks, a case could effectively be made that movies are a more viable medium for this kind of manipulation.[28] Certainly recent films (*Je t'aime, Je t'aime*; *The Silence*; *Belle de Jour*) have impressively expanded the number of minimal cues by whose means we may be able to locate ourselves in terms both of time and the relative subjectivity of the experience.

The matter of accomplishing "unnatural" visual events commanded much attention in the nineteenth century. Stage illusions were developed both for their own sake (in magic shows) and as aids to the popular thrillers. Investigations of perception eventuated in a number of parlor toys (like the Japanese magic mirror, trick opera glasses, the thaumatrope, the Zoetrope, the Phenakistoscope). The refinement of lens systems and of new lighting techniques encouraged imaginative projections of lantern-slide tricks. Soon after its invention photography was being used to manipulate the reality it pretended to report.

Apparitions and ectoplasm have always figured in stories. They were essential to the Gothic novel, and Mary Shelley assembled her monster back in 1818. Soon magical effects in prose flourished. Dickens, who used stage illusions in his private plays and public readings, liked to dissolve bodies from mist, as in *The Christmas Carol*: "Whether these creatures faded into mist, or mist enshrouded them, he could not tell. But they and their spirit voices faded together. . . ." Indeed, swirls became traditional with vampires. For example, Bram Stoker's *Dracula*:

> . . . the whirling figures of mist and snow came closer, but keeping ever without the holy circle. Then they began to materialize till— if God have not taken away my reason, for I saw it through my own eyes—there were before me in actual flesh the same three women that Jonathan saw in the room, when they would have kissed his throat.

27 Beach, *The Twentieth Century Novel*, 362–63.
28 Beach took such a position as early as 1932 in *The Twentieth Century Novel*.

The eighties and nineties saw many transformations: youth to age, beast to man (and back), good to bad, visible to invisible (and back), ugliness to beauty. Marie Corelli's *The Soul of Lilith* (1897) could as easily describe an H. Rider Haggard heroine, or for that matter the ending of *Lost Horizon*.

> Lilith—his Lilith was withering before his very eyes! The ex-
> quisite body he had watched and tended was shrunken and yellow
> as a fading leaf,—the face, no longer beautiful, was gaunt and
> pinched and skeleton-like—the lips were drawn in and blue—and
> strange convulsions shook the wrinkling and sunken breast.

What elements did these strange creatures reconcile? Within our present context we might say that time was bound and then released in *She* (1887), *The Picture of Dorian Gray* (1891), and *The Soul of Lilith*, while mirror images of morality (with overtones of the unadmitted self) are given a public face in *Dr. Jekyll and Mr. Hyde* (1886), *The Island of Dr. Moreau* (1896), *The Happy Hypocrite* (1896), *The Invisible Man* (1896) and *Dracula* (1897). Such a body of sports would add an interesting footnote to the history of the unconscious, and perhaps an additional level of "simultaneous experience."

As naturalism pared its style into a sparer prose, the possibility of certain sorts of effects was diminished by tighter reins on metaphor. In an introduction to *Maggie: A Girl of the Streets*, Joseph Katz notes an early Sullivan County sketch whose techniques Crane came to eschew as "clever and witty expedients." Four men are sliding down a passage in a cave. "The swirling mass went some twenty feet and lit upon a level, dry place in a strong, yellow light of candles. It dissolved and became eyes."[29]

Henry James, on the other hand, didn't shy away from a dissolve. He would even incorporate it with a "dream balloon." In *The Lesson of the Master* (1888), Paul Overt is listening to the novelist St. George describe a young lady in whom both are interested.

> It seemed [to Paul] to show the art of St. George's admired hand,
> and he lost himself in gazing at the vision—this hovered there be-

29 Crane, *Maggie: A Girl of the Streets.*

fore him—of a woman's figure which should be part of the glory of a novel. But at the end of a moment the thing had turned into smoke, and out of the smoke—the last puff of a big cigar—proceeded the voice of General Fancourt, who had left the others and come and planted himself before the gentlemen on the sofa. "I suppose that when you fellows get talking you sit up half the night."

The device of giving visual evidence to thoughts had its counterpart in the dream balloons of cartoonists and in theatrical Vision Scenes. In prose, such scenes were common. For Winston Churchill in *The Crisis* they even had a kind of conversational currency in which *ideal* figured.

> . . . he was the ideal which you had in mind. The impression of him has never left it.
>
> "Hold the image of Abraham Lincoln in front of you. Never forget him."

A more fleshed-in Vision could develop something of the quality of a painting by David (himself an enthusiast of the theatrical panorama), as in *The Scarlet Pimpernel*:

> Before her mental vision there was absolutely nothing but Armand's face. Armand, whose life was in the most imminent danger, and who seemed to be looking at her from a background upon which was dimly painted the seething crowd of Paris, the bare walls of the Tribunal of Public Safety, with Focquier-Tinville, the Public Prosecutor, demanding Armand's life in the name of the people of France, and the lurid guillotine with its stained knife waiting for another victim . . . Armand! . . .

More profoundly, the Vision Scene could take a sounding on desire. In *Death in Venice*, von Aschenbach breaks off from staring at a man in Bavarian costume standing on a portico, after which

> He felt the most surprising consciousness of a widening of inward barriers. . . . Desire projected itself visually. . . . He beheld a landscape, a tropical marshland beneath a reeking sky, steaming, monstrous, rank. . . . Hairy palm trees rose . . . mammoth milkwhite blossoms floated. . . . Among the knotted joints of a bamboo thicket the eyes of a crouching tiger gleamed—and he felt his heart throb

with terror, yet with a longing inexplicable. Then the vision vanished.

George Heym (1887–1912), a German writer, has at least one short passage which both externalizes the dream and holds with equal vividness the body of the dreamer. Doctors are performing an autopsy.

> And while the blows of the hammer resounded on his head, a dream, the remnants of love in him, awoke like a torch shining into his night.
>
> In front of the large window a great wide sky opened, full of small white clouds that floated in the light, in the afternoon, quiet, like small, white gods. And the swallows travelled high up in the blue, trembling in the warm July sun.
>
> The dead man's black blood trickled over the blue putrescence of his forehead.[30]

As early as Georges Méliès, Vision Scenes were incorporated into motion pictures. Edwin S. Porter used the device, and it frequently appears in primitive animation from Emile Cohl to Felix the Cat. When film drew back from the techniques of theatrical staging, the balloons within a photograph widened to encompass the entire frame, thence to become the *audience's* vision.

Just how far the new technologies (first still photography and then the movies) restructured our senses of time, perception, interior fantasy, and the unconscious will never be sorted out. But there is ample evidence among writers that these new media figured persistently in novelists' ideas about the mind's operation. Noxon quotes Proust's notion of memory as accessible in the way a photographer "goes deliberately into his darkroom to develop the latent images in leisurely contemplation."[31] Thomas Dixon impressed his image of rape on the retina. Something of the same notion that moments of heightened emotion, violence, and death will impose some kind of tangible perpetuity on the physical environ figures in the period's spiritualism, which also used photography to document the ectoplasm.

[30] Heym, "The Autopsy," translated by Michael Hamburger, in Stephen Spender, ed., *Great German Short Stories.*

[31] Noxon, *op. cit.*, 17.

Terry Ramsaye, who himself says at one point "Thus it appears that Memory lives in mental motion pictures,"[32] quotes an undated editorial from the St. Louis *Post Dispatch* which underlines the feelings for time travel which motion pictures encouraged.

KINETOSCOPE MARVELS

The kinetoscope, we are told, has recently been made to run backwards, and the effects of this way of running it are truly marvelous. In his remarkable romance, *Lumen*, the imaginative French astronomer, Flammarion, conceives of spiritual beings who, by traveling forward on a ray of light, see, with the keen vision of the spirit, all that ray of light carried from the beginning of creation. . . .

It now seems that the kinetoscope is to make this wonderous vision possible to us. . . .[33]

Nicholas Camille Flammarion was a French astronomer-author who wrote a book in the early seventies about an interstellar race, *Masters of Time and Space*. During the nineties it was widely circulated in the United States in two editions.

Ramsaye also notes a meeting between H. G. Wells and the English inventor Robert W. Paul. After reading *The Time Machine* (1895) and conferring with its author, Paul submitted a British patent application (Number 19984, dated October 24, 1895). He proposed an elaborate theater in which spectators shifted and moved on platforms "to create the impression of traveling" while viewing a screen which would project enactments of time past, present, and future. The entertainment was to include lantern slides and films, along with color changes and weather effects. Even the idea of close-ups is prefigured, for the projection equipment would be mounted on "suitable carriages or trollies, upon rails provided with stops or marks, so as to approach to or recede from the screen a definite distance and to enable a dissolving effect to be obtained . . . in order that the scenes might be gradually enlarged."[34]

Ramsaye inquired of Wells whether direct experience with motion pictures motivated his descriptions in *The Time Machine*.

32 Ramsaye, *op. cit.* I, xlvi.
33 *Ibid.*, 159–60.
34 *Ibid.*, 152–58.

Wells could not recall, but if he had not seen a movie, he was surely writing one, including slowed, speeded, and reverse movements.

> Mrs. Watchett came in and walked, apparently without seeing me, towards the garden door. I suppose it took her a minute or so to traverse the place, but to me she seemed to shoot across the room like a rocket.

> As I returned, I passed again across that minute when she traversed the laboratory. But now her every motion appeared to be the exact inversion of her previous ones. The door at the lower end opened, and she glided quietly up the laboratory, back foremost, and disappeared behind the door by which she had previously entered.[35]

In *The First Man on the Moon* (1901), Wells manages even to accelerate vegetable growth on the lunar surface in the manner of time-lapse photography: "Every moment more of these seed-coats ruptured, and even as they did so the swelling pioneers overflowed their rent distended seedcases and passed into the second stage of growth."

The mind was becoming a camera system. Marie Corelli, a novelist of ambitious and sometimes extraterrestrial proclivities, explained in *The Soul of Lilith* the process that was to lead to Gus's execution in *The Clansman*. The speaker is a mindreader.

> "As the stars pattern heaven in various shapes . . . so you have patterned your brain with pictures or photographs of your past and your present. All your past, every scene of it, is impressed in the curious little brain-particles that lie in their various cells,—you have forgotten some incidents, but they would all come back to you if your were drowning or being hanged; because suffocation or strangulation would force up every infinitesimal atom of brain-matter into extraordinary prominence for the moment. Naturally your present existence is the most vivid picture with you.

The same equation is voiced in *The Little Colonel's Knight Comes Riding,* written for young girls by Annie Fellows Johnston:

> Again that flashing look that made his eyes deepen so wonderfully and curved the cynical lips into an altogether gentle and winning

35 Noted in Ramsaye,152–54.

smile. It seemed to photograph itself on Lloyd's memory, recurring to her again and again in the most unexpected moments.

George DuMaurier was very clear about the sources of "dreaming true" in *Peter Ibbetson* (1891):

> It was something like the "camera-obscura" on Ramsgate pier; one goes in and finds one's self in total darkness; the eye is prepared; one is thoroughly expectant and wide-awake.
>
> Suddenly there flashes on the sight the moving picture of the port and all the life therein, and the houses and cliffs beyond; . . . gay Liliputians walk and talk, their white teeth no bigger than a pin's point. . . . Not a detail is missed. . . . And what color it is! And all is framed in utter darkness. . . .
>
> It is all over; you come out into the open sunshine, and all seems garish and bare and bald and commonplace. All magic has faded out of the scene; everything is too far away from everything else; everyone one meets seems coarse and Brobdingnagian and too near. And one has been looking at the like of it all one's life!
>
> Thus with my dreams, compared to common, waking, everyday experience. . . .

It sounds like Walker Percy's *The Moviegoer!* DuMaurier explains the process in detail.

> Evidently our brain contains something akin both to a photographic plate and a phonographic cylinder, and many other things of the same kind not yet discovered; not a sight or a sound or a smell is lost; not a taste or a feeling or an emotion. Unconscious memory records them all, without our even heeding what goes on around us beyond the things that attract our immediate interest or attention.

With practice, Peter Ibbetson is finally able to transcend the time-bind of personal past into something like a racial memory, thus turning himself into an early version of the time machine. With his companion (who shares the dream although she sleeps elsewhere) Peter has "hobnobbed with Montaigne and Rabelais" and "slummed with Francois Villon." "We have even just been able to see, as in a glass darkly, the faint shadows of the Mammoth and the cave bear, and of the man who hunted and killed and ate them." But the mammoth is "blurred and indistinct like a composite photograph."

DuMaurier also points up a sense of the dreamer as spectator:

> I knew perfectly who I was and what I was, and remembered all
> the events of the previous day. I was conscious that my real body,
> undressed and in bed, now lay fast asleep in a small room on the
> fourth floor of a hotel garni in the Rue de la Michodière. I knew
> this perfectly; yet here was my body too, just as substantial, with all
> my clothes on; my boots rather dusty; my shirt collar damp with the
> heat, for it was hot.

Yet the dream is drama, and drama involves its audience, so the
event is simultaneous.

> Soon I discovered by practice that I was able for a second or two
> to be more than a mere spectator—to be an actor once more; to
> turn myself [Ibbetson] into my old self [Gogo], and thus be touched
> and caressed by those I had so loved.

Parker Tyler has contrasted two ideas about the movies: the
Siegfried Kracauer sense of film as reproducing the even and open
ended "flow of life," and Suzanne Langer's equation of movies
with the dream, "the dreamer himself and those perceived in
dreams seldom obey gravity and material bounds strictly; they
fade in and out as material bodies may do in film. . . ." (Tyler
finds both attitudes a Janus-faced representation, erring commonly in their assumption that the dominant function of the
medium is reportorial.)[36] Nevertheless, the two dispositions are
highlighted in DuMaurier's conceit, for his own vision is one continuous shot, more like the camera obscura than a movie: "In a
dream there are always breaks, inconsistencies, lapses, incoher-
ence, breaches of continuity, many links missing in the chain. . . .
There was nothing of this in my dream." Perhaps for this reason,
the dreams of DuMaurier-Ibbetson are curiously placid and emotion free, but for bliss.

Marcel Proust not only developed his images, he noted how
the position of his body is "loyally preserving from the past an
impression which my mind should never have forgotten, brought

---

36 See "Masterpieces by Antonioni and Bergman," in Tyler, *op. cit.* In *The Interpretation of Dreams*, Freud notes the editing predisposition of the dream, a technique
of implying causality through the ordering of events in time.

back before my eyes."[37] DuMaurier, too, prescribed a particular supine position to achieve "dreaming true," predating the James-Lange theory of emotions as expressed in William James's *Psychology: Briefer Course*.

Proust represented the dream as the route to the past. To explain the "shifting and confused gusts of memory" he notes how we "isolate the successive positions of a [horse's] body as they appear upon a bioscope." Even the conflict between personal and manufactured dreams is clearly delineated in the recollection of a magic lantern assembled in the writer's bedroom. Its projections intruded the recent past with dissettling images, thrown across the window curtains or on a door handle, unwelcome in a room which had until then been singularly composed by Proust-Swann's personality.

So memory, drawing on the innermost resources, becomes a private movie in which the projections of parlor toys are an intrusion. (One is reminded of the prancing skeleton in *Persona*.) Until commercial films had defined their own form, they composed the bottom half of society's double bill.

The notion that movies could prove a vehicle uniquely able to project human reserves, which were difficult enough to admit and even harder to externalize, grew in the silent period. As late as 1929, Pirandello (who had written *Shoot*, a novel about a cameraman) said, "The screen play should remain a wordless art because it is essentially a medium for the expression of the unconscious."[38] Interesting that the unconscious, like the camera obscura and early film, should be soundless. It remained for twentieth-century forms, the modern tradition, to organize that quality of drama which Mann had begun to suspect in the fearful dream of von Aschenbach:

> . . . if dream be the right word for a mental and physical experience which did indeed befall him in deep sleep, as a thing quite apart and real to his senses, yet without seeing himself as present in it. Rather, its theatre seemed to be his very soul.

---

[37] This and subsequent quotes from Proust are from the Overture to *Swann's Way*.
[38] *The Bioscope* (Feb. 6, 1929), 26.

Part Two
Graphic Arts

5

Mr. Griffith, Meet Windsor McCay

The animated cartoon, the movie, and the comic strip were born simultaneously; although each appeared independently of the other, they embodied in three related forms the single deep-seated trend underlying the entire nineteenth century.
—Pierre Couperie

Newspaper comics rivaled dime novels as early, mass-circulated ephemera. Their appearance accompanied the development of the motion picture. After the creation of the animated cartoon, the most successful comic artists worked both fields. Beyond this phase, film historians tend to overlook comics until the adventure strips of the 1930's developed a new generation of hard-edge melodramatists who pilfered movie techniques.

That much, of course, is true. Harold Foster (*Prince Valiant*), Alex Raymond (*Flash Gordon*), and Roy Crane (*Captain Easy*) all constructed realistic narratives that paralleled Hollywood Western, crime and adventure stories of the Depression years. Their champion was Milton Caniff, who developed *Terry and the Pirates* into a personal style that made special point of silhouetting, strong color, black-white contrasts, chiaroscuro lighting, and inventive camera angles, particularly a Jean Renoiresque arrangement of close profiles against middle and background action. Such a strip is often used by motion picture instructors as a teaching aid because of its faithful adherence to the orthodoxies by which smooth continuities are accomplished in film editing.

However, a number of additional relationships emerge between film and the comics if we broaden our perspective to view the strip artist and the filmmaker as confronting common problems of space and time within the conventions of narrative exposition.

The comic strip—a combination of sequential panels with a story line and a consistent set of characters—emerged from the circulation wars of Pulitzer and Hearst during the nineties.[1] Just as movement was the element which drew nickelodeon audiences to the feats of the Lumières, Edison, and Méliès, color helped to insure strip cartoons their "readers." Strip cartooning appeared in the Sunday Supplement, itself a product of new, high-speed rotary presses. In the *Morning Journal* of October 17, 1898, Hearst boasted

> Bunco steerers may tempt your fancy with a "color supplement" that is black and tan—four pages of weak, wishy-washy color and four pages of desolate waste of black.
> But the JOURNAL'S COLOR COMIC WEEKLY!
> Ah! There's the dif!

The increasing demands first of lithography and then of photo-lithography had forced refinements in printing presses and freed ilustrators to work again with pen and ink. Photoengraving allowed that same freedom, for after the introduction of the half-tone in the eighties photography bypassed the need for engraving tools and intermediaries in preparing graphics for publication.

Printers found in the broad fields of the cartoonists' drawings (for example, the nightshirt of the Yellow Kid) a field for experimentation in color combinations and drying solvents. In the early comics color was often the domain of the pressmen.

Created in 1905, Winsor McCay's *Little Nemo in Slumberland*

[1] What is called the comic strip should not be confused with cartooning itself. The Egyptians drew cartoons of animals on limestone flakes and papyrus. Punch appeared on broadsheets and pamphlets in seventeenth-century England: the first comic books. Sequential cartoons are early too. The Yale library has books of drawings which depict the adventures of Jonathan Swapwell and of Jeremiah Saddlebags in the California gold country. The latter (*Journey to the Gold Diggins by Jeremiah Saddlebags*) has varied angles, distances, and panel sizes. *Harper's* ran a monthly comic section from the early 1850's. The Wilhelm Busch *Max und Maurice* comic books date from 1865. They were translated by Rev. Charles Timothy Brooks of Salem for American distribution in 1870 and became the forerunners of many pairs of mischievous children, most especially the *Katzenjammer Kids*. A. B. Frost began as a comic illustrator with *Out of the Hurly-Burly* by Charles Heber Clark. Frost's *Stuff and Nonsense* (1884) contains full-page collections of sequential pen-and-ink drawings of comic, mimed action like "The Fatal Mistake—A Tale of a Cat." The comic weekly *Judge* started in 1881, and *Life* in 1883.

was probably the first strip to manipulate color with consistent hues and thoughtful locations for them. (When we look at reproductions of the early Sunday pages we must bear in mind that we see but half the publication, like watching *Accident* or *The Red Desert* in black and white.) The comic-strip artist could enlist the techniques and conventions of the nineteenth-century illustrators and editorial cartoonists. The requirements of his editor and audience assigned him to a representational form. By introducing the element of time, the chronological paneling demanded a story.

The early filmmakers shared similar restrictions. Their images were representational, their urban audience common. The first writer-directors turned to the same conventions of music hall comedy, dime novels, and theatrical melodrama for characters and plots.

However, in contrast to film, a comic page poses the dimension of time on a visible linear continuum. Even after the reader has proceded from picture to picture, the panels continue to relate to one another on the page in a kind of spread-out, timebound Cubism. The picture on the screen vanishes at the moment of its perception. The cartoon panel can be called back and rerelated to its neighbors by a movement of the eye. This is why comics differ essentially from the animator's storyboards and why they share two filmic impulses that have been generally discrepant in the movie theater until recently: toward single, replaceable images and toward multiple, simultaneous representations.

The representational painter faces the problem of reconciling objects' "local color" with the range of tonal gradation needed to suggest depth. The photographer resolves this problem in the mechanics and the chemistry of his craft, although he must decide where and how to "place" the gray scale or color scale overall. The cinematographer captures movement (which implies space) as well as calling upon the devices of the still photographer. The painter "places" his objects in space by modeling; the photographer mechanically records his light source or its effects.

In contrast, the early cartoonist was deprived of almost everything. With the printing techniques at his disposal he could only suggest perspective by a vanishing point, foreshortening, and the obscuring of smaller distant objects with larger near ones. He could shade primitively with straight- and cross-hatches. The colored inks were flat; he could not simulate depth with the luminosity of glazes. These limitations thrust the early cartoonist into self-apparent, visible stylizations. With the illustrator's tradition of caricature as his other resource, fantasy became the cartoonist's mode.

For example, note Winsor McCay's maneuvering of perspective "laws" in Figure 10. Little Nemo has been magically enlarged for this episode in preparation to confront the guards. His proportions are defined relative to the size of the Lilliputian guides. How much larger then the guards seem when the perspective promises that their size should have diminished. The partial torso of the far-right figure is monstrous.

Space is also defined by its enclosure. Early backgrounds and settings tend to be open (*Mutt and Jeff, Happy Hooligan, Krazy Kat, Abie the Agent*) with parsimonious application of visual cues to help the reader fill in detail. A common practice is to place the action in an interior where wallpaper, doors, windows, and minimal decor can efficiently define period and locale (*Newlyweds, The Captain and the Kids, Buster Brown*).

Since the graphic artist is not held to the perspectives and the conventions of the proscenium, or to a theatrical audience's vantage, he is free also to explore the space around his subject. (Similar mobility on the part of the moving-picture camera does not occur for one or two decades—first on the part of D. W. Griffith, then with the efforts of German and Russian directors of the 1920's.)

Early comics tend toward "medium shot" distance, but this is not necessarily the case, nor is the point of view always static. Some sequences of panels are surprisingly filmlike, both in the character of their movement and in the optical definition of their field. The pan of Figure 11 is from an 1896 English halfpenny children's sheet called *Chips*. There is a gyroscopic circling and pullback in Figure 12, a 1912 English *Comic Cuts*.

Winsor McCay is particularly striking in these optical effects. At least two years before he attempted film animation, McCay was employing strikingly "visual" techniques in a daily comic strip called *Dream of the Rarebit Fiend*. In one adventure he executed an impressive trucking shot (Figure 13). An episode from 1906, the previous year, is even more remarkable (Figure 14). A man leaps from a bridge, apparently depressed by Hearst's unsuccessful campaign as candidate for mayor of New York City. The perspective "drops" earthward to keep the leaper centered in the lower part of the frame during his sequential revolution. With each panel the angle of the bridge shifts and with it the relative visibility of such details as the cable, tower, undergirding, and siding. Then in the second line of the strip, the figure reverses his direction like an early film trick and returns to his original perch. No panel's perspective matches any of the others. (Struck by similarities to camera frames, a film purist might argue that the man seems to be revolving in the same direction both up and down and that the boat remains unaccountably centered throughout. The point is not that an artist is copying another medium, but that he has found a like solution to a similar problem.)

Movement within a frame while the view stays stationary was not only a Mélièslike way of performing for the orchestra seats. It could provide its own bases of humor by noting change in something of the manner of the Dioramas, which showed time passing through lighting effects. A good example is the four panels of a 1905 strip by J. R. Bray (Figure 15), where his intention is furthered by the stationary pose of *Mr. O. U. Absentmind*. Bray became a movie cartoonist, and his *The Debut of Thomas Cat* (1916) is said to be the first movie color cartoon (although Méliès hand drew colors for some of his early pixilation).

Another method of showing movement was to relate a subject's position to some fixed point on the horizon. This was sometimes more of a "follow shot" effect, as in the illustrated adventure of *Peck's Bad Boy* by Dougal dating from somewhere in the early 1900's (Figure 16). Note the positions of the boat relative to the sails, city skyline and lighthouse.

When the viewer's position (as with a movie camera) changes relative to a moving subject, the sophistications heighten and film effects are even more striking. In a very early conception of *Hair-*

93

FIG. 10. Winsor McCay's *Little Nemo in Slumberland* (1905) began to maneuver the laws of perspective in a manner later filmmakers were to imitate. (From *Penguin Book of Comics*.)

FIG. 11. Some comic-strip panels are almost filmlike in their movement. Note how the point of view of this strip—an English halfpenny called *Chips*, published in 1896—"pans" from one panel to the next. (From *Penguin Book of Comics*.)

95

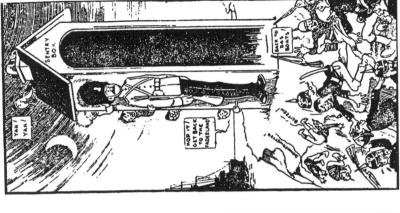

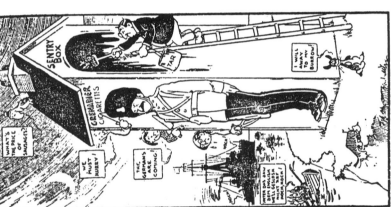

THE MULBERRY FLATITES REPEL THE GERMAN INVASION!

FIG. 12. In the above three panels the cartoonist circles and then pulls back the point of view, a feat cameras could not yet accomplish when this British *Comic Cuts* was published in 1912. (Note that the letters on the sack carried by the Jigglike character in the first panel stand for pounds [L], shillings [S], and pence [D].) (From *Penguin Book of Comics*.)

96

FIG. 13. An impressive "trucking shot" executed by Winsor McCay in 1907. (From the author's collection.)

FIG. 14. In *Dream of the Rarebit Fiend* (1906) McCay again alters perspective by centering the leaping man in the bottom of each frame as he jumps from a bridge and then rebounds to his original position—as if a camera were following his movements. (From the author's collection.)

FIG. 15. J. R. Bray, like *Méliès* before him, indicates movement in time by altering the effects—in this instance, rain—surrounding a stationary figure. (From *Good Old Days.*)

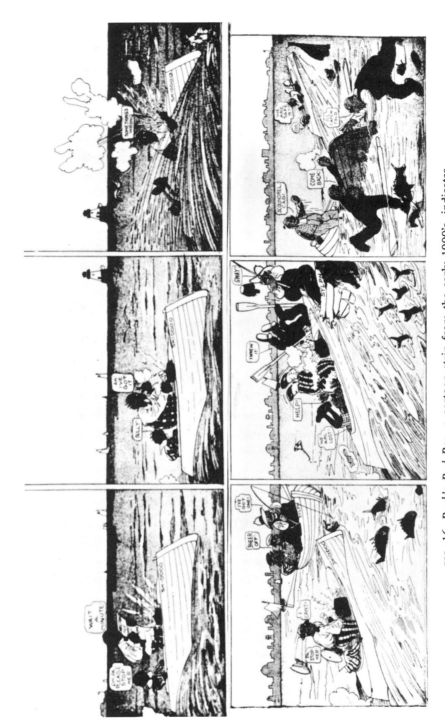

FIG. 16. *Peck's Bad Boy*, a cartoon strip from the early 1900's, indicates movement by relating the subject's position to some fixed point on the horizon. (From *Good Old Days*.)

100

breath Harry (here he was the *Boy Hero*), C. W. Kahles moves his camera to follow Harry and a polar bear (Figure 17) from an igloo across the snow to the One and Only North Pole, then up and around the pole. The strip is dated September 29, 1907. Kahles is not successful in adjusting the position of the sun and background to his mobile vantage.

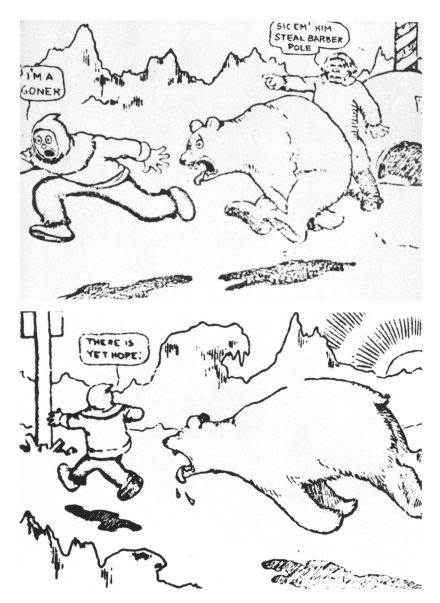

FIG. 17. C. W. Kahles, in *Hairbreath Harry* (1907), moves his "camera" to follow Harry and a polar bear from an igloo across the snow to the North Pole, then up and around the pole. (From *Good Old Days*.)

Winsor McCay is far more subtle in the maneuverings of his lines of perspective (Figure 18) as he follows Flip, in a December

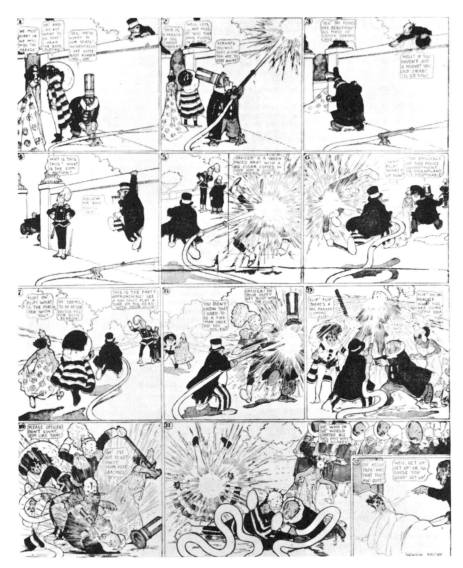

FIG. 18. Note the subtle maneuverings of perspective in this Winsor McCay *Little Nemo in Slumberland* strip from December 10, 1911. (From *Good Old Days*.)

103

10, 1911 strip, from atop a wall, around an entrance, and into a palace yard, then pulling into a tighter shot of the ensuing debacle. But the shadows of Flip as he runs across the lawn indicate that McCay has not taken the changed positions of the sun altogether into account.

In an airship adventure (Figure 19), Nemo's passage relative

to the Statue of Liberty is documented by a view that poses extreme close-up against long shot as the camera draws off into a space independent of any visible foundation. In such a collection of drawings one finds the vision of an early cartoonist at its most stunning; he literally invents a place from which to view his adventure with the consistencies of an as yet nonexistent aerial camera shot.

104

FIG. 19. Long before aerial photography Winsor McCay posed extreme close-up against long shot. (From the author's collection.)

Contemporary humorists like Jules Feiffer and Charles Schultz (and Bob Newhart and Shelly Berman) both satirize and indulge the weaknesses of much of the early comic convention: the tendency to use posturing figures as anchors of characterization for spoken gags. *Mutt and Jeff*, the second daily strip (preceded three years earlier by Clare Briggs's *A. Piker Clerk* in the Chicago *American*) set the pace. Visually, where "primary movement" occurs, it is usually done to carry the humor (Figure 20), but this *Comic Cuts* (1890) also betrays the paucity of the approach,

"You women don't know how to hang pictures—takes a man to do it!"

"I think I'll put it here, or—a little farther over."

"A trifle farther yet—this is the spot; now just hand me a hook and some string, and I'll have this picture up in a jiffy. I tell you, I understand hanging pictures right down to the——

—ground!"

FIG. 20. *Comic Cuts*, a British cartoon from 1890, uses posturing figures to set the characterization for spoken gags. (From *Penguin Book of Comics*.)

which needs a kicker like McCay's bridge leap. What *happens* to a character was most often evidenced in cause-and-effect drawings; it is characteristically violent, direct, simple, and naïve. *Krazy Kat* (who had originally intruded into another 1913 strip as a minor character) was the first and finest effort to draw its strength from inventive variation on the clichés. Our animated equivalents are the *Tom and Jerry's* and *Roadrunners*.

Until Holman's *Smokey Stover* in 1935 (which still appears in midwest papers), characters tended to stay obediently within their frames, however they might behave otherwise. The matter of getting from one panel to the next posed problems similar to the shot-to-shot transitions of the narrative film. The usual procedure was to continue a previous situation or action at a later moment, but there is some evidence of the cartoonist's ability to visualize what film editors describe as a pickup or cut-in. A Griffith device, the cut-in amounts to singling out a portion of the previous shot in enlarged detail for the next image. At least one cartoon instance can be located in a 1907 strip by Opper (Figure 21).

FIG. 21. In 1907, Opper uses a Griffith device, the cut-in, by singling out a portion of one frame for enlargement in the next. (From *Penguin Book of Comics*.)

Similarly, the Griffith cut-away directs the viewer's attention by intercutting a view motivated by its surrounding scenes but not visible in them: Shot 1, a girl looking out the window; Shot 2, her view of the villain approaching; Shot 3, the girl withdraws. The same technique is evident in a 1908 episode from a French feature by Louis Forton called *La Bande des Pied-Nickelés* (Figure 22). (This sort of author-reader ubiquity is common and far more inventive in many nineteenth-century novelists, and Doré "changed

The news that the famous Pieds-Nickelés gang had finally fallen into the hands of the police had spread among the crowd like a trail of gunpowder. An indescribable mob pressed close to the winding-drum of the balloon in order to get a better view of the famous bandits. From the nacelle, Croquignol, Ribouldingue, and Filochard looked down, without the slightest enthusiasm, at the crowd of rubbernecks for whom their arrest was one more attraction among the other attractions of the festival.

With all his colleagues on ha Mirette gave the order to have balloon brought down. "We're su fellas," sighed Ribouldingue. "Be five minutes have passed the cops have collared us."

The nacelle came down very slowly, and soon it was only about a hundred yards above the earth. The Pieds-Nickelés saw the two policemen, who were greeting their arrival with their most mocking smiles, and the words, "Okay, you guys, this time we've got you for good!"

"Not yet, you idiots," sneered Filochard, when the balloon was only fifty yards up. And taking from his pocket an enormous cutlass, he abruptly cut the cable holding the captive balloon. A roar of mingled surprise and stupefaction burst from twenty thousand mouths. The nacelle, no longer held by a cable, had leaped . . .

. . . with a bound to a great hei Hanging joyfully over the nacelle, three buddies waved their hats, ing, "So long, Cops! It's our turn make fun of you mugs, you me heads! See you again soon, you s pletons!"

FIG. 22. The viewer's attention, in this French cartoon of 1908, is directed by intercutting a view motivated by its surrounding scenes but not visible in them—a cut-away device later employed by Griffith. (From *Penguin Book of Comics*.)

angles" repeatedly in his bloody *L'Histoire de la Sainte Russe* of 1854.)

Winsor McCay carries the techniques of visual transitions far beyond any other artist of the period. Little Nemo pursued a continuous dream each Sunday. In the final panel he returned to his bed and woke. Thus the transition is predictably one of both time and space. What film editors were later to term "matching action" often carries Nemo out of his dream. A continuity of movement is achieved by juxtaposing two shots in which the posture of the subject is identical. This device is evidenced in Figure 10, but a better example can be seen in Figure 23.

Slumberland is a world with some of the qualities of environmental transience that were later enjoyed by *Krazy Kat*. In Figure 24, when Nemo and Impy, his chum, flee from a forest skyward over farm and city, McCay keeps their legs in the same positions while "cutting" from exterior to exterior, yet preserving the same perspective lines throughout. Similar freedom of movement through space does not appear in the film until Buster Keaton's dream sequence as a projectionist in the 1924 *Sherlock Jr.*, to be followed by Buñuel's *Un Chien Andalou* in 1928, and Maya Deren's experimental *Meshes of the Afternoon* (1943). Note again the matching of screen position in the transition back to the bed.

Balloons appear as early as fifteenth-century woodcuts and are common in the drawings of Rowlandson. As with sound film, ballooned comics enjoy certain narrative freedoms that mime lacks. Balloons tend to be "lip-sync," although there have been surreal exceptions; *The Spirit*, a unique Sunday hero of the 1940's who inhabited the Philadelphia *Record*, tended to talk through his nose. Balloons are characteristically "close to the mike" with strong presence, however discrepant this may be with the perspective of the picture (Figure 13). In film this would have the effect of a cheaply dubbed track—an Italian spectacle of the late show. Among comics the very incongruity can work toward humorous ends or toward intimacy. A talky strip is like a talky film, but an inventive writer can create private vocabularies, expressions, and verbal mannerisms consistent with the visual stylizations. Even

FIG. 23. Winsor McCay achieves a continuity of movement by juxtaposing two shots in which the posture of the subject, Little Nemo, is identical. (From the author's collection.)

FIG. 24. Again the brilliant Winsor McCay, here showing movement through space by keeping Nemo's and Impy's legs in the same positions while "cutting" from exterior to exterior, yet preserving the same perspective lines throughout. (From *Penguin Book of Comics*.)

the visualized dream balloon of Porter's *American Fireman* (Figure 6) had its counterpart in an 1847 Töpffer (Figure 25).

Although his panels were devoid of plot, Töpffer made use of the "simultaneous" character of the comic both as narrative sequence and as a single-paged graphic totality (Figure 26). In recent years, this kind of experimentation has taken place more often in the comic book than by way of the syndicated newspaper

FIG. 25. Compare this 1847 Töpffer cartoon with the dream balloon in Edwin S. Porter's film shown in Figure 6. (From *Penguin Book of Comics*.)

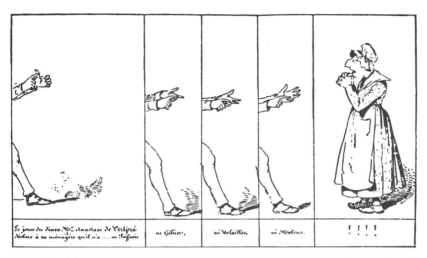

FIG. 26. Although his panels were plotless, Töpffer made use of the "simultaneous" character of the comic both as narrative sequence and as a single-paged graphic totality.

features. Indeed, Sunday Supplement titles have never fully recovered from the publishers' decision in the 1940's to reduce matrixes by a third or more in order to fit tabloid formats, regardless of whether any given paper chose to use that smaller size fold or not. Given the requirement of the same number of panels, the consequence has been either to retain balloon size and diminish figures to heads or long shots, or else to reduce everything with consequent loss of detail and graphic effects.

Happily, the development of the super-hero action comic books pointed another route. No tradition or syndicate enforced a requisite number of panels per page. Besides, as the stories attenuated their moments of violence (like Eisenstein's approach to catastrophe on the Odessa steps), new strategies toward the page as an entire drawing helped to arrest and glorify the moment by slowing time down to an epiphany of special effects. The films, again laggard, began to realize an equivalence in the slow-motion violence of *Bonnie and Clyde* and *The Wild Bunch.*

Although they are beyond the confines of this study, I cannot resist discussion of more recent comic accomplishments. We find

113

our modern-day Töpffer in the artists for such Marvel Comics as *Doctor Strange* (Figure 27). As in Töpffer, four panels read chronologically "against" a fifth. The crystal ball carries us down to the crouched Dr. Strange at lower right. It is replaced in the last picture by Nightmare. On the top of the page, the balloons pace our comprehension of the pictures. On the right-hand page two sets of balloons appear. Alternate readings are equally valid because the action is concurrent. Lightning-pointed arrows and spurs on the balloons underline the intensity of Nightmare's speech. Note the trapezoid shaping of the panels. On the original a blue field borders the left page to emphasize the astral character of the experience. Its facing page is edged in black. Roy Lichtenstein may have "stripped the narrative" from the comic, but the story was moving so slowly anyway that it is rather like making freeze frames out of Andy Warhol's *Empire*.

The Marvel Comics Group has been the last decade's focus for innovation in layout and "simultaneous" continuities, with its half-burlesqued super-heroes like Hulk, Sub-Mariner, Thor, Spiderman, The Torch, and the Fantastic Four. Emphases are on movement, violence, sci-fi special effects, and the physiognomy of muscled heroes, with that awed adulation of the gluteous maximus that has magnetized comic artists since Alex Raymond. As in contemporary theater, there are few good parts for girls. More important, the ignorance of middle-aged film faculties toward such material only underlines a sensibility gap which usually means that students are ahead of their teachers when it comes to putting films together. The new direction in underground comic artists like R. Crumb seems to include extensions of the Marvel layouts allied with surreal-pornographic content that unfortunately, would not yet survive exposure in a G-rated book.

In the Marvel Comics Group major fights—say between super-villains—may take pages, accompanied by unique combinations of Jewish pop and arcane phrases (Figure 28). Or a sequence may exploit fast reverse angles (Figure 29), drawing the heavy into extreme close-up while Captain Marvel struggles with his cap. Tension is accentuated by alternating captionless panels with Marvel's speech (panel 3) and thoughts (bubbled balloons).

FIG. 27. A modern-day Töpffer can be found in Marvel Comics' *Doctor Strange*, where four panels read chronologically "against" a fifth. (From *Doctor Strange*, No. 182, Copyright Marvel Comics Group, 1974.)

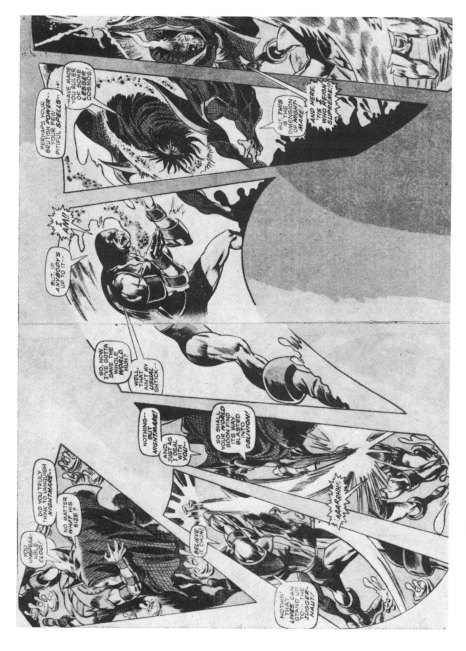

FIG. 28. Juggernaut fights Nightmare, accompanied by unique combinations of Yiddish pop and arcane phrases. (Copyright Marvel Comics Group, 1974.)

116

FIG. 29. Extreme close-ups and fast reverse angles heighten the tension as Captain Marvel struggles with his helmet. (Copyright Marvel Comics Group, 1974.)

117

Sometimes the panels are simply devices for contracting space (Figure 30) while at the same time preserving the continuity of movement in an economic graphic language. Years ago Sergei Eisenstein argued for a "dynamic" motion-picture border which might flexibly adapt to the demands of its composition.[2] I always thought Eisenstein's presentation somewhat tongue-in-cheek, but finally—satire and all—it has been realized in the comic book. In Figure 31, Captain Marvel is slipping into something called the Negative Zone. (Perhaps he has been caught in a reversal processor.) His moment of transition is noted in silhouette in the center of the page. Its frame is borderless, breaking into the "fading" close-up of upper right. The arrowed figuration of the top borders point to his "negative" color-contrasted image in the last panel. Note how two of the five Marvel figures and most of the balloons obtrude across panel borders. Smoky Stover has made it into the 1960's!

The early strip cartoonists provide convincing evidence of imaginative approaches to many problems of graphics and story which found similar resolution in the early motion pictures. Current comics show attitudes toward story and multiple imageries that parallel other media. While the comic books retain storylines, their graphics show far more concern for compounding the techniques of exposition than they do in smooth editing effects.

The comic strip has consistently maintained close relations to fantasy. It can never manufacture an equivalent to the camera's photographed surfaces. The epidermis of reality in cartooning is halftoned, doubletoned, Bendayed and stippled. Yet like many art forms the comics' imaginative potential has developed from those technical "limitations" that distinguish it from the reality it purports to document.

In their earliest period Winsor McCay seems to have realized the most profound possibilities among the fantasy-prone predelictions of comics. His strips, tied as they so often are to the world of dreams, indulge not only bizarre characters and behaviors, but lovingly elaborated systems where transformations, changes, dis-

---

2 See "The Dynamic Square" in Eisenstein, *Film Essays and a Lecture*.

118

FIG. 30. Captain Marvel fights Tam-Bor, and the panels are simply devices for contracting space while preserving the continuity of movement. (Copyright Marvel Comics Group, 1974.)

119

FIG. 31. Captain Marvel slips into the Negative Zone, the artist adapting—
Eisensteinlike—picture borders to content in Dynamic Frame. (Copyright
Marvel Comics Group, 1974.)

tortions, aberrant perspectives, and defiances of gravity itself are executed with grace and brilliance.

One of McCay's most winning qualities is evidenced in the progress of Little Nemo. Initially, he is a shy, anxious intruder into Slumberland. Gradually, Nemo familiarizes himself with the world's people and terrain. As the strip progressed through its decade Nemo penetrated deeper and deeper into his dream—by submarines and airships in interplanetary and subterranean travel to magic countries where increasingly he was required to fall upon his own resources. By the end of the strip's life Nemo has become more self-possessed, less a victim of the whims of his companions. He begins to learn the secrets and some of the meanings in his dreams, and his adventures have helped him to grow up.

6

The Picture
in Our Heads

Marshall McLuhan makes special point of literacy as a moment in human history that redefined what had been social (that is, oral) tradition into private perceptions of space and of the passage of time. In like vein, describing effects of the novel on European culture, Leslie Fiedler finds literacy internalizing myth and fantasy within the "dreaming mind of man."[1]

Both McLuhan and Fiedler were discussing consequences of print, which became, with the advent of mass production techniques, a democratized mode of individual awareness. However, print was not unique in this respect, for during the same period—the sixteenth through the nineteenth centuries—other modes developed as well. First on the fairgrounds and city streets and then in the home, toys, tricks, and optical games gradually refined their own expository language. This visual syntax emerged in strength at the end of the Victorian age. In hindsight it seems to presage a great drama of postliteracy, but the traditions were lurking in the wings with preliterates during all that time.

The intentions of this chapter are to define various kinds of nineteenth-century "viewings" and other optically affected perceptions. We shall discuss first optical systems, then their effect on private and public entertainments. Finally, some attention will be given to the audiences.

Lenses appear early in the European past. The lorgnette evolved from the viewing glass and dates at least as far back as Louis XIV (as mentioned in the *Memoirs* of Saint-Simon). With shifts away from ordinary glass higher quality optics developed in the early

---

1 Fiedler, *Love and Death in the American Novel*, 41.

122

nineteenth century. Abbe and Schott pioneered new achromatic systems beginning in 1886.

Spectacles were common by midcentury, and their possible effects on artists offer a bypath which cannot be pursued here. (For example, Tennyson's misperceptions that led him "down the ringing grooves of change": he thought that railroad tracks had a channel or rut on their surface.)[2]

More important to our own considerations is the use of optics to affect our vantage so that (1) by option we see not normally but differently; (2) in some measure we can control where and how we do see beyond the normal limitations; and (3) our relation to the objects of our scrutiny assumes a kind of "closeness" which is unique to the contrived perception and which disappears when that experience ceases.

So we are led to lens systems. The telescope is said to have been constructed in Holland around 1600. The simple Galilean telescope (significantly, the French called it *lunette d'approche*) was commissioned to military use immediately. Small viewing devices based on the Galilean principle were used by the eighteenth-century aristocracy, made of porcelein and Wedgewood imitation, mounted on walking sticks, beautifully boxed and sculptured in ivory. They appear in the animal drawings of Grandville. A portrait, *Jeunne Dame au Théâtre*, from the time of Louis XVI, pictures her with a lorgnette.

The nineteenth century developed collapsible viewing glasses that raised capacities for focus and magnification while remaining portable. Opera glasses appear with increasing frequency in the art and literature of the time. Edgar Allan Poe wrote a story called

2 Trollope says he first met Dickens when the latter was thirty-three (which would be about 1845), and that Dickens was "to a very slight degree near-sighted" although "he never used a glass." A study of centenarians made in the eighties reported that out of fifty subjects (most were in comfortable circumstances), "thirty-five, including a number who used glasses, were reported to have the enjoyment of good sight." (These pieces of undated intelligence come from a scrapbook of newspaper clippings located in the Rose Hawley Mason County Historical Museum, Ludington, Michigan.) Certainly the opportunity to correct those misunderstandings that arise out of personal failure defines perception in the most specific terms. For a discussion of the so-called "perceptual theory of artistic change," see Richard Wollheim, "Art and Illusion," in Harold Osborne, ed., *Aesthetics in the Modern World* (New York: Weybright and Talley, 1968).

The Spectacles in 1844. It concerns a handsome young man with poor vision who falls in love with a woman he sees at the opera. While studying her as best he can, the lady examines *him* carefully with opera glasses. Finally a meeting is arranged. The youth discovers his lady is rather old, marries her daughter, and buys a pair of spectacles.

Binoculars were common by our period. In a review of Buffalo Bill's 1886 opening at Madison Square Garden, "the elk sniffed the air, and passed before Mrs. Belmont. She raised her opera glasses. The elk turned his head toward Congressman Belmont. The wily red man then approached. The elk turned on him, the redskin ran, and the crowd roared."[3] From the west side of Van Ness Avenue James Stetson watched the San Francisco fire through binoculars. Use of binoculars (or the single-tubed spyglass)[4] figures commonly in novels with opera and theater scenes. An 1897 treatise on magic (Figure 32) numbers among its tricks a pair of opera glasses so constructed that "The practical uses of the glasses are apparent. Our engraving shows a plain view of a theatre, with the stage, boxes and seats. The gentleman in the box and the one on the right of the center aisle both appear to be observing the actor on the stage, but in reality they are observing the lady on the left of the center aisle."[5]

A developing concept, that one may magnify a field to isolate it for special attention, is reflected in *The Opera Glass*, a title for at least two periodicals: "A Musical and Dramatic Magazine" with "Glimpses of Musical and Dramatic Life" (Boston, 1894)[6] and an 1897 newspaper published in Galveston, Texas.

Here then are close-ups with a vengeance, occurring quite as naturally and functionally as those in prose or pictures, close-ups which happen easily, without recourse to photography. If we consider the actualities of vision by binoculars and telescopes, certain graphic aspects of the experience become apparent. The field is

3 New York *Herald*, probably November 25, 1886.

4 A September 2, 1861, cartoon in the New York *Illustrated News* shows correspondent "Bull Run" Russell watching a battle through a spyglass.

5 Hopkins, *Magic: Stage Illusions and Scientific Diversions*.

6 *The Opera Glass: A Musical and Dramatic Magazine*. Issues are located in the Lincoln Center of the Performing Arts Collection, New York City.

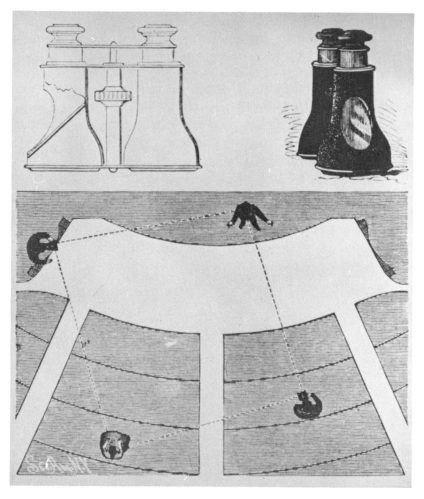

FIG. 32. Trick opera glasses from a book on magic published in 1897. The gentleman in the box and the one on the right of the center aisle both appear to be observing the actor on the stage, but in reality they are observing the lady on the left of the center aisle.

125

spherical, like stage, cartoon, and sometimes literary vision scenes and close-ups. The picture is two-dimensional, flatter as the image size increases, a consequence of the optical properties attending magnification. Choice of composition is the prerogative of the viewer. (We make our own close-ups.) The compositions need be neither symmetric nor orthodox. A tree may thrust itself into our field. Out-of-focus shapes can edge the scene or foregrounds intrude. These increase our sense of candidness, even of secrecy. Finally, the "shot" is quite as mobile as we wish to make it. Swimmers, aerial balloons, and spear carriers: we can follow them, let them exit the frame, swish from one image to another. Popularly, pan shots predate movies by more than a century.

Spurred by the advent of photography, then by military need and the development of photolithography, the history of lenses and lens systems in the nineteenth century traces an entire new matrix for man's perceptions. (See Appendix IV.) Many period toys and common public amusements were outgrowths of simple lens systems, constructing an enclosed "world" in which the illusion of its reality was accomplished both by a viewer's isolation from other frames of reference and by the peculiarities of optics. A good example is the peep-egg.

Adapted in the Victorian era from sixteenth-century peepshows, peep-eggs were fashioned of alabaster. Each came equipped with a double convex lens mounted on its top.

> Inside, three surfaces fixed in a metal spindle supported the scenes, which might be brought into view by two knobs which protruded from either side. The scenes were lit either by sunshine or artificial light shining through the translucent alabaster. A peep-egg in the collection of the Barnes brothers at Mousehole shows wonderfully plastic changing views of the Clifton Suspension Bridge and Nightingale Valley.[7]

The illusion of reality in such experiences was a function of three elements. False perspective was secured by way of mirrors and miniature drops and frames. The viewing lens converged vision on a designated field. Diffused illumination provided "fill

---

[7] Cook, *Movement in Two Dimensions*, 27.

light" to further the effect. Variations in the light immediately effected variation in the scene: the "movement," the "wonderfully plastic changing views of the Clifton Suspension Bridge."

A stylized and simple form of naturalism was sufficient to create that sense of a self-consistent, separate world (or at least another place on this one) which is where stories begin. The bridge from individual toy to public show is evidenced in such a transition as that from peep-egg to peepshow. In the process, single scenes gave way to graphic displays. These events were broken down into component parts.

Communal peepshows (they might number as many as twenty-six lenses) constructed stories out of pictures that were raised and lowered by the operator sequentially into the machine. The shows sound like the earliest motion pictures: *The Mail Coach Setting Off from the Post Office*; *The Coronation of George IV*; *Queen Victoria's Visit to the City of London*; *Napoleon's Battle of the Pyramids*; *The Mutiny on the Bounty*; *The Opening of the Thames Tunnel*; *The Coronation of Queen Victoria*.[8]

The nineteenth century saw a variety of efforts to integrate stroboscopic inventions with viewing systems, each anticipating the motion picture. The stories of these toys and novelties are well recounted in many studies;[9] a small sidelight is the evidence of unsuccessful efforts to promote nonprojected viewing systems so as to merchandise home equipment. From today's vantage these devices seem almost like animate (as well as animated) creatures scuttling after security on the parlor table. A study of some of the early British patents[10] notes odd amalgams of different media

8 *Ibid.* Compare these views to the lithograph-inflected melodrama scenes described in Chapter 2.

9 See Terry Ramsaye, *A Million and One Nights* I: Quigley, Jr., *Magic Shadows*; Ceram, *Archaeology of the Cinema*; and Cook. Several inventions are demonstrated in two 16mm motion pictures: *Biography of the Motion Picture Camera* (produced by Les Films du Compas and Roger Leenhardt, distributed in the United States by A. F. Films; twenty minutes) and *Origins of the Motion Picture* (produced by the U.S. Navy, M.F. 11 8634, twenty-one minutes). Early animation devices including the Phenakisticope, Reynaud's Praxinoscope, and a recreation of the Théâtre Optique appear in *Animated Cartoons—The Toy that Grew Up* (produced by Les Films du Compas and Roger Leenhardt, A. F. Films, seventeen minutes). Some of Méliès' tricks are reenacted by his son in George Franju's *Le Grand Méliès*.

10 Hopwood, *Living Pictures: Their History, Photo-Production and Practical Working*, Appendix I.

(like a notch for the buggy whip in the first automobiles, or spurs on World War I pilots):

Bonelli, G., and Cook, H., No. 2063, Aug. 19, 1863
A series of small views are mounted on the edge of a disc and viewed through a microscope.

Claudet, A. F. G., No. 711, Mar. 23, 1853
A series of views are seen through stereoopticon eyepieces, which are alternately eclipsed by a reciprocating slide.

Melville, A. A., No. 14917, Nov. 17, 1886
A "living picture book" of drawings, apparently actuated like the mutoscope and bound radially.

Another curiosity was the effort to accomplish with stage machinery effects more easily managed by projection. Hopwood[11] notes the invention of a Mr. Beale of Greenwich. Mr. Beale painted a human bust on a screen, replacing the face with a hole. Behind the hole drawings of a face were brought into view, each lit when it was in place. The light was extinguished during the transition from face to face. (A similar device was called the Electric Tachyscope, made with photographs, and attributed to Ottamar Anschuetz of Lissa, Prussia. Figure 33.)

Many optical toys were simple, graphic displays, like the cylindrical mirror, a polished, metal cylinder which reflected a "corrected" image back from a series of distorted drawings called polyoptic pictures. They could be minimally enlivened by bending. Otherwise movement had the repetitive, ritualized quality of the Zoetrope and Phenakisticope; that is, cyclical actions whose attraction rested in the novelty of the motion and the bizarreness of the drawings.

Historically, cyclical repetition figures in one major aspect of the motion pictures: animation. There we even bring anticipations of repeated movements into the plots. Otherwise the general pattern of movie prehistory suggests that once a technique extends itself into the domain of story (abdicating cyclic repetition and assuming narrative continuities), the medium is likely to become

11 *Ibid.*, 19.

FIG. 33. The Electric Tachyscope, an invention attributed to Ottamar Anscheutz of Lissa, Prussia.

129

public or at least shared.[12] Such a passage from individual view to social performance can be traced in the transition from peepshow to multiple peepshow, from Phenakisticope to Plateau's Lantern Wheel of Light, from Zoetrope to Projected Praxinoscope.

Another instance of this tendency is included under Appendix V, The Phasmatrope. Introduced in Philadelphia on February 5, 1870, by Henry R. Heyl, the Phasmatrope was an adaption of the skeleton wheel of the Zoetrope, but it projected photographs onto a "life size" screen. Taken in the wet-plate period, the pictures were mounted on glass. Waltzing figures and acrobats were posed to simulate cycles of movement. (It might be argued that the individual-to-social disposition worked in both directions: movies to Mutoscope, lantern slides issued as postcards. On the whole, however, these seem to be only merchandising efforts to expand already existing markets.)

After the nursery, the nineteenth century was a parlor age—a condition explained by the absence of central heating as well as any other single element. There on the table beside a velvet-covered photograph album (and rivaled only by the player piano in popularity), the stereograph was a pastime for rainy days and gaslit evenings.

Stereographs grew out of the application of photography to a machinery that provides the illusion of binocular vision by presenting the brain with two images to merge into a "three-dimensional" picture. A "Stereoscope" was invented by Sir Charles Wheatstone in 1838, using drawings. Sir William Brewster applied the concept to photographs in 1850.[13]

The stereograph became commercially popular in the United States between 1865 and 1873. From the 1880's until 1920 wide-

---

12 The cyclic quality of photographed movement came either from its early animal motion subjects (Marey, Muybridge) or from the cylindrical design of the machinery, like the invention of Coleman Sellers. Coleman Sellers was a Philadelphia mechanical engineer. In 1860 he photographed his sons hammering in a series of sequential poses. The pictures were revolved on a paddle wheel. Viewed through a peephole the pictures simulated a continuous movement. For the public equivalent of Colonel Seller's invention, see Appendix V.

13 Darrah, *Stereo Views*. Almost all my factual information on the Stereograph (but not the cards) comes from Darrah's book. Curiously, we can train our vision to "see" stereograph cards successfully without recourse to the viewing machines. We had to

spread mass production and distribution broadcast stereograph cards across the United States. Elmer and Ben Underwood introduced sets of slides in a highly successful business venture that started in 1882. These sets were sold door to door by thousands of young men, as well as through direct mail, advertised in the newly popular national magazines. By 1900 four major companies used the same techniques.

The stereograph related narrative devices of the lantern slides to inexpensive distribution practices and the privacy of the home. Using a simple viewing device, designed in 1859 by Oliver Wendell Holmes, stereographs successfully combined the peep-egg quality of a private, three-dimensional world with the continuities of a story set. They are a little-read chapter of Victorian theater.

Originally marketed as interesting or amusing individual views, the stereograph set then structured simple chronologies, recounting trips and explorations. Soon, however, subjects were also invented and posed in sequences. Milburn, Underwood, and other publishers exploited the "humorous stereograph" cartoon series.

> Best known, and indeed today a collector's item, are sets of twelve (occasionally ten) cards of "The New French Maid." In sequence, the girl is hired, catches the eye of the husband, in an embrace, has her floured handprints transferred to his coat, is caught by the poor unsuspecting wife, and so on until a less beautiful and much older maid replaces her and a repentant husband promises to stray no more. There are several variations on the set.[14]

Another series was *Journey into Hell*, issued from 1868 to 1874. Numbers in the series varied from six to twenty, twelve being the most common. "The scenes show the pleasures and pains of hell and, in the larger sets, the riotous earthly pleasures of sins

invent a mechanical contrivance in order to create cards which could then dispense with the viewer. Unfortunately, commercial appeal of stereography has waned, except for the little round cards which are sold today with children's toy viewers. However, for new approaches to the medium see Harold A. Layer, "Figurative Photo-Sculpture With 3-D Pointillism," *Leonardo*, V, 55–58 (1972); Harold A. Layer, "Space Language: Three Dimensional Concrete Poetry," *Media & Methods* (Jan., 1972), 34–36; Harold A. Layer, "Exploring Stereo Images: a Challenging Awareness of Space in the Fine Arts," *Leonardo*, IV, 233–38 (1971). The last article has an impressive collection of additional references.

14 *Ibid.*, 153.

that lead one there. The figures are scaled skeletons and dolls staged in elaborate settings and recorded by so-called 'table-top photography.' "[15]

The English stereographic photographers of the 1860's posed Victorian poetry and novels. R. Soning did *She Stoops to Conquer*. M'Clashon made a series under the title *Realties of the Waverley Novels*. Lake Price issued *Robinson Crusoe and His Family* and *Don Quixote in His Study*. In America, Kilburn made *The Vision of Sir Launfal*. Echoing the "scenes" of cartoonists and chromolithographs, many religious cards illustrated *The Life of Christ* and biblical allegory. Courtship-and-marriage sets were popular between 1896 and 1910. Most were prepared in ten- or twelve-card series.

The accompanying illustrations are excerpted from one such set (Figures 34–40). While all are medium shots, the camera set-ups vary, as does the distance. No. 15 "The Wedding March," is the only into-the-lens composition, although all the cards are characteristically organized so that some diagonal lends credence to the third-dimension illusion. No. 16, "The Wedding," readjusts to a side view, while No. 17, "Placing the Wedding Ring," moves back to a front vantage on the minister. No. 18, "The Blessing," reverts to the positioning of No. 16; No. 19, "The Bridegroom's Kiss," parallels the setup for No. 17 only slightly more distant. No. 20, "The Mother's Kiss," and No. 21, "The Father's Congratulations," recomposes the party from the same angle, varying it only slightly from No. 19 (if one notes the position of the potted palm on the left). A single event has been broken down into sequential components, each photographed from an appropriate camera set-up, and the entire sequence is designed to vary perspective in terms of an overall organization.

An 1898 set, made by T. W. Ingersoll, enacts another event, this time drawing on a Negro stereotype to show an unsuccessful rabbit hunt (Figures 41–43). In order, the slides are titled: (a) *Sam Black Gets a Shot at "Bre'er Rabbit"*; (b) *"Lordy Dad! Be Yous Kilt?"*; and (c) *"Oh Golly, But Dat Ol' Gun Done Kick."* While (a) and (b) are shot from the same position, following

[15] *Ibid.*, 154.

132

one another in "quick" succession, note that the camera pulls in to (c) in order to examine the fallen figure in greater detail. (While the positions of the birches remain unchanged, the rifle has curiously reversed itself in the snow.) This series is accompanied by paragraphs printed on the backs of the cards, each descriptive of the preceding cards where possible. Thus the backing on (b) accompanies the circumstances of (a), while (a) is simply a prologue and (c) adjusts to accommodate both (b) and itself:

> (b) Sam Black is a good shot. Many a 'coon and 'possom has fallen victim to his marksmanship and today he did not miss one of the four rabbits that crossed his path during the first three hours of the hunting expedition. But then Sammy junior began to feel tired, or maybe he didn't care to be loaded down with any more dead rabbits, so he begged dad to return home. Dad assented, but when they were only a mile from the cabin, there was a rabbit sitting up right before them and dad made ready to get it.

With the introduction of new printing techniques, Lithoprint Stereograms were introduced in 1898, halftone and usually multi-colored. Cards could be sold for as little as a penny each, seventy-five cents a hundred. (Photographed cards had been marketed at a quarter apiece.) Millions of lithoprints were sold through Sears, Roebuck and Montgomery Ward, the majority between 1904 and 1916.

A public equivalent of the stereographic three dimensional privacies existed in the forms of Panoramas and Dioramas, entertainments that attracted figures like Louis Daguerre and Robert Fulton. In various degrees they can be said to have evolved from elements of the camera obscura, lenses, and the peepshow.

The camera obscura (Italian for darkened room) was sketched by da Vinci; it is said that Daniel Barbaro's book on perspective (1568) was the first to point out that a sharper image could be procured if a convex lens were inserted in the chink of a window blind, thus creating an elementary projection system.[16] Such a system provided a primitive auditorium and screen. The eighteenth century's developing interest in effects of light, which grew in part

[16] Ivins, *Prints and Visual Communication*, 117.

15. The Wedding March.

FIGS. 34–40. A selection of seven stereograph cards from a set depicting a wedding sometime in the 1890's. (From the author's collection.)

16. The Wedding.

17. Placing the Wedding Ring.

18. The Blessing.

135

19. The Bridegroom's Kiss.

20. The Mother's Kiss.

21. The Father's Congratulations.

from artists' uses of the camera obscura to study perspective,[17] encouraged experiments with illumination behind glass. When the glass had been painted on one side the image was rendered translucent. Its quality could be affected by manipulation of the light source, as with Victorian stage sets.

Injections of movement and duration (*time* as an element of the experience) into the Panorama dates from the very beginning. Its inventor, an Edinburgh painter named Robert Barker, exhibited in London a view of the British Navy on a 16×45 foot canvas which "revolved slowly round the spectators seated in the center. . . . Placed in semi-darkness in the middle of a circle . . . the audience gazed across a gulf of as much as 12 feet at a continuous, moving view of an entire region. . . ."[18]

Panoramas created jointly by Daguerre and Charles Marie Bouton employed both light and movement. In their case the auditorium itself moved, passing the audience

[17] John Baptista Porta proposed the camera obscura's use by artists, and some painters even had darkened coaches equipped with miniature versions of the camera obscura introduced through the cab tops for use in the field. It was likely used by Vermeer. Coke, *The Painter and the Photograph*, 6.

[18] Cook, *op. cit.*, 22–23.

89 (a). Sam Black Gets a Shot at "Br'er Rabbit."
Copyrighted, 1898, by T. W. Ingersoll.

FIGS. 41–43. Stereograph cards from 1898 by T. W. Ingersoll. (From the author's collection.)

90 (b). "Lordy, Dad! Be Yous Kilt?"
Copyrighted, 1898, by T. W. ng

91 (c). "Oh! Golly, But Dat Ol' Gun Done Kick."
Copyrighted, 1898, by T. W. Ingersoll.

from one part of the picture to the other and from one picture to another and giving the impression that the image was animated. . . . The impression was strengthened by perceiving the light and shadows' change, as if clouds were passing over the sun. . . . While gazing . . . the spectator's attention was disturbed by sounds underground. He became conscious that the scene before him was slowly moving away and he obtained a glimpse of another and very different prospect, which gradually advanced until it was completely developed and the cathedral had disappeared.[19]

Later exhibitions of Panoramas and Dioramas sometimes revolved the audience itself and reenacted volcanoes, military engagements, and church services, the latter to the accompaniment of organ music.

All such performances, of course, show unity of time and space, but soon we note a developing sense of sequence and selection of detail, as well as the introduction of movement within a scene. In *The Burning of Moscow*, by Jean Charles Langlois, for example, an overhead view from one of the Kremlin towers gave the audi-

19 *Ibid.*, 36–37. The description comes from a contemporary account.

ence a clear vantage on the spreading fire. Then the Emperor and his guard fled, passing along an adjacent alley and exiting from view.

Any intervention between the spectator and his illusion was further diminished by construction of auditoria so as to rationalize the audience's physical relation to the event, to place them *in* it (Figure 22). In 1832 Carl Wilhelm Gropius built the interior of his Berlin theater to simulate a ship from which *The Bay of Naples* might be viewed in passage. Two years earlier Langlois had resurrected parts of an actual battleship, the *Scipion*, to house his Parisian audience to *The Battle of Navarino*.

Many contemporaries appear to have viewed Panoramas and Dioramas as serving the educational function of the documentary film. (They still figure, of course, in Museum of Natural History exhibitions.) One "cyclorama" was described in detail in 1895. Simulating the Battle of Gettysburg, the exhibition was painted by M. Paul Philippoteaux, based on photographs of the terrain (Figure 44). The spectators viewed an altogether circular canvass —abetted by sod, fences, and cut-out figures—from a central platform, themselves supplying the continuity as they followed the battle from incident to incident.[20]

In a manual way Philippoteaux' efforts enlarged photographs into great displays on auditorium surfaces. Long before, however, photography's rite of passage from private view to public event had transpired through the intermediary of projection.

Projection equipment (like cloud machines) had been used increasingly in nineteenth-century theater to further illusions and to smooth continuities. The dimming of houselights during scenes also helped to direct spectator attention and to distinguish the stage from the rest of the theater. In a darkened theater, the projected image became more demanding of attention. With the appearance of the incandescent light, magic lanterns grew safer and more reliable.

The integration of auditorium and photography came at least as early as 1857. In his Panoramas of *The Fall of Sebastopol* and *The Battle of Solferino*, Charles Langlois projected photographs.

[20] Hopkins, *op. cit.*, Book 2, Ch. 7.

140

FIG. 44. An 1895 Diorama, painted by M. Paul Philippoteaux and based on photographs of the terrain, depicting the Battle of Gettysburg.

By the end of the century the ambitious Chase Electric Cyclorama combined projection, cycloramas, photography, and lighting effects to make rapid scene changes. (One of their programs was the Chicago Fire.) Projection apparatus was mounted in the center of the theater, suspended from the ceiling (Figure 45). An operator was equipped with "eight carriages, upon which are mounted the lanterns, cinematographs, kinetoscopes, and all arrangements for imparting life to the scene and producing the transformations."[21]

21 *Ibid.*, 360–61.

141

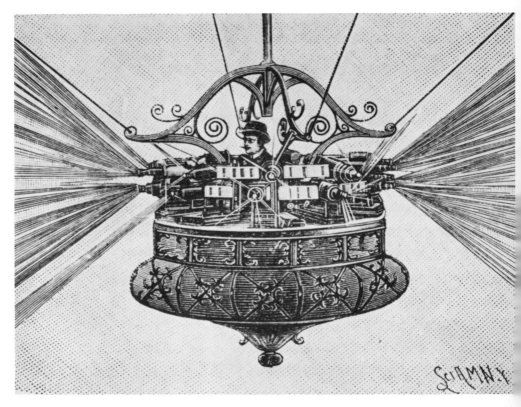

FIG. 45. Projection apparatus mounted in the center of the theater and suspended from the ceiling.

An 1887 show, *A Trip to the Moon*, was done in Berlin and the United States. It is interesting both as an antecedent to the Méliès film of 1902 and because it combines slides, painting and stage lighting effects to realize a sequential exposition. This early planetarium commenced with the reproduction of a solar eclipse as witnessed from Lake Havel near Berlin on August 19, 1887. Accompanied by a lecture, optical lanterns traced the paths of crescent and corona. Another slide, separately projected, simulated the movement of waves by manipulating three glass parts so as to vary the combinations of their painted undulations. Sunlight was represented by electric foot and border stagelights, controlled by a rheostat.

The second scene showed the moon viewed from five thousand miles. This was replaced by scenes of Mount Aristarchus and Cape

Laplace as if from a height of two and a half miles. Then the earth was seen from the moon's surface. The performance was climaxed by a solar eclipse as witnessed from the moon, followed by a return to earth, with a view of the Tyrolean highlands. "A sunset on the Indian Ocean and moonrise on the first scene concludes the lecture. A series of stereopticon views of great beauty are interspersed between the mounted scenes, thus furnishing a continuous performance."[22]

Fictional stereographic sets had been preceded early in the sixties by lantern slides, which posed live models against painted backgrounds to assemble narrative sequences based on popular songs, plays, poems, and stories. Techniques included the montages dear to still cameramen to show flashbacks, dreams, and before/after contrasts.[23] Pictures, like the later song slides, are assembled with an eye for composition and with a thoughtfulness of detail and decor which compares much to its own favor with the sparse and painted flats of early films.

Early in the nineties motion pictures were preceded in vaudeville houses by the "Illustrated Song" and the "Animated Song Sheet."[24] Song slides continued in popularity through the decade. According to Ramsaye,

> The production of series of slides often entailed considerable dramatic staging, travel for backgrounds and casting and costuming.
> When Charles K. Harris made his slide series for *Ionda, Can't You Love Your Joe?* he sent a photographer into Alabama and Tennessee for settings and real Southern Darkies. As many as sixty persons appeared in the ensemble scenes.[25]

[22] *Ibid.*, 353.

[23] Ceram includes a slide from *The Scent of the Lilacs* with a Vision Scene. A set entitled *The Drunkard's Revenge* (also in Ceram) consistently poses stagebound variations of the medium shot, but there are also interiors, exteriors, and an establishing shot. The story highlights "important moments." The merchandising of lantern-slide sets was enhanced with the application of chromolithography to glass plates by the J. L. Theobald Co., again in the sixties. A description of a set called *The Fireman* is in Cook, p. 91. It sounds very like Edison's catalogue copy for *Life of an American Fireman*. She speaks of the men setting out on their horses, the rescue of women and children, and a reward for the heroic firemen. There is even a close-up: the horses' "tossing manes and mad eyes against a background of leaping flame, purple and white-hot with the prey it has already consumed."

[24] Grau, *The Business Man in the Amusement World*, 135.

[25] Ramsaye, *op. cit.*, 102–3.

In 1907 Harris' song *The Best Thing in Life* was staged as a song-and-picture drama in three acts, using twenty-eight slides ranging from a clubroom interior to Madison Square in a snowstorm. *Hello Central, Give Me Heaven* was illustrated with scenes from a Chicago telephone exchange.

Song slides were usually accompanied by a local singer. (In the cheapest nickelodeons there was a phonograph instead.) Most often produced in a set of sixteen 4×5 dry-plate negatives, they were first provided free to theaters and later sold. Ballads were most popular. Models for the slide sets included Norma Talmadge and Mabel Normand. Theater patrons, often immigrants, used the song slides to learn English as well as American etiquette, styles, and music. Singers included George Jessel, Eddie Cantor, Al Jolson, and even Harry Cohn, later president of Columbia Pictures.

In *Only a Message from Home Sweet Home* (Figures 46–61),[26] slide 1 establishes the location; 2 is an interior of a hotel bar. In the same sequence of time 3 pulls in to the "reckless crowd," while 4 seems to be a literal enlargement of a portion of 3. Slide 5 then makes a transition to the loved ones down on the farm, whose sequence continues through 6, 7, and 8. Slide 9 is a new area of the bar (echoing a film device of moving characters when the camera is off them during a time-paralleled interim). Slide 10 returns the crowd to the location of 1. Note that it, like 12, seems surely to have been photographed on the same occasion. (Regard the composition of the figures and of the attendant at the far left entrance.) Jack, the son, is back in the final scene, tying the two storylines together.

The slides are better composed, in a more venturesome collection of locations, than is photography in the early films. More important, their narrative composition is in advance of the motion picture. Camera movement is more functional (slides 2–4). The parallel construction involving two sets of characters anticipates the Griffith Biograph films by several years. Finally, the evidence that the hotel bar exteriors (slides 1, 10, 12) were photographed

---

[26] Carroll Fleming, words; Edmond Florant, music, 1905.

1

FIGS. 46–61. *Only a Message from Home Sweet Home*, a set of sixteen song slides from 1905. *1* establishes the location; *2* is the interior of a hotel bar; *3* the "reckless crowd"; *4* appears to be an enlargement of *3*; *5–8* shows the loved ones down on the farm; *9* is another room at the bar; *10* returns to the bar exterior and was probably photographed at the same time as *1*; *11* is a shot of the home; *12* shows Jack's departure; *13–16* once again, back home on the farm. (Reproduced from John W. Ripley, "All Join in the Chorus," *American Heritage*, June 1959.)

2

3

4

5

6

7

8

152

9

10

154

11

12

13

14

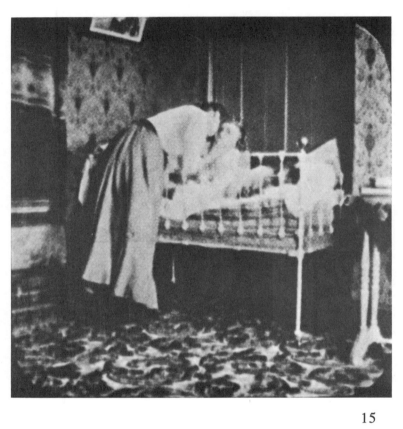

15

16

at the same time is clear indication of premeditated "editing." The sixteen-view narrative has been predesigned (scripted), and one sequence of movements has been broken up into fragments isolated by other locations. The song slide may have been dislocated by the phonograph, player piano, and a new antiballad temper in *Alexander's Ragtime Band* (1911), but its narrative continuities resurfaced in the motion picture.

The extension of drama into slide entertainment was furthered by Alexander Black, an amateur photographer who lectured on the camera in the early nineties. In 1894 he scripted and filmed in slides *Miss Jerry,* an adventure story about a girl reporter. Projecting his slides at the rate of four per minute, Black dissolved from one scene to the next, keeping background in the same position while characters "moved" from before to after poses. Miss Jerry was Blanche Bayliss, a popular model for the illustrator A. B. Wenzell. Interiors and exteriors were filmed with a hand camera. Arc lights, reflectors and diffusing screens were used.[27]

The increasingly elaborate magic lanterns tried in various ways to smooth transition techniques. In his *Motion Picture Handbook*, Richardson discusses the construction of dissolve and color wheels.[28] Another simulation of the passage of time was effected by dissolving different slides of the same scene, each separately colored so as to accomplish sunrises and sunsets.[29] A contemporary advertisement cites a "Hughes Special Biurnal with Diaphragm Shutter for rolling curtain effect, and a Malden dissolving top." There was also the Hughes Living Picture Photo Rotoscope, which

27 Ramsaye, Ch. 7. Black describes *Miss Jerry* in "Photography in Fiction," *Scribner's*, XVIII (September, 1895), 348–60. A second production, *A Capital Courtship*, is discussed in Black, "The Camera and the Comedy," *Scribner's*, XX (November, 1896), 605–10. Interestingly, Black rejected an offer from B. F. Keith to put the performance in a theater chain, believing his plays to be essentially "a lyceum rather than a theatrical feature, . . . he chose to avoid a general audience that would look for livelier dramatic elements." The productions *do* appear to be rather talky, period comedies. Black later became an editor for Hearst's Newspaper Feature Service.

28 Richardson, *Motion Picture Handbook: A Guide for Managers and Operators of Motion Picture Theatres.*

29 Jenkins and Depue, *Handbook for Motion Picture and Stereopticon Operators,* 42.

projected a few sequential pictures and "will give with oil four
foot pictures, with limelight 11×14 foot pictures."[30]

Projected slides accompanying the early motion pictures eased
the introduction of the new form. One impetus to convert the
Kinetoscope into a projected image for an audience came from the
demands of penny arcade owners who wanted an equivalent to
Henry Reno Heyl's magic lantern shows of the seventies.

Jenkins and Depue advise a movie projectionist to "have each
picture announced by a special slide in an auxiliary lantern."[31]
Hopwood notes, "To fill up the time during the change of film it
is desirable to have some arrangement for the projection of ordinary slides and this course is to be recommended as heightening
the effect of Living Pictures by contrast with a motionless one."[32]

As narrative continuities appeared among the visual entertainments of the nineteenth century, they seem to have amplified and
consolidated their techniques in response to various pressures.
Where illustrative of prose, lyrics, and drama (lantern slides, song
slides, stereograph cards), the visual tradition developed "sets"
and "series" which drew on the continuity devices of the primary
source. Where the event was an historical or travel experience
(Dioramas, Panoramas, the planetarium), time remained continuous, if truncated. Movement was introduced for the sake of
"realism," and subjective vantages to increase audience empathy.

Private entertainments were generally supplanted by one or
another kind of projection system. However, attendance at a
public performance was no less personal. Indeed, as the entertainments began to tell more elaborate stories, they became, like fiction
and melodrama, increasingly *experienced*.

In part this audience intimacy was manipulated by stories of
greater complexity, tales that encouraged identification by use of
plot and character. However, the depths of response to projected
images, especially when viewed in a darkened room, ought in
itself not be underestimated. Olive Cook quotes an authoress of
the early 1800's.

30 Hopwood, *loc. cit.*
31 Jenkins and Depue, 72.
32 Hopwood, *op. cit.*, 212.

I used to see [the magic lantern] cleaned by daylight and to handle all its parts, understanding its whole structure; yet such was my terror of the white circle on the wall, and of the moving slides, that to speak the truth, the first apparition always brought on bowel-complaint; and, at the age of thirteen, when I was pretending to take care of little children during the exhibition, I could never look at it without having the back of a chair to grasp, or hurting myself to carry off the intolerable sensation.[33]

The intensity of such an intimacy (Proust hints at it in his introduction to *Swann's Way*) suggests a degree of empathy often sought by art; the nineteenth century bypassed literacy to bring it within the purview of new audiences.

Whatever the event, the picture in our head remains the same size. A story exists from the pages of the *Weekly Wisconsin*, printed sometime during 1884. Through an unhappy accident that followed the efforts of a student of Mesmer to show his skills, a young man is suspended, like Rip Van Winkle, throughout the century. On waking he is bewildered by gas lighting and the telegraph and discomfited with the friction match and the idea that "the sun will paint our portraits." However, when he watches with the aid of a field glass while a train approaches, "his hands shake . . . partly with excitement."

With the introduction of lens systems the relation of audience to performance assumes heightened qualities of psychological "closeness" unparalleled by earlier events. Some elements of the experience echo our earlier description of binoculars: circumscribed vision, a secret sense of special privilege, and the ambiguity of a "view" curiously incongruent with one's literal distance from the subject. Such qualities all affected a spectator, leaving him curiously vulnerable. Compounding those pressures were formal elements of a structured experience (in the case of viewed or projected stories) which *directed* one's attention and regulated its duration. Increasingly, such controlling principles drew as heavily on visual information as they did on the narrative traditions of prose and theater.

---

33 Cook, *op. cit.*, 19. The writer is Harriet Martineau.

7
Art, Photography, and the Shape of Things to Come

Cross influences between painting and photography operated long before the printing press had its way upon either. This chapter will detail effects both of photography and of printing on the graphic arts. After that we shall try to sketch in brief outline the character of several narrative visual elements which foreshadow like practices in the motion picture.

Almost from the time of its inception photography became an adjunct to the graphic artist, a diary to his memory and a reinforcement of his committment to surface detail.[1] However, it was not the painter alone who equated lenses with perception. Earlier we have noted the preoccupation of writers like Proust and Du-Maurier with visual qualities in memory. The idea of mental "close-ups" even penetrated psychology. Rudolf Arnheim describes as the voice of a new era a 1909 representation by the psychologist Edward B. Titchener on the nature of his personal images of thought:

---

[1] The best study of early artist-photograph relationships is Van Deren Coke, *The Painter and the Photograph.* A contemporary account of conflicting aesthetics can be found in Alexander Black, "The Artist and the Camera: a Debate," *Century,* LXIV, No. 6 (October, 1902), 813–22. Honoré Daumier had known affinities with photography. Homer, Eakins, and Remington used photographs. Degas copied a Muybridge drayhorse. Thomas Eakins worked with Muybridge at the University of Pennsylvania. In fact, Eakins developed a single-lens camera designed to replace Muybridge's multiple-lens approach to animal motion. The Eakins machine used a pair of revolving disks. As a subject moved across the field these discs sequentially exposed separate images, each overlapping the previous one, all on a single negative. The 1874 exhibition which gave rise to the name Impressionism was staged in a photographer's studio. Marcel Duchamp learned from the motion studies of Marey. The photographs of Bragaglia influenced Balla's Futurist paintings, both in composition and as motion studies. The Rome Futurism exhibit of 1911 financed a display of photos so that painters could study the state of the new art.

164

My mind, in its ordinary operations, is a fairly complete picture gallery,—not of finished paintings, but of impressionist notes. Whenever I read or hear that somebody has done something modestly, or gravely, or proudly, or humbly, or courteously, I see a visual hint of the modesty or gravity or pride or humility or courtesy. The stately heroine gives me a flash of a tall figure, the only clear part of which is a hand holding up a steely grey skirt; the humble suitor gives me a flash of a bent figure, the only clear part of which is the bowed back, though at times there are hands held deprecatingly before the absent face. . . . All these descriptions must be either self-evident or as unreal as a fairy-tale.[2]

In the popular mind photography became an easy paradigm for perception and mental process. Thus Marie Correlli, a successful lady novelist of the period, explained in *The Soul of Lilith* (1897) how a Near Eastern mystic reads minds:

Consider yourself the photographic negative, and me the sensitive paper to receive the impression. I may offer you a blurred picture, but I do not think it likely. Only if you wish to hide anything from me I would advise you not to try the experiment.

By this date blurred pictures were less likely because the faster exposures of Etienne-Jules Marey and Eadweard Muybridge were correcting the impressions. Just as contemporary prose stylists sought to capture the specifics of action by spelling out its elements in more accurate detail, painters now began to investigate movement's components.

Capacities to arrest figures in motion hardly originated with photography. In the early eighteenth century Houbraken attributed to Rembrandt an ability to catch a moment at any given instant with observation so fine that it might be retained until the occasion called for it.[3]

The suggestion of action rather than its arrest had been pursued by a variety of techniques. Rodin represented sequential moments, like two stages of action in the same figure. In Delacroix movement is indicated in the self-evidence of brush strokes and their

2 Titchener, *Lectures on the Experimental Psychology of the Thought-Processes* (New York; Macmillan, 1926), 13, 21. In Arnheim, *Visual Thinking*, 107.
3 Gombrich, *Art and Illusion*, 345–46.

varied direction.[4] (Later painters like Van Gogh and Dubuffet used brush strokes not only dynamically, but to call attention to the medium itself.) However, after *Scientific American* reported Muybridge's animal locomotion studies with photographs on the October 19, 1878, cover, movement became subject to new scrutiny. This condition is readily apparent if we contrast action drawings in several illustrations.

Movement figures in many engravings, but its appearance accelerates in frequency as pictures were used to serve the subjects of journalism: explosions, disasters, and riots. An 1865 woodcut forecasting ground tremors in California presents stick-figure characters (Figure 62), in contrast to Everett Shinn's *Street Scene at a*

[4] See Tyler, "Film as a Force in Visual Education," *Sex, Psyche and Etcetera in the Film.*

FIG. 62. An attempt to capture movement is illustrated in this 1865 woodcut forecasting ground tremors in California. (From the *San Francisco Chronicle.*)

166

Fire. Done for the *Century* in February, 1891, Shinn's drawing shows how far movement unbent in the interim (Figure 63). Shinn is not only far more "real" in his detail of behavior, but, like a photographer, crops out the blaze itself, the better to isolate the drama of the firemen. More noted for his western illustrations, Frederic Remington, who made use of Muybridge's animal photographs, provides an 1890 instance of arrested movement in *Touchdown: Yale vs. Princeton* (Figure 64).

Three years later Vachel Lindsay came to the New York School of Art, where the emphasis rested on "capturing action" in drawing. Lindsay speaks with special affection in this regard about his teacher, Robert Henri, leader of the Revolutionary Black Gang which later became the Ashcan School.[5]

Lindsay was one of the early figures to write insightfully (if sometimes hysterically) about motion pictures, and a doctoral dissertation proposes that this early training influenced the poet's approach to criticism.[6] While the idea may be more apparent than real (Lindsay seems inclined to praise moments of film that remind him of *any* older art), he does seem thoughtfully aware of special graphic possibilities to photographed movement: "Even in a simple chase picture, the speed must not destroy the chance to enjoy the modelling."[7]

In a vein similar to Remington and Shinn, the "dynamic framing" of George Bellows (himself influenced by Robert Henri) in *Stag at Sharkey's* (1907) encourages us to anticipate the next point in time.

These examples illustrate not only a growing perspicacity toward movement, but also a correlary to that interest, namely, new qualities of graphic composition. Figure 62 shows a symmetry of design that belies the actions purported to be "caught." It has the look of spectacle staging in nineteenth-century theater at its most ambitious. Such an approach to surface reality was drastically affected by photography.

The nineteenth-century photograph replaced engravings, which

---

[5] Wolfe, *Vachel Lindsay: the Poet as Film Theorist*, 61–63.
[6] *Ibid.*, 64.
[7] Lindsay, *The Art of the Moving Picture*, 116.

FIG. 63. Everett Shinn's *Street Scene at a Fire* (1891) eliminates the fire altogether, the better to capture the drama and movement of the firemen. (Reproduced from Walt Reed, *The Illustrator in America*.)

168

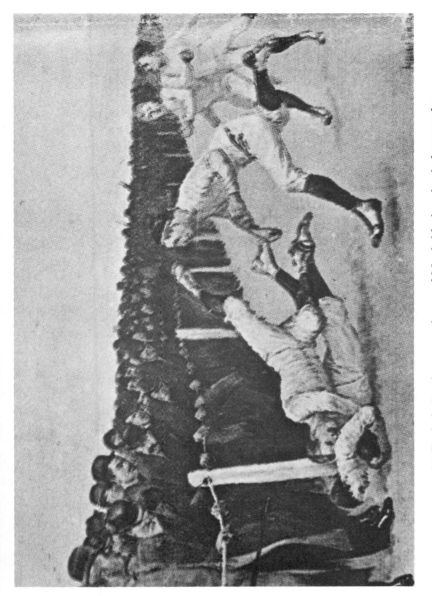

FIG. 64. Frederic Remington made use of Muybridge's animal photographs in his study of movement. In *Touchdown: Yale vs. Princeton* (1890) note how the action is arrested "photographically."

had failed to report with satisfactory accuracy on the details of surface and line that we now come to expect unquestioningly from graphic materials. William Ivins notes how early printmakers tended to "rationalize their own pictorial accounts and [to] overlook or disregard what appeared to them to be mere irrationalities in the pictorial accounts given by their predecessors." These very rationalizations "most frequently took the form of an endeavor for symmetry, which produced regular shapes that not only lost all verisimilitude of lines and edges but introduced a balanced arrangement of parts and forms, which, however satisfactory to mental habits, resulted in a very complete misrepresentation of the actual facts."[8]

The very essences of photography, its "limitations," encouraged new approaches to graphic form, and like dispositions accompanied the early motion picture. As the early photographs were generally defined by studio settings, the movies grew from compositional conventions of the proscenium. Even the exteriors of the Lumières mostly indulge simple sorts of design, except when a physical exigency (for example, the placement of a railroad track) forces more interesting complications of movement. (As soon as the camera got outside, compositions with strong diagonals figured, too, in still photography.)

A major problem faced by early still cameramen was bulky equipment, coupled with slow emulsions and lenses. In spite of this, and saddled, literally, with the wet plate collodion process, Matthew Brady and his associates introduced to photography, and soon to art, a new wealth of compositional complications detailed by war. By necessity Brady was limited to military camp snapshots, ruins, and the static spontaneities of corpses. Yet it is these very holocausts, like the ruins of Charleston and Richmond, whose restrictions on camera placement, combined with Brady's sense of image and of open form, to render pictures that remain fresh today.

In 1871, Richard Leach Maddox discovered how to replace the earlier solution of guncotton, alcohol, and ether with gelatin. The new dry plates were not only manageable in a way that the

8 Ivins, *Prints and Visual Communication*, 41–42.

cumbersome portable darkrooms could never be, they also achieved an emulsion speed by way of the gelatin-bromide solution, which permitted exposures of much less than a second. This put the camera adventitiously into the hands of the photographer, and introduced an age in which visual candor seized on arrested motion to instigate new compositional interest.

If we look at any photographic record of the eighties and nineties, we are often most struck by the accomplishments of amateurs. Some photos, of course, are poor in design, and others have been doctored by publishers who reconstructed from ancient "originals" what amount to different pictures by cropping and often through enlarging portions of the pristine print for the sake of better composition or more striking vantage. This has always been the prerogative of publishers' art departments, but more important it was the very scheme by which painters of the late nineteenth century put photography to use and by which, in turn, many photographers reclaimed their medium in the 1920's. In any case, the hundred-year-old photographs of fishing trips, school classes, and sandlot baseball games often seem to have a quality of space about them that is almost incongruous with the costumes and the textures of another age.

An 1888 photograph like Jacob Riis's famous *Bandit's Roost* maintains its ominous record of a society separated from us now by time as well as class (Figure 65). In the long run, however, what seem most affecting are the lines of wash strung across Mulberry Street at oddly coherent intersections of angles, and the fence and distant tenement walls that backstop our perspective.

There is a particular compositional scheme recurrent in the paintings of Edgar Degas which is clearly derivative of photography. A serious student both of the new medium and of the Japanese prints, which had entered Europe during the 1860's, Degas injects a strong quality of complementary movement in such paintings as *Place de la Concorde* (*le Vicomte Lepic et ses Deux Filles*, 1873–74); in *La Voitures Aux Courses* (c. 1871); and *Aux Cours, Jockeys Amateurs Pres d'une Voiture* (c. 1880). All show the most planned, photolike "accidents."

In *Place de la Concorde*, for example, the direction of the

FIG. 65. Jacob Riis's famous photographs of New York's Lower East Side (this one dates from 1888 and is called *Bandit's Roost*) could almost be a set for Brecht's *Three-Penny Opera*.

horse and carriage reinforces the gaze on the part of the left figure who is cropped so as to be "caught" half in, half beyond the frame (Figure 66). Despite the contrary direction of glance on the part of the Vicomte's two daughters and their dog (whose figure seems especially arbitrary in the arrangement), all attention is artfully centered on the Vicomte.

This manipulation of distinct fields of movement did not adapt itself so readily to the stage, where motion was inclined to be simplistic and (begging the production of epic grandeurs), generally useful only to motivate a character or to advance the plot. In the motion picture its premeditated appearance comes with D. W. Griffith (who of course liked to advance plots too). By the time of a Biograph short like *The Lonedale Operator* (1911), Griffith has transcended theater rubrics to design and execute complications of movement and staging more like Degas than Belasco. A simple example illustrates the point.

In Figure 67 a train draws into a railroad station. When it has slowed to a stop (Figure 68), an attendant moves into the foreground. (He is relaying some moneybags to the Lonedale outpost.) As this business is transacted, conductors descend from the rear of the train. A baggage cart then moves down the platform into the midground field (Figure 69), there to pick up a large case from a loader in a baggage car. Concurrent with this, passengers exit from the rear and new riders ascend (Figure 70). The original attendant exits, the train pulls off (Figure 71), and finally the baggage cart moves away in a contrary direction with its load.

Elementary as these negotiations may appear, they demonstrate a level of visual sophistication new to the motion picture. The screen is engaged in a number of events which simultaneously command its area in something beyond simple compositional form, balancing one another's movements and presaging future plot. Griffith has learned to prepare for later events with compositional repetitions that will underline his intention.

Soon afterward, when the train pulls into the Lonedale station, his composition is repeated in reverse. Blanche Sweet enters to receive the money (Figure 72), and while she negotiates this two

FIG. 66. Edgar Degas was a serious student of both photography and Japanese prints. In *Place de la Concorde* (1873–74) he injects a strong quality of complementary movement which is clearly derivative of photography.

174

FIGS. 67–73. In *The Lonedale Operator* (1911) D. W. Griffith illustrates movement in a way novel in cinema. In Figures 67–71 a train pulls into the station, baggage is loaded, passengers exit, new riders ascend, and the train pulls out. In Figures 72–73 composition and movements are reversed: Blanche Sweet enters to receive the moneybags and two rail-riders exit behind her. Griffith has learned to prepare for later events with compositional repetitions that will underline his plot. (From the author's collection.)

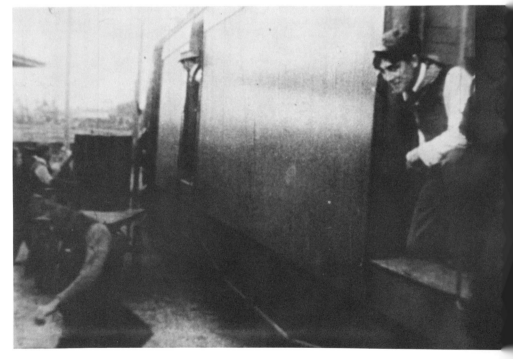

177

ruffians who have been riding the rails exit behind her (Figure 73). Visually, this is the little payoff for the earlier scene's business—Griffith's equivalent to what the pulp author of Uncle Wiggley called "laying pipes."

Another device which could be used both to direct a viewer's attention and to define foreground-background relationships was the element of focus, again a consequence of lenses, particularly of those lens designs whose longer focal length shrank the depth of field (see Appendix IV).

If we compare the Degas *Portrait de Desiré Dihau* (Figure 74) with a painting by another artist interested in photography, Camille Corot, we find variant approaches to focus. In Corot's *La Cathédrale à Travers les Arbres* (1865–70; Figure 75), the foreground leaves go "out of focus" to lend attention to the cathedral. In Degas, foreground focus is sharper. Corot, during his later years, characteristically drew on a palette of green-grays, adjusting the variant light values in emulation of the film emulsions of his day.

178

FIG. 74. Preoccupations with focus colored Impressionist imagery. Note how sharp the foreground is in Degas' *Portrait de Desiré Dihau*, how fuzzy the dancers.

The idea of cutting out a portion of the human figure by the boundaries of the frame again has historical antecedent. In Jan van Eyck's *Music Making Angels*, from the Ghent alterpiece (c. 1432), we can spot the smallest detail of an obscured angel working the bellows of an organ while another's face is halved by the upper right arch. Such a scheme encourages our sense that the reality of a picture extends beyond its frame. It is evident, too, in

179

FIG. 75. Camille Corot was also interested in photography, and in his *La Cathédrale à Travers les Arbres* (1865–70) he makes the foreground leaves go out of focus to lend attention to the cathedral.

artists as divergent as Donatello (*Herod's Banquet*) and Dürer (*The Prodigal Son*), but it appears with increasing frequency among the late nineteenth-century artists: Pissarro (*La Causette*, 1892), Renoir (*Baigneuses*, c. 1885), Seurat (*Le Cirque*), Degas (*La Femme aux Chrysanthèmes*, 1863), Gauguin (*Nature Morte et Profil*, 1886), and—most famously—Toulouse-Lautrec (*At the Moulin Rouge*, 1882).

A further photolike disposition in nineteenth-century painting which later reappears in the cinema is the angle of view as it is used to serve narrative purpose. In such Degas perspectives as the low-angled *Les Musiciens à l'Orchestre* (c. 1868); (Figure 76), with its sharper focus on the foreground and the many high-angled "shots" of dancers, there exists an obvious equation between how the painter chooses to see his subjects and his attitudes toward them. Steep perspectives are found too in DuMaurier, as early as the illustrations for a *Legend of Camelot* in *Punch* (1866), recalling similar designs by the pre-Raphaelites.

Charles Dana Gibson carried this approach further, for he constructs visual circumstances in which the audience may be privy to attitudes unknown by some of the subjects. This technique had some correlation in the theater (including the melodramatic "aside"), but even the toned-down acting encouraged by Belasco was more heightened and stylized than a drawing required. In this respect two noteworthy Gibson drawings were done for *Life: Reading the Will* (Figure 77) and *A Love Song* (Figure 78).

As with prose, as soon as the viewer is encouraged to assume a point of view that is both unique and judgmental to the story, he (with the illustrator) has become "involved." The election of "angle" is a matter of consequence. We are an accomplice with the reader of the will, just as the composition of *A First Night* (Figure 79) enables Gibson to require a kind of spatially maintained omniscience from us in its "high shot" vantage. Whereas Toulouse-Lautrec's *Jane Avril* might have been seen from a box, Gibson's is a new angle, not open to rationalization by theater seating.

In an earlier discussion of the close-up as a prose device in Flaubert, mention was made of photography as a possible causal

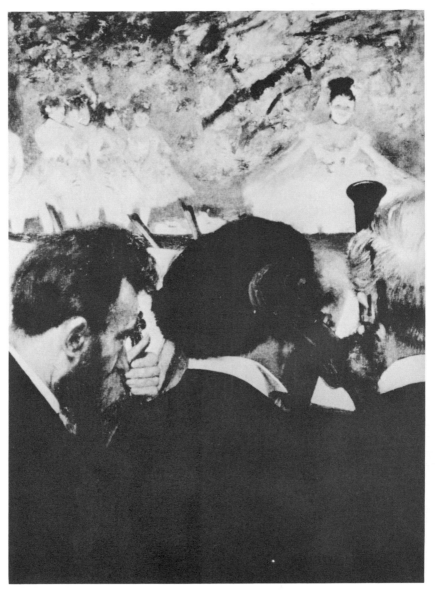

FIG. 76. A further photolike disposition in painting is the angle of view. Degas' *Les Musiciens à l'Orchestra* (c. 1868) locates its point of view close to the stage apron from an orchestra seat, a technique undertaken also by Daumier. (Property The Louvre.)

182

FIG. 77. Charles Dana Gibson constructs visual circumstances in which the audience is privy to attitudes unknown by the subjects. The above illustration is called *Reading the Will*. (Reproduced from Charles Dana Gibson, *The Gibson Book*.)

FIG. 78. *A Love Song*, also by Gibson, encourages the viewer to assume a point of view that is both unique and judgmental, in short, to become "involved." (From Charles Dana Gibson, *The Gibson Book*.)

FIG. 79. The composition of *A First Night* enables Gibson to require a kind of spatially maintained omniscience from the viewer in its "high shot" vantage. (From Charles Dana Gibson, *The Gibson Book*.)

agent. Photos of sculptured heads may be viewed, like architectural details, as close-ups. Of course the very fact that *any* photograph of *any* size will be seen by its audience from vantages quite different from the camera lens' purview itself simulates something of the ambiguity attending movie viewing. Even more detailed photographs can be located in the Eugene Trutat book on photography and natural history which has animal studies at close vantage.[9] Marey's motion studies include picture sequences of the umbrella of the medusa, the dorsal fin of the sea horse, and the comatula.

Among painters the detail study, as in early drawing books, has figured for centuries. Yet other techniques of lending emphasis through the magnification of selected portions of a field have been

[9] Trutat, *La Photographie Appliquée à l'Histoire Naturelle*.

184

used as well. Big heads, for example, gave caricature a means simultaneously to indulge two "angles" on one subject. Caracci, first to use the word caricature, drew big-headed people, and they also figure in seventeenth-century woodcuts illustrating plays of religious burlesque. The technique lends satiric importance to a figure. It is common in the comic valentines of 1825–40 and can be found among illustrations of novels like *Wuthering Heights*.[10]

In large measure the graphic elements noted so far brought their effects into public consciousness because of technological innovations in printing. (Specifics of this revolution are outlined in Appendix VI.) Their result was the introduction of photography on a mass scale to the reader by invading his newspaper and magazines with pictures. At the same time the invention of line engraving gave the illustrator exceptional new freedoms and fineness of line, evident in the work of such men as Charles Dana Gibson.

Released to earn livings in the service of journalism, photographers separated their identities from painters, while usurping the domain of portraiture. On the other hand, artists learned to distinguish their own perceptions from that of the camera. One particular preoccupation—multiple-angled views done within a single composition—warrants special consideration because it foreshadows the cinema's later concern with time-space interrelationships.

Various media seem in our period to have confronted the matter of simultaneity and to have evolved solutions to its expression by different conventions. The techniques of multiple staging answered some of the plot demands of melodrama. Parallel editing served similar purpose for narrative prose. Slides and stereographs had Vision Scenes and other kinds of multiple exposure.

Something of the same tendency appears among illustrations and photographic layouts. The idea of such compositions is not new, but what does appear innovative is the increasing use of the several-picture form to resolve problems of space, time, and multiperspective vantages.

10 Laderman, "On the Uses of the Past and of the Too Recent Past," *Vanity Fair* (October 19, 1961). Reprinted in *Artforum* (1970), 56–58.

Following the lead of O. G. Rejlander, who made a famous composite photograph in 1857 called *The Two Paths of Life* (Figure 80), Henry Peach Robinson did similar several-negative prints for years and wrote *Pictorial Effects in Photography* (1869) to explain his work. "Trick photographs" were popular at the end of the century, like the famous three-faced photo of Toulouse-Lautrec painting himself. Many such techniques, especially bodiless heads and dimunitive figures, were preempted by Méliès in his early movies.

Inventions of the time, like the telegraph and the telephone, encouraged a sense of simultaneous occurrence. The *Daily Graphic* of March 16, 1877, pictured on its front page a telephone speaker and the worldwide audiences to his words (radio being uninvented as yet). Another sketch, similarly designed, promoted the idea of telephones both for social and business use.

Simultaneous views served a special purpose in advertising because they promoted multiple display for a product or procedure. In the 1897 Sears Roebuck catalogue we find "masthead" artwork, which usually introduces a new subject, serving this end. Equally interesting is the dramatic contrast in size and (sometimes) angle of view between the components. Thus in the timepiece section a watch and chain, suspended from the lettering, are larger than the human figures, and the picture includes an "insert" of the mechanical department (Figure 81). A similar illustration promotes the Minnesota sewing machines, which circle the globe at the equator, the compositions adorned by Pucklike children on whose shields are emblazoned the company's emblem (Figure 82).

A domestic do-it-yourself impulse toward multiple-image arrangements can be found among the hand-colored lithographs, which were combined with metallic embossing to produce fancy package labels. Free of advertising, these were collected by customers for scrapbooks (Figure 83). German lithographers printed large sheets with separable motifs (flowers, birds, letters) which might be cut up by the collector for artistic arrangements.

The garish chromolithographic posters which proclaimed Victorian melodramas would represent, in many pictures, their stars (or one performer in various make-ups) and moments of high

FIG. 80. *The Two Paths of Life* (1857), a famous composite photograph by O. G. Rejlander, attempts to resolve problems of space, time, and multiperspective vantages.

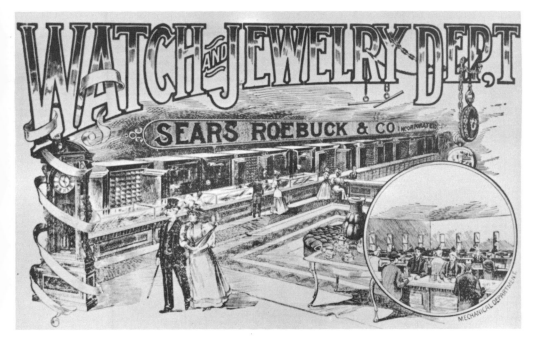

FIG. 81. Simultaneous views served a special purpose in advertising because they promoted multiple display for a product. (From an 1897 Sears Roebuck catalogue.)

FIG. 82. A similar illustration promotes the Minnesota sewing machines, which circle the globe at the equator, the compositions adorned by Pucklike children on whose shields are emblazoned the company's emblem. (From an 1897 Sears Roebuck catalogue.)

FIG. 83. Multiple-image arrangements can also be found among the hand-colored lithographs, which were combined with metallic embossing to produce fancy package labels. Free of advertising, these were collected by customers for scrapbooks. (From Frances Lichten, *Decorative Art of Victoria's Era.*)

excitement, arranged in no necessary order except as the composition determined.[11] An 1880 poster for *The World* (Drury Lane) has eight elements, each done from a different angle (Figure 84). As dime novels became successful, they absorbed the theatrical poster to illustrate high moments in their lurid stories (Figure 9).

Chromolithographs were also prepared to mark events of public interest. One made by Kurz and Allison uses before-and-after "shots" of the battleship *Maine* in Havana Harbor, plus inserts of Admiral Montgomery Sicard and one of the ninety *Maine* survivors, Captain Charles Sigsbee (Figure 85).

The engraved certificate was another form for multiple-image display, running back to the eighteenth century in the United States. (We might consider everything that goes on on the back of a dollar bill.) A less remarked location for imaginative approaches to many-pictured compositions was the Victorian valentine. Many angles and perspectives are evident in the work of Esther Howland (c. 1860), made of several pages, ornamented with scraps and embossed paper (Figure 86). Similarly, wrappers dating as far back as the Civil War show multiple views. Another location for several-imaged compositions was the picture postcard, which, like the Vision Scene, might leap forward or back in time (Figure 87). An interesting wood engraving by Winslow Homer assimilates the early Christian convention of ovaled portraits with theatrical Vision Scenes (Figure 88).

Early motion pictures adopted similar multiple-image techniques from the trick photography of the still camera and the Vision Scenes of the theater. Their narrative use figured later in the tryptich screens of Abel Gance's *Napoleon* (1925). Durgnat notes how Claude Autant-Lara "split his Cinemascope image into two for *Construire un Feu* (1927)."[12] The multiple screens of Expo '67 renewed the tradition. Many experimental films and

---

[11] A similarly cavalier approach to design appears in *The Great Train Robbery* (1903). Its close-up of an outlaw firing into the camera lens was to be located at the beginning or end to "heighten interest."

[12] Durgnat, "Fake, Fiddle and the Photographic Arts," *The British Journal of Aesthetics*, V, No. 3 (July, 1965), 285.

FIG. 84. Garish chromolithographic posters advertising Victorian melo-dramas represented moments of high excitement, arranged in no particular order except as the composition determined. An 1880 poster for *The World* (Drury Lane) has eight elements, each done from a different angle. (From Maurice Disher, *Melodrama: Plots That Thrilled*.)

191

FIG. 85. Chromolithographs were also prepared to mark events of public interest. One made by Kurz and Allison uses before-and-after "shots" of the battleship *Maine* in Havana Harbor, plus inserts of Admiral Montgomery Sicard (left) and one of the ninety *Maine* survivors, Captain Charles Sigsbee (right). (Reproduced from *American Heritage*.)

special effects sequences have additionally made varied use of overlayed and bypacked images. Their tradition stems more directly from Cubism.

No nineteenth-century esthetic investigation has been more lasting in effect than the study of variant perspectives which began with Paul Cézanne and continued, somewhat different in intent, with Picasso and Braque. Their direction finally led to a sophisticated combination of the Eakins-Muybridge camera with the time preoccupations that haunted the pre-World War I artistic world.

Dating from the 1890's, Cézanne began to "build up his pictures in staggered planes of color superimposed one atop the other

FIG. 86. Many angles and perspectives are evident in the work of Esther Howland (c. 1860), made of several pages, ornamented with scraps and embossed paper.

perpendicularly, and thus obtained a self-created spatial recession that owed nothing to nature, nor did it hollow out the picture surface."[13] His work does not, like Degas and others, echo the photograph. Rather, as Merleau-Ponty notes, Cézanne's distinctiveness lies in the differences:

> By remaining faithful to the phenomena in his investigations of perspective Cézanne discovered what recent psychologists have come to formulate: the lived perspective, that which we actually perceive, is not a geometric or a photographic one. The objects we see close at hand appear smaller, those far away seem larger than

[13] Raynall, *Cézanne*, 62.

FIG. 87. Another location for several-imaged compositions was the picture postcard, which, like the Vision Scene, might leap forward or back in time. (From the author's collection.)

FIG. 88. An interesting wood engraving by Winslow Homer assimilates the early Christian convention of ovaled portraits with theatrical Vision Scenes. (Reproduced from the *San Francisco Chronicle*, December 21, 1969.)

they do in a photograph. (This can be seen in a movie, where a train approaches and gets bigger much faster than a real train would under the same circumstances.) To say that a circle seen obliquely is seen as an ellipse is to substitute for our actual perception what we would see if we were cameras; in reality we see a form which oscillates around the ellipse without being an ellipse.[14]

Merleau-Ponty elaborates this distinction between the realities of the lens and those of the eye by citing the artist's portrait of Mme. Cézanne: ". . . the border of the wallpaper on one side of her body does not form a straight line with that on the other; and

14 Merleau-Ponty, *Sense and Non-sense*, 14.

195

indeed it is known that if a line passes beneath a wide strip of paper, the two visible segments appear dislocated."[15]

In forsaking the apparent realities of "what we would see if we were cameras," Cézanne finally denied Alberti's 1435 geometrical rationalization for pictorial space and cleared the way for multiple vantages on a *single* subject. Art heralded the spatial ubiquities of edited film,[16] abstracting the image in the process. (Cézanne said, "I see overlapping planes before me and sometimes lines that seem to fall away.")[17]

Taking cues both from Cézanne and from those exaggerations and twists of line and shape he found in African sculpture, Picasso, working with Georges Braque, continued this imaginative journey. Their efforts resulted in a series of paintings, soon called Cubist, in which flat and variegated surfaces sometimes intercut, sometimes overlapped in multivaried perspectives on the same object. Their pictures dislocated space and paralleled contemporary efforts of writers, players, and cinematographers to ellipsize time down into the moment. For in restructuring pictorial space, Picasso and Braque also presented their objects as they would be perceived at different points in time. Thus if we examine such a painting as Picasso's *Accordionist* (1911), we note that what is discernible in the figure and the instrument seems to vary in terms of camera angle (portions of the hands and the keyboard are closer shots than the rest), while at the same time the position of the instrument swings in the temporal arc of a musician's performance (Figure 89).

It as if Duchamp's *Nude Descending a Staircase*—painted at about the same time, and, he says, influenced by photography—had been drawn from many vantages on the stairs, and the images had been fully superimposed as well as overlapped.

Insofar as the painter found himself subject to temporal sequence, Cubism freed him from straight-ahead exposition in a way strikingly like the impulses of Ford Maddox Ford and Joseph Conrad. Let us reconsider an earlier quotation from Ford:

[15] *Ibid.*

[16] I want to acknowledge here the emphasis on this commonality of concern placed by Gerald Noxon, "Cinema and Cubism," *Society of Cinematologists*, II (1962), 23–33.

[17] Raynall, *op. cit.*, 62.

FIG. 89. Picasso's *Accordionist* (1911) dislocated space and paralleled contemporary efforts of writers, players, and cinematographs to ellipsize time down into the moment. (Reproduced courtesy The Solomon R. Guggenheim Museum, New York.)

It became early evident to me that what was the matter with the Novel, and the British Novel in particular was that it went straight forward, whereas in your gradual making acquaintanceship with your fellows you never do go straight forward. . . . To get . . . a man in fiction you could not begin at his beginning and work his life chronologically to the end. You must first get him with a strong impression, and then work backwards and forwards over his past. . . .

Life does not say to you: in 1914 my next-door neighbor, Mr. Slack, erected a greenhouse and painted it with Cox's green aluminum paint. . . . If you think about the matter you will remember in various unordered pictures how one day Mr. Slack appeared in his garden and contemplated the wall to his house.[18]

Compare, then, a representation by E. A. Gombrich of Picasso's approach as it eventuated in Cubism:

If we think of an object, let us say, a violin, it does not appear before the eyes of our mind as we would see it with our bodily eyes. We can, and in fact do, think of its various aspects at the same time. Some of them stand out so clearly that we feel we can touch and handle them; others are somewhat blurred. And yet this strange medley of images represents more of the "real" violin than any single snapshot or meticulous painting could ever contain.[19]

The parallel is clear, and, curiously, both authors refer to various pictures (or snapshots) which must be handled into place. The writers are evocative of Titchener's mental gallery, and Gombrich even echoes Marie Correlli's blurred picture. In some common fashion all these people, perhaps abetted by the idea of photography as mental process, appear to describe an identical kind of visual introspection. Further, their manipulation of the materials coincides. Picasso, like Conrad, could be said to have edited images some time before the invention of the Moviola. However, unlike Conrad, all his pictures were of the same subject.

Plato seized on one aspect of the problem in *The Republic*: "You may look at a bed from different points of view, obliquely or directly, from any other point of view, and the bed will appear

18 Ford, *Joseph Conrad: A Personal Reminiscence*, 192–93.
19 Gombrich, *The Study of Art*, 432.

different, but there is no difference in reality. And the same of all things."

Yet there is a difference, for Plato's bed does not change with the passage of time. Picasso confronted a filmic problem by recognizing that a moving subject (like a musician) could be represented on a two dimensional plane as altering both its shape and perspective. One must fragmentize the material into discrete components, then create in their recomposition his own new space-time continuum.

Part Three
The Movies

8

Ten Cent
Palace Life

The most extraordinary revolution recorded since entertaining
the public was a line of endeavor.
                                                    —ROBERT GRAU

At first the business of motion pictures competed not only with
traditional public entertainments, but also with an entire new
coin-operated industry (see Appendix VIII) for its nickel-and-
dime audience. The expansion of nickelodeons relegated many
other entertainment media—like the player piano and the phonograph—to the home.

We err if we envision all urban, laboring-class audiences as
alike. Clearly, there were heterogeneous interests which had to be
sorted out by experience as movies developed if tastes were to be
served. Joe Batten has interesting accounts of two London events
attended by workers at the turn of the century. At Conway Hall,
for example, the music of Haydn, Mozart, Schubert, Schumann,
Beethoven, Mendelssohn, Dvořák, Brahms, and Franck was spon-
sored by the South Place Ethical Society. "An audience that was
almost pure Dickens and mainly of the working classes, artisans
and shopkeepers from the neighborhood, patriarchal Jews and
their families, and earnest students following the music with open
scores on their knees."[1] In contrast, at the Britannia at Hoxton,

> The evening began at seven o'clock with a five- or six-act drama.
> This was followed, some time between nine thirty and ten, with
> variety, consisting of four to six turns. Before these appeared there
> would be a new influx to the audience, the half-timers admitted at
> half-price. As they entered . . . after the variety, a rollicking farce

1 Batten, *Joe Batten's Book*, 11.

203

would bring the curtain down somewhere near midnight. The drama
served was of the like of *The Silver King, The Colleen Bawn,* or *The
Grip of Iron,* whilst the farce might be *Box and Cox* or *White-bait
at Greenwich.* During the pantomime season the theater was
crammed from pit to gallery with mothers and children, the noise
was deafening and the smell of oranges all-pervading.[2]

Descriptions of audience response to nickelodeons suggest that
these patrons more likely paralleled the half-timers than the South
Place Ethical Society. The economics of nickelodeon operation
were itemized in a 1907 *Saturday Evening Post* by Joseph Medill
Patterson (who returned from World War I to found the New
York *Daily News*).[3] Quoting one manager that "This is like a
Klondike," Patterson spelled out the budget for a weekly entertainment which, Blue Laws permitting, ran every day of the year to
an audience made up by 35 percent children:

Wage of Manager	$25
Wage of Operator	20
Wage of Doorman	15
Wage of Porter or Musician	12
Rental of Films (two reels; changed twice a week)	50
Rent of Projecting Machine	10
Rent of Building	40
Music, Printing, "Campaign contributions," etc.	18
Total	$190

Most of the nickelodeons consisted of 199 kitchen chairs, their
number defined by regulations which in major cities required an
annual five hundred dollar fee for theatrical licenses if an audience
numbered two hundred or more. Thus at its admission price, a
nickelodeon had to service a weekly attendance of thirty-eight
hundred to reach its break-even point. Yet it was a "Klondike,"
and prices did not long remain at a nickel.

2 *Ibid.,* 13–14. Descriptions of Lottie Collins, George Lupino, and Tararaboomdeay
follow.
3 Patterson, "The Nickelodeons," *Saturday Evening Post,* Nov. 23, 1907. Antholo-
gized in Butterfield, *The Saturday Evening Post Treasury.*

One indication of the amount of money to be made in films at its earliest period can be found in the evidence of pirated dupes: illegal prints of circulated titles. In 1905 one man sold shares in an organization formed for this very purpose. He had accumulated forty thousand dollars before he was stopped by the Film Theft Committee, a vigilante group formed within the budding production industry.[4]

By 1911, 11,500 movie houses contracted with one or more of the 150 rental exchanges for different film programs each week. (Figures of the Motion Picture Patents Company dating from December 18, 1911, locate 6,236 of its licensees, 5,205 non-licensees, and an assortment of legitimate theaters which sometimes used films.)[5] Business growth was also indicated by the development of advertising as a promotional tool to film exhibition. By about 1905 film companies were distributing such materials with their "feature" releases, including stills and lithographic sheets. The pictures often bore little relation to the movies.[6]

In many respects early entertainment films seem rather like their contemporary phonograph records; that is, little documentations of events either of public interest or echoing the popular idea of artistic merit. There were turn-of-the-century cylinders of Tennyson reciting *The Charge of the Light Brigade*, Barnum speaking on the circus, Sir Henry Irving reciting Shakespeare, and Coquelin as Cyrano. Commander Peary described the discovery of the North Pole. Lord Baden Powell explained the purpose of the Boy Scouts. The bugler who sounded the Light Brigade charge at Balaclava played his call again "on the original bugle."

Similarly, the early films of Edison documented the vaudeville acts with which they were sometimes interspersed on music hall bills: Crissie Sheridan doing a Butterfly Dance, Buffalo Bill firing a rifle, Charles Sandow, Annie Oakley, and a simulation of the Sioux Indians' Ghost Dance. Perhaps an historical event was first reenacted in the execution of Mary, Queen of Scots, done in August, 1895.

4 Jobes, *Motion Picture Empire*, 45.
5 Cassedy, "Monopoly in Motion Picture Production and Distribution: 1908–15," *Southern California Law Review* XXXII, No. 4 (1959), 374 note 287.
6 Jobes, *op. cit.*, 48.

All of these might be fairly described as "event" documentations, episodes short and stable enough to accommodate the limitations of the early cameras and emulsions. Soon, however, longer reels became possible, and duration was accompanied by dramatic requisite. To make the difference between "making the nut" and hitting a Klondike, the theater managers pragmatically discovered what drew. In some measure, at least, different localities, as with the automated coin machines, "required different attractions." The needs were transmitted from the theater men through the exchanges to the movie makers. One "studio manager" reported his concensus to Patterson:

> The people want a story. We run to comics generally; they seem to take best. So-and-so, however, lean more to melodrama. When we started we used to give just flashes—an engine chasing to a fire, a base runner sliding home, a charge of cavalry. Now, for instance, if we want to work in a horse race it has to be a scene in the life of the jockey, who is the hero of the piece—we've got to give them a story; they won't take anything else—a story with plenty of action. You can't show large conversations, you know, on the screen. More story, larger story, better story with plenty of action—that is our tendency.[7]

A story may be either contrived or implicit in the materials of documented "life." Indeed, the more "real" events have traditionally supplied the most popular entertainments. Some of the early successful films, for example, were prizefights, either photographed in actuality or staged for the cameras.[8] Terry Ramsaye describes early boxing films and their successes with the same rationale used by Richard Leacock in explanation of his approach to *cinéma vérité*.[9] Both have a built-in dramaturgy. (Ramsaye thinks the first movie prizefight—Michael Leonard, the "Beau Brummel of the prize ring" vs. Jack Cushing—the father of the story film, since it was staged for maximum effect. Certainly the production date of July, 1894, precedes the filmed demise of Mary.)[10] Finally,

[7] Patterson, *op. cit.*

[8] Ramsay, *A Million and One Nights*, Chapters 8, 16, and 24 *passim*.

[9] Leacock, "The Frontiers of Realistic Cinema: The Work of Ricky Leacock," *Film Culture*, Nos. 22–23 (1961), 12–23.

[10] Ramsaye, Ch. 8.

Ramsaye notes that Enoch Rector tripled the reel capacity of the Kinetoscope to record the fight.[11]

Five years later the Jeffries-Sharkey match (November 3, 1899) used artificial illumination (purportedly a blistering pattern of four hundred arc lamps) in order to perpetuate itself as a movie. This film was hailed as being seven miles in length, with 264,000 pictures, and toured the road like the later *The Birth of a Nation*.

In 1910, *The Youth's Companion* editorialized against the filmed prizefight exhibitions—while at the same time praising an Indian massacre pageant staged at Hadley, Massachusetts. If the magazine's claims are accurate, theater managers responded quickly to threats of boycott.[12] This might indicate a disinclination to alienate the growing middle-class clientele, or it could mean that nonfiction fisticuffs were losing their appeal in the box offices. The latter explanation seems unlikely.[13]

In any case, the first decade of this century developed into a period when story films emerged as the increasingly dominant entertainment on the American scene. Where, earlier, the theater stage became a screen, the movie now defined itself as a great, versatile, spellbinding dramatic performance.

Sedulous records of prizefights, real or staged, escaped reliance on contrived continuities. Other events were less fortunate, especially when stable cameras could not record them in their entirety. According to Gessner, the first use of shot juxtapositions and contrasting camera placements took place in a film of a sporting event.[14] Two British photographers, G. A. Smith and James A. Williamson, recorded moments of the 1899 Royal Henley Regatta. These shots were intercut with others, which were filmed from a boat and caught the cheering crowd on shore. There is another

11 *Ibid.*

12 *The Youth's Companion*, August 4, 1910.

13 Another example of the continuous film with its own dramaturgy was the simulation of railroad trips by Hale's Tours. These are fully described in an admirably researched article by Raymond Fielding, "Hale's Tours: Ultrarealism in the Pre-1910 Motion Picture," *Cinema Journal*, X, No. 1 (Fall, 1970), 34–47. Another kind of documentary with its own built-in drama is the pornographic film. I have, as yet, been unsuccessful in tracing down the story that pornography was shot as early as 1904 in Buenos Aires bordellos. The Institute for Sex Research at Indiana University has no films in its collection earlier than 1916.

14 Gessner, "The Moving Image," *American Heritage*, XI, No. 3 (April, 1960), 30–35.

short film by Williamson, dating from 1901, which cuts together separate shots from different camera placements while yet maintaining a simple, fictive continuity. It is titled *Englishman Swallows Photographer: Eaten Alive.* In the first shot a man gestures toward the camera to the effect that he does not want to be photographed. He approaches the lens until his open mouth seems to encompass it. In shot two the photographer, swallowed, passes down inside the throat. In a final scene the original subject draws back from the camera and chews vigorously, seemingly well pleased.

Since efforts were first undertaken to organize movie history, the matter of accurately evaluating old material has been complicated beyond measure by film's impermanence and its destruction through wear and mishandling. These forces continue to operate, although matters have been somewhat alleviated by increased support to agencies for film archival storage and restoration. A Los Angeles cinematographer and author, Kemp Niver, has contributed enormously to our general knowledge of film's beginnings by way of a ten-year program undertaken in order to restore to projection form those films which were submitted to the Library of Congress between 1894 and 1912. Niver painstakingly copied these titles from the bromide paper prints that accompanied copyright submissions.

In addition, he has prepared an index of this material, categorizing and describing each film.[15] Besides this work, Niver assembled a collection of twenty-six reels drawn from the same material, which are available for rental and purchase.[16] The one hundred early motion pictures included in this series are noted chronologically in Appendix IX.

No one would claim that these short films represent all the significant titles produced within the dates of our study. Indeed, many of these earliest films are probably lost forever, and other popular titles, made by such men as Méliès, Porter, and Griffith, have been purposely omitted from the anthology. Nevertheless,

[15] Niver, *Motion Pictures from the Library of Congress Paper Print Collection 1894-1912.*

[16] Available through any of the regional offices of Audio-Brandon Films, Inc., and through Pyramid Films, Box 1048, Santa Monica, Calif. 90406. Pyramid also sells another publication written by Niver, *The First Twenty Years*, 176 pp., $7.50.

the Niver reels contain what is undoubtedly a representative cross-section of popular and influential films of the time. Their very success is marked by the efforts of producers or distributors to enlist copyright protection.

This Niver material will be used here to highlight some of my early premises. It was suggested in the Introduction that motion pictures during their formative years cannibalized much substance and many forms from contemporary media. The following section outlines such material as it is evidenced in Niver. Its nomenclature reappears in the General Index as subheadings under media listings (like *theater*). In consequence, interested readers may pursue the book's argument by comparing like references.

If the films themselves are not accessible to the reader (several are available through other sources as well),[17] he is referred to Niver's "Program Notes" prepared to accompany the series.[18] For dates and production information on each cited title, see Appendix IX. Occasional films which have not been included in the Niver series are identified, when possible, by director and date.

COMPOSITION

Angle of Shot. The idea of sequential "angles" is a consequence of the appearance of multishot compositions which do not simulate theatrical staging of "scenes." Two separate-angled shots appear in *Terrible Teddy, the Grizzly King.* See also the foregoing discussion of the Royal Henley Regatta (1899), and the James Wiliamson film, *Englishman Swallows Photographer: Eaten Alive* (1901).

Audience Attention Directed by Manipulation of Light. There is a "firelight" source in *The Seven Ages.* The light intensifies and diminishes in *The Tunnel Workers* for dramatic purpose. In *Fools of Fate* (which precedes *Pippa Passes*) Griffith has an actress carry and extinguish a lantern in a darkened room for expository purpose.

Audience Enjoys Spatial Ubiquity During an Event. Any se-

17 See, for example, the offerings of Blackhawk Films in Davenport, Iowa.
18 Niver, *In the Beginning.*

quential angle change beyond a proscenium staging accomplishes this, but we begin to move *around* a continuous event as early as *Life of an American Fireman* when the camera perspective shifts from interior to exterior during the rescue. See also *Jack and the Beanstalk*, for we cut (dissolve) from Jack's escape to his mother simultaneously waiting below.

Foreground-to-Background Relations. Many of the chase films (*The Great Train Robbery*; *Rounding Up of the "Yeggmen"*) have vigilante groups sneaking up on unaware bandits. The use of a premeditated close shot/medium shot compositional device for dramatic purpose is harder to locate. Perhaps movies, like the woodcut artist Thomas Bewick, first used it successfully to achieve pathos. The contrast of foreground and background is implicit in *The Birth of a Nation* (1915) at the end of the famous scene entitled "While the women and children weep a great conqueror marches to the sea," although Griffith's camera, technically, has panned from a hilltop to the deep panoramic composition of Sherman's March to the Sea. Ten years later Chaplin placed himself outside the dancehall for another pathetic effect in *The Gold Rush*.

Figures Cropped at Picture Borders. As early as *Elopement on Horseback* a mounted rider half circles to exit in a close shot cropped in a screen-right composition.

Mise en Scène. The matter of set dressing, props, and design, as they are functional to the exposition, is arguably one of degree (the railroad employee tries to hide behind a cabinet in *The Great Train Robbery*) and predelineation (Porter's interiors in *Rounding Up of the "Yeggmen"* are more believable than anything thus far, but they are still obviously sets). Decor that contributes to character delineation and to the plot as well may be another Belasco-to-Griffith carryover. Mary Pickford's use of props in such films as *The New York Hat* (1909) define her uniquely Edwardian self. In *The Lonedale Operator*, Blanche Sweet balances along a railroad track and fingers the branch of a willow tree to spell out Griffith's gallant estimation of blonde womanhood.

210

Omniscience of the Audience. Uncle Tom's Cabin has stagelike actions accessible to audience view and unknown to some characters, as does *Jack and the Beanstalk.* See, too, the capture of the bandits in Porter's *The Great Train Robbery* (1903).

Planes of Action. By the accident of passersby and their relation to the camera on the plaza, the camera movement of *Circular Panorama of Electric Tower* leads to quite complicated lines of human movement. Preconceived actions of some intricacy are apparent during the chase sequence in *Rounding Up of the "Yegg-men."*

Visual Assumption of a Character's Point of View. Grandpa's Reading Glass and *A Search for Evidence* both include one-shot "subjective" camera angles.

CONTENT

Adaptations: Play to Film. *The Kiss* (May Irwin/John Rice) excerpted theater from *The Widow Jones* (1896); Joseph Jefferson did scenes from *Rip Van Winkle* in the same year. Coquelin was filmed in moments of *Cyrano* in 1900, with accompanying phonograph records.

Dime Novel to Film. *Kit Carson* (American Mutoscope and Biograph, 1903) figured in dime novels, and Niver's index synopsizes many dime-novel plots; for example, Biograph, *The Redman and the Child* (1908); Gaumont, *Raid on a Coiner's Den* (1904). However, the appearance of a character invented by hack writers may first occur in Louis Feuillade's *Fantômas* series, although Fantômas is more properly pulp than dime novel.

Literature to Film. Méliès made *Faust et Marguerite* in 1897 and *Guillaume Tell et le Clown* in 1898. *La Danse du Feu* (1899) was based on *She.* G. Albert Smith made *The Corsican Brothers* in 1898.

News Events to Film. There is the actuality film itself for example, Robert W. Paul, *Persimmon Wins the Derby of 1896 for Edward, Prince of Wales*, released June 3, 1896. Reconstituted history may commence (barring the prizefights) with Edison, *The*

Execution of Mary, Queen of Scots (1893). J. Stuart Blackton made *Tearing Down the Spanish Flag* (1897). Méliès did *L'Explosion du Cuirass "Maine" dans le Rade de la Havana* (1898) and *L'Affaire Dreyfus* (1899).

Vaudeville to Film. Edison filmed Mae Lucas, solo dancer of *A Gaity Girl* (c. September, 1894) and, during the 1894–95 season, Buffalo Bill, Annie Oakley, Mme. Bertholdi, a contortionist, Sandow, a slapstick barbershop scene, etc. Niver's index devotes a section to vaudeville acts; the earliest is an exhibition dance, copyright September, 1897: Edison, *Charity Ball*.

Fantasy. Méliès is germinal to the traditions of fantasy. Titles of some of his earliest films (1896) suggest that he had assumed this direction from the beginning: *Seance de Prestidigitation*; *Un Bon Petit Diable*; *Escomotage d'une Dame Chez Robert Houdin*; *Le Fakir*; *Mystere Indien*.

Melodrama. Like comedy, melodrama seems to be as early to film as the story itself, preceded only by the Méliès/Porter fairytales. Stereotyped characters, simple morality, resolution through action, spectacle, etc., are all apparent in *Life of an American Fireman*, *Uncle Tom's Cabin*, and *The Great Train Robbery*.

Spectacle. Méliès did *Le Christ Marchant sur les Flots* in 1899 and *Eruption Volcanique à la Martinique* in 1902. See also Porter's race between the *Robert E. Lee* and the *Natchez* in *Uncle Tom's Cabin*.

EDITING TO EFFECT SMOOTH CONTINUITIES

Change of Angle. See *Angle of Shot* under *Composition* above.

Cut-in. The second of the shots in *Gay Shoe Clerk* is a close-up detail of the earlier one. See also Figures 90–91 from *The Lonedale Operator*.

Matching Action. On a primitive level there are two sequential shots of a clerk fitting a shoe to a lady customer in *Gay Shoe Clerk* in which the movement appears to carry across the splice. In *The Widow and the Only Man* the same elemental effort links long

FIGS. 90–91. An example of a cut-in from Griffith's *The Lonedale Operator* (1911). Figure 91 is a close-up of the monkey wrench seen in Figure 90. (From the author's collection.)

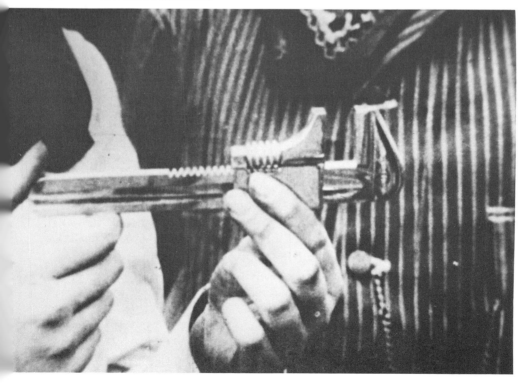

shot to medium close shot to long shot as the widow admires a flower bouquet.

Matching Screen Position. Cut-ins are usually matched into a point of focal interest from the previous shot. See Figures 90–91.

Matching Screen Direction. The movements of the firewagons match effectively in two sequential shots from *Life of an American Fireman*. They are put to more sophisticated use in *Rounding Up of the "Yeggmen,"* where three shots trace an escape, matching the direction of movements against changes of locale. It is difficult to be sure where matched movements are not happy accidents. Griffith mixes up a stroll of Blanche Sweet and Frank Grandin in *The Lonedale Operator*, but later there is a very effective pairing of movements as the villains sneak away from the train (Figures 92–93).

EDITING TO EFFECT TRANSITIONS

Flashback. D. W. Griffith's *After Many Years* (1908) enlarges the dream balloon to the full dimensions of the screen, although the time of the "thought" is presumably the present. *The Birth of a Nation* affords an interesting example of the transition from dream balloon to flashback. As reported by Seymour Stern, Margaret Cameron cannot forget the death of her second brother, Wade. "As Margaret moves to another part of the garden, she sees the death of . . . Wade, killed during the bombardment of Atlanta. A 'balloon' vignette of Wade appears, as he lies prostrate on the earth near a fence, refugees streaming past him, and closes his eyes in death. *Note*: in the prints from 1915 through 1921, the vignetted 'balloon,' similar to the 'dream image' later used in German silent films, appeared in the upper lefthand corner of the screen, while Margaret's embittered face appears in close-up to the right. The double printing of the two shots on one frame was successful, but, unfortunately, not permanent. As the years passed, the vignetted 'balloon' began to fade before it was actually due to fade out, and after 1921, Griffith had the shot of Margaret's face, alone, reprinted. Then a vignetted close-up of Wade's, as in the 'balloon,'

FIGS. 92–93. An effective pairing of movements as the villains sneak away from the train, from Griffith's *The Lonedale Operator*. (From the author's collection.)

was intercut as a separate shot—the way it appears today. As the vignette fades off, the continuity cuts back to Margaret."[19]

Reordering of Time in the Chronology of Exposition. The idea that fictive chronology exists independent of the sequence of its production is operating in *Life of an American Fireman* from the use of "stock shots." By the time of *The Girls and Dolly*, Griffith was shooting the material altogether out of sequence in order to complete at one time all shots necessary to any given set. However, I am unaware of any radical manipulation of straight-ahead time until *Intolerance* (1916); even there, each story proceeds in its own straight-ahead fashion.

Sound Carryovers. The fire alarm in *Life of an American Fireman* wakens the firemen in the next shot.

MOVEMENT

Audience Approaches Subject. This is a common Méliès device; for example, *A Trip to the Moon* (1902).

Pan Over Static Subject. Porter accomplishes extensive movement in *Circular Panorama of Electric Tower* and in *Panorama of Esplanade By Night*.

Required Compositional Change. Such a camera-to-subject movement is faked in *The Twentieth Century Tramp*, although the background is merely sky. There is minimal camera panning-to-follow in *The Great Train Robbery* and more extensive movement in *Rounding Up of the "Yeggmen."*

Significant to Exposition. Clearly, any mimed action furthers a story. Perhaps "significance" which contributes otherwise to character delineation appears with those bits and business of minimal acting movement which Griffith translated from the Belasco stage. See *Mise en Scène* under *Composition* above.

Time Slowed or Accelerated. See the speed-ups in *Mr. Hurry Up of New York* and Zecca, *Slippery Jim*, (c. 1906).

19 Stern, "Griffith: 1—The Birth of a Nation," *Film Culture*, No. 36 (Spring-Summer 1965), 86.

216

PLOT DESIGN

Choice of Significant Movement for Scenes. As a stage device, this is carried over by Méliès, *L'Affaire Dreyfus* (1899); *Cendrillon* (1899); and Porter, *Jack and the Beanstalk. Life of an American Fireman* interjects the same impulse into a less stagey story. It might be proposed that the history of the dramatic film could be traced in terms of what different directors have thought significant movements to be.

Contrast. Both *The Ex-Convict* and *The Kleptomaniac* compare experiences as they are affected by the characters' roles in the social scheme.

Employment of Technique to Intensify Climax. In *The Lonely Villa* (1909), Griffith intercuts his parallel stories, diminishing shot lengths to build the climax.

Establishing Shot. In *The Widow and the Only Man*, William Bitzer introduces his main players in close-up, then goes to an establishing shot of the widow's enemies. In *The Skyscrapers*, F. A. Dobson pans New York City, then details construction workers on the job riveting great steel girders.

Events Separate in Space Ordered in the Same Composition. Méliès uses a split screen in *Faust aux Enfers* (1903). Parallel action is enclosed in a single frame by way of a split screen in *At the French Ball.* A cross-sectional view of three rooms, each separated by a wall, is illustrated in *Anthologie du Cinema.*[20] Méliès used six simultaneous matted images of his head in the fantasy *Le Melomanc* (1903). A split screen in *The Twentieth Century Tramp* affords another interesting effect. While its intention is the illusion of a bicycle rider flying above the city, the perspectives of each shot do not coincide. The rider is a simulated follow shot, while the lower portion of the screen shows a pan across the New York skyline. The effect is oddly like a "live" Cubist painting: a curious, primitive, and unwitting oneupmanship on Picasso.

Parallel Action. This structure is germinal in *The Great Train*

[20] See illustration in Bessy, "Méliès," *Anthologie du Cinema*, 19.

Robbery, and developed by *The Ex-Convict* and *The Kleptomaniac* into alternating cut-backs to maintain two storylines.

SPECIAL EFFECTS

Diffusion of Borders. Grandpa's Reading Glass diffused the edges of the glass to give the impression to the audience of viewing through it.

Dissolves, Double Exposures. Attributed to Méliès, the first superimpositions are said by Bessy to appear in *La Caverne Maudits* (1898).[21]

Dissolves for Place Change and Time Passage. The device is implicit in Méliès' use of the dissolve as an equivalent to a theater curtain; *see L'Affaire Dreyfus* (1899) and *Cendrillon* (1899).

Frozen Movement. There is a simulation of a theatrical Picture Scene at the beginning of the death of Little Eva in *Uncle Tom's Cabin.*

Musical Accompaniment. Pianos and pianolas often accompanied the nickelodeons. Saint-Saëns wrote an accompaniment to *The Assassination of the Duc de Guis* (1908).

Projection of Thoughts, Wishes, Past, Future. See *Jack and the Beanstalk* and Tom's death in *Uncle Tom's Cabin* (Figure 7).

Simulation of Natural Effects. Uncle Tom's Cabin has snow and lightning.

Transformations. Méliès made *La Danse du Feu* in 1899, based on the aging scene in *She.*

In summary, the appearances of film narrative techniques themselves arrive unsystematically and reexpress like devices among other entertainment media. Within the motion picture field they surface throughout the period of our inquiry. Many are traceable to the earliest days of filmmaking. It is sometimes unclear whether early appearances are arbitrary or even accidental.

21 *Ibid.,* 50.

By Griffith's time (from 1908 onward), some elements were becoming more functional to the story, like parallel editing and matted close-ups. Additionally, he introduced staging techniques (for example, lighting effects) and capitalized on the tighter controls over actors and efforts toward maximum effect with minimal movement which had been developing on the stage.

More important, Griffith honed down existing film continuity techniques to tell a *continuous* story whose effects often grew out of the pacing he accomplished by controlling shot lengths and movements with a new sophistication. (Nonetheless, there are many Griffith films which fail to satisfy in these respects.)

A good number of the earliest story films were comic chases. A major contribution from Griffith appears to have been the successful integration of the chase format into melodrama; he made the chase a rescue. Although his efforts after characterization are self-consciously evident, possibilities for accomplishing strong audience involvement through titles, acting business, and mimed speeches were clearly limited. Indeed, the weakest of Griffith's one-reelers suffer from this defect, while his railroad and automobile stories are the most successful. (By 1916, Mack Sennett was parodying the whole scheme in *Teddy at the Throttle*, reinjecting comedy.)

In any case, a picture like *The Lonedale Operator* (1911), a successful but hardly unique achievement, integrates many of the previously noted narrative techniques. This short film, available for rental or purchase from many sources, will be used here as an indication of the coherence which had been brought by the end of our period to previously fragmented and isolated devices.

SYNOPSIS

A charismatic—peers like him and children respect him—railroad engineer, Frank Grandin, is introduced. He meets a girl, Blanche Sweet, and they go for a short walk, concluded with a waist shot in which she playfully twists his ear in affectionate, virginal response to his amorous impulse. Grandin returns to his train; Miss Sweet goes back to the Lonedale station where an elderly gentleman (her father?) complains of a headache. Blanche replaces him and waves goodby to the departing Grandin (Figures 94–96).

At another station along the line a worker receives a gold shipment and puts it aboard an arriving train (Figures 67–71). Two bums hide beneath a car on the train. When the train arrives at Lonedale, Blanche receives the gold (Figures 72–73) and carries it to the office. The bums climb out, exit behind the building (Figures 92–93), and decide to steal the money.

Blanche sees them through her window. She locks two intervening doors and frantically telegraphs for help. A distant operator awakens, takes down her call, and rushes outside to inform Grandin, who has just arrived in his train. Grandin hurries back to Lonedale. Blanche faints and recovers. The train rushes along its route. The bums break down the doors; they are about to attack Blanche when she points something at them. They draw back, startled and intimidated. Grandin arrives with his assistant. The bums are apprehended and Blanche displays her weapon: a monkey wrench (Figures 90–91).

[*Note*: The "laying of pipes" is apparent in Griffith's construction. Early in the story Blanche Sweet idly picks up an object (which we cannot see, but realize later is the wrench) and sets it aside. Further, Griffith carefully "paces out" for us the distances and the obstacles which the bums must surmount to reach Blanche. We know how frighteningly small the hindrances are and how far Frank Grandin must travel to reach her.]

COMPOSITION

Angle of Shot. The engineer in his speeding locomotive. Blanche's view of the villains.

Audience Enjoys Spatial Ubiquity. Griffith cuts to either side of a locked door when the villains attack.

Foreground-to-Background Relations. See Figure 71 or 72.

Figures Cropped at Picture Borders. Trains periodically bleed off into the screen edges (Figure 71).

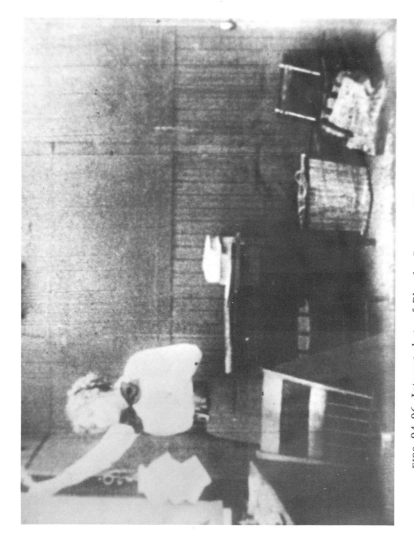

FIGS. 94–96. Intercut shots of Blanche Sweet and Frank Grandin waving goodby to each other in Griffith's *The Lonedale Operator*. (From the author's collection.)

221

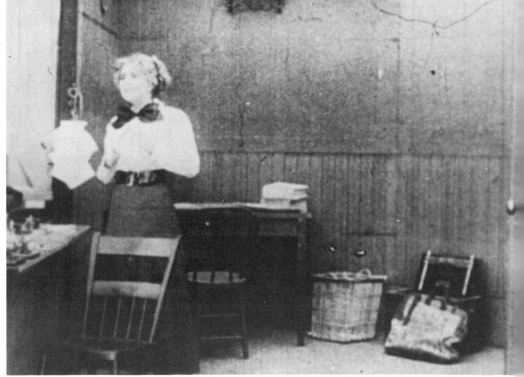

Mise en Scène. A wall clock and background typist in the gold shipment office, a calendar fluttered by a breeze as Blanche anxiously telegraphs—all further Griffith's intended moods.

Planes of Action. See Figures 67–71 and discussion in Chapter 7, pp. 173–78.

Visual Assumption of a Character's Point of View. Blanche twice looks out her window, to be replaced by the camera's taking over of her view: first, to see the departing Frank Grandin and then to spot the bums.

CONTENT

Rescue by telegraph is at least as old as *The Long Strike*, written by Boucicault in 1866. Samuel F. B. Morse, one of America's earliest daguerreotypists, clicked out "What hath God wrought?" in 1844.

EDITING

Cut-in. See Figures 90–91.

Matching Screen Position. See under this title, p. 214.

Matching Screen Direction. See under this title, p. 214.

MOVEMENT

Significant to Exposition. See discussion of *Mise-en-Scène,* p. 216.

PLOT DESIGN

Ellipsis of Time. See the country walk by Blanche Sweet and Frank Grandin.

Employment of Technique to Intensify Climax. As the hero approaches and the villains break down the door, Griffith cuts with increasing speed from one story to another. The villains even reach the office, but they are too dumb to tell a monkey wrench from a revolver.

Parallel Action. Griffith juggles the structure of a girl imperiled in her office, *and* the villains breaking in, *and* a distant telegraph operator, *and* a hero riding to the rescue.

Griffith both expanded notions of "breaking down a scene" and remained within something of a stagey theatrical tradition. Increasingly, he makes use of close shots to emphasize details, to suggest objects of thought or concentrations of interest (by the time of *The Birth of a Nation*), and to magnify detail from an earlier composition (a cut-in). That the device of the significant detail was not unknown to the pre-Biograph Griffith is evident in his play *A Fool and a Girl*, which was registered for copyright in 1906.

Plot elements from *A Fool and a Girl* crop up periodically in Griffith films. In Act V, Griffith describes the response of his heroine, Effie, to a song which has special sentimental meaning to her:

> Hand organ begins playing "La Gala Drina." This instrument must be of the very best class, and skillfully handled for its effect. After a few bars of the song, Effie's hand appears on doorway above her head, only the hand being seen by the audience. As the music plays, the hand slowly drops. The organ plays but one verse. At end of verse, the hand is down. Music stops, pause, and enter Effie.[22]

There is an extreme close-up of hands sculpting a bar of soap in Griffith's *Betrayed by Hand Prints* (1908). Another close-up (of a triggering device) appears in *At the Alter* (1909). Griffith seems generally to conceive his closer views as an accommodation of audience need for additional information. Like opera glasses at a stage performance, they are enlargements. Perhaps because of the size and design of the set, the Ford's Theater sequence in *The Birth of a Nation* carries this technique to impressive lengths; here the director, spatially more mobile, is able to aim his attentions in a variety of *directions*, emanating from no common stance: audience, stage, and Lincoln's box.

The idea of the close-up seems curiously to permeate many

[22] Griffith, *A Fool and a Girl: a Dramatic Composition of Five Acts*, copyright 1906 (unpublished manuscript).

phases of dramatic exposition. Close-ups not only simulated binoculars, they were the first significant way to use what a character himself saw by combining gaze with motive. They encouraged the director to point up material neither character nor audience might otherwise have thought to notice (like Mae Marsh's hands in *Intolerance*, 1916.) The close-up (sometimes called an *Insert* in this period, contrary to the industry's later use of that term in a more specialized sense) had affiliations with the Vision Scene. Thus an early text on film construction and technique requires that an insert be "interpretive" rather than "explanatory."[23] The author includes as inserts static objects (like letters), portions of preceding scenes, and "visions" which "simulate the more subtle mental processes or thought and fantasy—such as reflection, introspection, dreams and hallucination—that have a simultaneous dramatic bearing on the conduct of the character and on the psychological development of the story."[24] Operating on these principles, Griffith took the first steps (Margaret Cameron in the garden is a good case) to integrate the material and mental continuum (Kracauer) or "simultaneous experience" (Edel) into an integrated visual continuity that becomes the audience's own perception. In consequence, a viewer must begin to make his own decisions about the validity of what is shown.

At this juncture Griffith sets the stage for German and Russian experiments to follow within a decade. Through them, the camera/audience finally established a coherent viewpoint which encouraged independence from the subject matter; that is, a shot was not required to follow action or mime in slavish commitment to reportorial values.

At the same time dramatic exposition could be heightened and intensified by raising story intentions to more complicated conceptual levels. The better films of the twenties were less like documentaries of performances that existed somehow independent of the medium. In large part this happened because the interior and exterior worlds of film, director, and audience started to become codified and then integrated.

23 Phillips, *The Photodrama*, 58.
24 *Ibid.*, 60–61.

Visual subjectivity (the camera/audience's assumption of a character's point of view) developed from single shots into sequences, which might even *move* in the manner of a character himself in motion. This psychic ubiquity was accompanied by the incursion of both Impressionism and Expressionism as aesthetics to be reconciled somehow into film's photographic essence. The ensuing problems encouraged development in editing, particularly in sophistications about the visual relations between shots. One instance of this was matching action, which grew well beyond those primitives impulses toward continuity between a medium or long shot and a nearer cut-in that we have seen thus far.

With the notion that a camera view might energetically change its perspective during an event which did not change locale (that is, require only a matching of screen direction between shots), new narrative possibilities ensued. If shots are cut together to maintain some continuity of movement, while at the same time varying how that movement is to be perceived (objective/subjective; protagonist/antagonist), the spectator's awareness of his own relation to the event becomes blurred into those purposeful ambiguities which constitute a large element in the modern art experience. This is a part of the accomplishment of movies like *Battleship Potemkin*, *Überfall*, *The Last Laugh*, and *Menilmontant*—films which helped to organize further confusions in the relation of the dreamer to his dream. But the roots were in Griffith. And Griffith thrived on the theater of his time. And everyone's roots encircled nineteenth-century entertainments, like a convoluted piece of *art nouveau*.

226

9

A Particular Phase of Perception

> Every art reduces reality to a particular phase of perception and translates the veracity of experience into a more or less homogeneous formal language.
>
> —ARNOLD HAUSER

It is not untypical for people to change careers, but an element curiously common to the backgrounds of several nineteenth-century inventors was the profession of painting. Robert Fulton worked as an assistant to Robert Barker, an Edinburgh artist who created the first Panorama. Both early and late in his lifetime, Louis Daguerre devoted his energies to the production of Dioramas and to painting. One of Daguerre's guests in Paris was a visiting American artist, Samuel F. B. Morse.

Nineteenth-century painting, of course, was like narrative prose and photography in translating the visible world to another idiom, one with fewer dimensions. Its execution required a particular expertise with regard to space, for space and light were what nineteenth-century painting was about. Perhaps those sophistications served as catalysts to combine scientific wisdoms with mechanical talents and produce the steamboat, the Daguerreotype, and the telegraph.

The Wizard of Menlo Park hinted at this spatializing disposition in an article on the invention of the phonograph (*North American Review,* 1888). Edison had been impressed by the effect of "certain musical notes and chords upon sand, when loosely sprinkled on a sounding board; in response to the sound waves the sand sifts itself into various curves, differing according to the pitch and intensity." Edison thought, too, of the fine lines of sand deposited on an ocean beach by a wave. "The sound waves, set going by a

227

human voice, might be so directed as to trace an impression upon some solid substance."[1]

The development of the phonograph followed lines similar to the motion picture. Both grew from efforts to "freeze" a moment of behavior for analytic purpose. In 1856, Leon Scott's Phonautograph channeled sound through a resonating chamber onto a diaphragm which traced the mechanical vibrations on lampblack-coated paper wrapped about a revolving cylinder. His device could be likened to Marey's motion-study machines. (Indeed, Marey and Doctor Rosapelly invented a mechanism to record graphically lip movement as well as portions of the palate and larynx, a scheme to teach speech to deaf mutes.)

What began in analysis ended with the re-creation of past events. The medium of recording is only now beginning to investigate those potentialities for time manipulation which have for years been shuffled on the film editor's table and processed in the motion-picture laboratory. Space is metamorphosed into length—a plastic ribbon, a spiraling groove.

In these concrete forms of linearity Buckminster Fuller finds soundings of the depths of our transition from the nineteenth to the twentieth century:

> The opening years of the 20th Century witnessed the transition of world technology from track to trackless, from wire to wireless, from pipe to pipeless and from dramatically visible structural stone strength to undramatically invisible alloyed structural strength. These years also witnessed the scientific transition from visible modelable geometric and mathematical computations to invisible non-modelable mathematical capabilities. The 20th Century's birth saw also the transition of art from starkly representional preoccupations through a gradually ephemeralizing impressionism to philosophic abstraction and thence to dephilosophized abstractional patterning idioms.[2]

---

1 At the time Edison was working to reconstitute the movements of Morse's telegraph onto paper tape. When the indented tape was quickly turned against the tracing point, it gave off a humming sound. "I saw at once that the problem of registering human speech so that it could be repeated by mechanical means as often as might be desired was solved."

2 Fuller, "Change as the Fundamental Norm," *Class* (Spring, 1970), 10.

Yet this change cannot really be quite as abrupt as are self-apparent distinctions between track and trackless. For that matter the electronic age has evolved its own kinds of linearities. The videotape is one, and computers are great monsters of tape and wheels. The 3M Company is a twentieth-century industry.

More important to the purposes of film, its cellulose, photo-chemical ribbons (like the shuffled chapters of *Lord Jim*, the super-imposed images of Picasso and Braque, the song slides to *Only a Message from Home Sweet Home*, and the matching panels of *Little Nemo*) can reorganize encapsulated time (with space a foot-dragging collaborator) by rearranging the tangible evidence.[3]

Fuller's last, long sentence touches on the consequences of time travel. As artists began to play H. G. Wells with their materials, the "dephilosophized abstractional patterning idioms" were inevitable. If you love space, then value time, for time is the stuff that space is made of.

No one would willingly limit twentieth-century art to the abstract. A painting like Chirico's *Melancholy and Mystery of a Street*, with its child rolling her hoop on a landscape, racing toward a shadow "where an unknown terror awaits,"[4] depends, like Nemo and the giants, on subtle manipulations of natural perspective[5] for its effect. The same sense of imminent terror just beyond what is to be seen figures in experimental evocations as diverse as *L' Avventura* and *Big, Two-Hearted River*.

Nevertheless, impatience with the emotional accuracies of objective, "straight-ahead" time and space characterized many separate aspects of our era of investigation.

Although we have been occupied with thin evidential traces in one narrow (if influential) tradition, the inclination to fiddle with

[3] The impulse to capture time so that it might be reexamined was not unique to narrative "entertainments." A random selection of similar efforts might include George Woodruff, coach at the University of Pennsylvania. He introduced backfield motion into football by plotting out movements of linemen, spare backs, and the quarterback into choreographies of sequential movement. Following on the success of the assembly line in industry, Frederick W. Taylor devised the time-study approach to a worker's execution of his job. Taylor graphically analyzed bricklaying, pig-iron handling, and industrial inspections, breaking the men's movements into special patterns.

[4] Kepes, *The New Landscape in Art and Science*, 18.

[5] I refer to dramatized perspective by extreme foreshortening and by scaling down the relative size of distant figures.

the unities was more pervasive than in drama alone. It included, of course, Einstein, Planck, and Bohr.[6] The final results defined a world in which, as Friedenberg said, "There is no longer any fixed reference point, and no perspective."[7]

Often the possibilities of restructuring past events were implicit in the medium. Lantern slides can be rearranged quite as easily as photographs. Yet the tendency is equally pronounced in prose, which evolved more from oral than from visual traditions. For that matter, the song slides only followed the continuities of their lyrics, however much they might take liberties in "visualizations."

All these arts, lasting and ephemeral, were in retrospect, groundswells. Finally, though, their isolate thrusts stood preempted by the motion pictures. Film supplanted the pulps, rendered stereograms obsolete, and dispatched the Panorama to the planetarium. It revolutionized theater, and cannibalized the music hall. In the end, it mated with radio to produce a bastard television whose social effects have moved far beyond our measure.

Why film?

As entertainment, motion pictures quickly evolved as products of acquisitive minds in a competitive, commercial jungle. They succeeded because they made money. They made money daily, continuously, like a gusher. The businessmen, themselves of the people, had come on a readymade, constant audience to which, even with minimal talent, they could easily adapt along occasional trends in "what the public wanted." As techniques of modern cultural exploitation became refined, the businessmen learned to help their public *conceive* of what it wanted. The consolidation of commercial film empires paralleled every other branch of the growing entertainment industries.

Early film audiences stepped off a city street into a renovated store. The moving picture did not simply entertain its audience, although it did that without straining mind or sensibility. It provided better audio-visual education than jugglers, lantern slides,

6 For a discussion of the imagistic bases for theory in modern physics, see Arnheim, *Visual Thinking*. After discussing post-Renaissance painting, he inquires, "Is not the change from corpuscular theory to field theory in physics an example of the same perceptual development?" (286).

7 Friedenberg, *The Vanishing Adolescent*.

230

coon shows, and even rotogravure sections. If you could not read English, you could understand the pictures, but the titles soon helped you to do both.

One of the first, great triumphs of the early movie was to engage not just middle-class, but noncosmopolitan markets into the same sort of learning relationship which had encouraged commercial success among the immigrants. As cities became central sources of cultural domination over the rest of the country, the motion picture contributed its share. Southern Europeans and Russian Jews had used the nickelodeon to find out how America acted. Now farmers and citizens of the small towns came to study the dress, action, and misbehavior of the cities.

At the turn of the century the phonograph discovered commercial nirvana when Emile Berliner practically adapted M. Charles Cros's theory about applying photoengraving to a disc stamper. Then, copying the printing press, he pressed records from heated Vulcanite. Likewise, the film industry duplicated its own materials on as wide a scale as necessary by the simple methods of contact printing.[8] Upon the growth of theater circuits, large-scale, simultaneous releases dovetailed with the techniques of commercial exploitation through national advertising. By 1910, the Victor Company spent a million and a half dollars annually for national advertising. Equal figures are not forthcoming from the film industry, but by 1911 the General Film Company divided its total net profits, after payment of dividends on preferred and common stock, as follows: Pathé-Freres, $164,965.92; Vitagraph Company, $149,919.35; Thomas A. Edison, Inc., $122,771.31; Selig-Polyscope Co., $109,703.03; Biograph Co., $104,907.61; Essanay Film Manufacturing Co., $102,316.70; Lubin Manufacturing Co., $101,370.65; Kalem Co., $90,833.31; George Kleine, $77,308.54; George Méliès, $31,483.56.[9]

Then there was the ease of execution which seemed to accom-

---

[8] The matter of reproduction is underlined by the activities of the early bootleggers, who made thousands of dollars monthly by producing illegal copies of current film titles. Bootlegging is still a flourishing business in the movie field, as well as in phonograph records and audio tapes.

[9] Cassady, Jr., "Monopoly in Motion Picture Production and Distribution: 1908–1915," *Southern California Law Review* (Summer, 1959), 362, note 209.

pany so many aspects of the film production process: "The thing is a Klondike." Movies simply swallowed up all the techniques of naturalistic artifice which had encumbered theater stages with sets and machines of increasing complexity and sometimes questionable dependability. To a theater audience, not to mention the stagehands, there was always some lingering doubt that a locomotive would arrive in time to miss the heroine tied to the track. On the screen one not only saw a real train, but the director could command its behavior down to as tight a rescue as anything dared by Hairbreath Harry. Furthermore, a cameraman could undercrank the pictures so they flashed across the screen with the speed of Barney Oldfield.

Too, the movies did their homework and learned the lessons of nineteenth-century entertainment—the tested genres, the timings of the stage comedians, the stereotypes that would predictably salivate a mass audience. They could combine Ned Buntline's melodrama with the actualities of Buffalo Bill Cody himself, trick riding and sharp shooting. Movement was the essence of the pulps. "You've got to give them story. They won't take anything else . . . a story with plenty of action." The manager of a nickelodeon said the same thing to Joseph Medill Patterson.

It was a "safe" reality for the audience, vicarious experience more real than real which guised the exaggerations of human perception in its secondhand conventions of narrative style. The movie performers were the audience writ large. They were unlike stage idols or burlesque performers, who either lived in another world or else, when you met them, turned out somehow different from your expectations. Movie actors were more like, say, the Austin High white jazz musicians of the twenties. With just a little bit of luck and some practice, you'd think you might have been one of them.

At the same time there developed a kind of sweep and awesomeness to stories of increasing ambition. Vachel Lindsay quotes Bernard Shaw to the effect that *Paradise Lost* would make a far better movie than Ibsen.[10] Then Lindsay finds Griffith's Ku Klux Klan dashing down the road "as powerfully as Niagara pours

[10] Lindsay, *The Art of the Moving Picture*, 69.

over the cliff."[11] The high-budgeted, Milton-type picture was more thrilling. Whatever the admission price (and it rose), audiences continued to nurse a secret satisfaction that they had shortchanged the management.

Finally, film did narrative better, combining the sequence of prose with the simultaneity of picture. As early as 1890, William James equated human thought with a flow of transitive ideas in which we have "states" corresponding to parts of speech, to emotional attitudes, and to "before" and "after" relations with time.[12] Novels managed that, the lantern slides and comics as well. But the motion picture was to thought as Bergson, the new philosopher, related memory to intellect; intellect transcended the orthodoxies of linguistic syntax. Like photography, intellect apprehended the material and rendered it into nonspatial terms. But memory? Memory was a good movie: ". . . to grasp, in a single intuition, multiple moments of duration, . . . frees us from the flow of things, that is to say, from the rhythm of necessity. The more of these moments memory can contract into one, the firmer is the hold which it gives to us on matter. . . ."[13] Whatever its substance, this was the form of the new art, one which enlisted an audience's unthinking will toward enforcing separate story strands into a simultaneous *now* with the stuff of Mary Pickford and Bronco Billy Anderson. It was the first great pop space/time victory. Picasso might interpret Einstein's theorem to a museum audience; in the darkness of a neighborhood Bijou other spectators learned something of the same lesson while they munched syndicated daydreams.

A curiosity of every age is its perception of what is real. At the Edison laboratory in West Orange, New Jersey, on the evening of October 21, 1915, the Metropolitan soprano Anna Case alternated her own voice with its recorded counterpart, and an audience detected no difference. Christine Miller undertook the same test with like effect. Half a year later a dramatic soprano, Marie Rappold, performed the experiment in Carnegie Hall before a

11 *Ibid.*, 75.
12 James, *Principles of Psychology*, I, Chapter 9.
13 Bergson, *Matter and Memory*, 303.

battery of critics. Behind curtains, the critics could not identify the "real" singer.

Increasingly, each trend and sway of popular culture now clouds a sense of "actuality" in the trappings and conventions of its own vicarious entertainments. Although film audiences soon became inured to railroad trains puffing straight into the orchestra, their continued confidence both in narrative continuity and in the photograph constantly insured a guileless credulence toward stories and attitudes of pure fantasy.

Commercial fantasy it was, but the security encouraged spectators, as in sleep, to draw on levels of consciousness as subterranean as the stories were "shallow." "To explore the most sacred depths of the unconscious, to labor in the sub-soil of consciousness, that will be the principal task of psychology in the century which is opening."[14] Bergson might have added art to science.

In the seventy-five year history of the commercial motion picture a great strength has been its ability to adapt narrative continuities to faddish new conventions, while discarding clichés quickly and effectively enough to maintain the confidence of a "mainstream" audience. So far this has been its salvation in the new countryside landscaped without fixed perspectives. For this experience a changing audience has emerged, the anxious, commercial-hip city dwellers of an electronic age. Film remains the art of these people. Its ubiquities of time and space soothe and reinforce them in the dark. Secure there, each viewer gives way to an *event*, to a *process* which smoothly corroborates his intuitions about worlds beyond those immediate frames edging the screen in his head. This is the melodrama of the twentieth century.

> No new century began yesterday.
> Avoid all delusions on that head.
> —New York *Tribune*
> January 2, 1900

14 Bergson, *Creative Evolution*, xii, 158.

Appendices

EARLY DEVELOPMENT OF AMERICAN SHEET MUSIC

The entire field of music publishing amply illustrates trends toward standardization, gargantuan size, mass distribution, and exploitation. Before the last twenty years of the century, sheet music was a function of companies which marketed piano instruction books and "serious" music, along with occasional issues from music stores and printing shops. In the eighties composers who had previously sold their tunes for pittances began to incorporate personal firms. In 1892 a Milwaukee author caught on with *After the Ball*, soon earning as much as twenty-five thousand dollars weekly on sheet music sales. He identified himself as "Charles K. Harris—Banjoist and Songwriter—Songs Written to Order."

The million-copy song was increasingly common in the new century. *A Bird in a Gilded Cage* sold two million copies in 1900 and *Meet Me Tonight in Dreamland* sold five million copies in 1909. In a success-ridden market, houses sought to secure popularity by tying titles to other vestiges of community interest. *Hello, Central, Give Me Heaven* came out in 1901. The new popularity of bicycles—established in the United States in 1903 by the introduction of models with equal-sized wheels, lower seats, and pneumatic tires—promoted *Daisy Bell (A Bicycle Built for Two)*; Kitty Hawk was followed by *Come, Take a Trip in My Airship*; *Come Josephine in My Flying Machine*; *Up in a Balloon*; and *Up, Up, Up in My Aeroplane*. The successes of Henry Ford were

235

solemnized in *The Little Ford Rambled Along*; *The Lady Chauf-feur*; *He'd Have to Get Under—Get Out and Get Under*; and *In My Merry Oldsmobile* (competitively).

Then there were the trend songs. After the Spanish-American War produced *Good-by, Dolly Gray*, Tin Pan Alley followed with *Good-by, My Lady Love*; *Good-by, Liza Jane*; *Good-by Rose*; and *Good-by, Good Luck, God Bless You*. There were Indian songs and Mary songs and Home songs and Summer songs and Moon songs.

As publishing empires grew they financed pluggers, men who bribed and cajoled orchestras and singers to perform material. They were planted as singing waiters, leaped up in vaudeville houses to repeat the choruses of their own material after a per-former had finished it, and sang in bars, nickelodeons, and beaches—even from trolleys and streetcars. Following a price war on sheet music between Macy's and Siegel-Cooper, a trust among the major publishers—American Music Stores, Inc.—effectively fixed sheet music prices at fifty cents.

For a lively history of this period, see David Ewen, *The Life and Death of Tin Pan Alley* (New York: Funk and Wagnall's, 1964).

II

Twenty Representative British and American Melodramas

1802 *A Tale of Mystery*, Thomas Holcroft (in Bailey).

1813 *The Miller and His Men*, Isaac Pocock (in Booth).

1826 *Luke the Laborer; or The Last Son*, John Baldwin Buck-stone (in Bailey).

1829 *Black-Ey'd Susan; or All in the Downs*, Douglas William Jerrold (in Moses and also in Rowell).

1832 *The Rent-Day*, Douglas William Jerrold (in Bailey).

1841 *London Assurance*, Dion Boncicault (in Moses).

1842 *Sweeny Todd the Demon Barber of Fleet Street*, George Dibdin Pitt.

1858 *My Poll and My Partner Joe*, John Thomas Haines (in Booth).

1858 *Ten Nights in a Bar-Room*, William W. Pratt (in Booth).

1860 *The Colleen Bawn*, Dion Boucicault (in Rowell).

1862 *East Lynne*, Mrs. Henry Wood (in Bailey).

1863 *The Ticket-of-Leave Man*, Tom Taylor (in Moses and also in Rowell).

1866 *Lady Audley's Secret*, C. H. Hazlewood (in Rowell).

1867 *Under the Gaslight*, Augustin Daly (in Booth).

1867 *Lost in London*, Watts Phillips (in Booth).

1868 *After Dark*, Dion Boucicault (in Bailey).

1871 *The Bells*, Leopold David Lewis (in Booth and also in Rowell).

1874 *Belle Lamar*, Dion Boucicault (in Leverton).

1882 *The Silver King*, Henry Arthur Jones (in Bailey).

1905 *The Girl of the Golden West*, David Belasco.

Sources to Cited Plays

Bailey, J. O. *British Plays of the Nineteenth Century* (New York: Odyssey Press, 1966).

Belasco, David. *Six Plays* (Boston: Little, Brown, 1929).

Booth, Michael R., ed. *Hiss the Villain* (London: Eyre and Spottiswoode, 1964).

Leverton, Garrett. *Plays for the College Theater* (New York: French, 1948).

Moses, Montrose J., ed. *Representative British Dramas Victorian and Modern* (Boston: Little, Brown, 1927).

Pitt, George Dibdin. *Sweeney Todd The Demon Barber of Fleet Street* (London: John Lane, 2nd ed., 1934).

Rowell, George. *Nineteenth Century Plays* (London: Oxford University Press, 1936).

III

Sub-Literature in the Nineteenth Century

From the time of the early primitive presses, chapbooks provided popular literature to Europeans. Although these appeared in the United States, the mass circulation newspaper proved a more workable medium for cheap fiction, a situation less feasible in England until the 1820's because of taxes and stamp duties imposed on advertisements. In this country newspapers could cram more words into less space, and they enjoyed special mailing rates.

The great, popular story weekly was the New York *Ledger*, whose editor, Robert Bonner, reached an annual income of $238,411 in 1868. Bonner spent large amounts of money on advertising, as much as $100,000 in a single year. By the late 1850's the *Ledger's* circulation was four hundred thousand.

Street and Smith bought a competitor, the *New York Weekly*, just before the Civil War. While its circulation was far below the *Ledger's*, the *Weekly* became the foundation on which Street and Smith built its dime novel business.

However, the first great success in the field was a new firm, Beadle & Adams, an outgrowth of the earlier Irwin P. Beadle & Company who had issued the first dime novel; Irwin was Erastus' brother. Erastus published ten-cent pamphlets and manuals of songs, games, jokes, and cooking in the new firm. During 1860, Number One of *Beadle's Dime Novels* was published: Anna Sophia Winterbotham Stephens' *Malaeska: The Indian Wife of the White Hunter*. It contained the phrase "bit the dust." Generally, Beadle hired the established story-paper authors. The two media continued without serious harm to one another until the eighties, when the popularity of the story paper declined.

Many stories were published first in the story paper and then reprinted as novels. Both forms pirated material. Sometimes shorter works were lumped into "novels" with minor changes.

Although some of the early prose pieces were garish in their descriptions and at least questionable in their morality, the general tenor of the dime novels was one of simple, romantic tales of (at first) far western heroes. A feeling for sensational images of the west was fostered in late 1869 when E. Z. C. Judson published *Buffalo Bill, The King of the Border Men* in Street and Smith's *New York Weekly*. Judson wrote as Ned Buntline. (A buntline is a rope at the base of a square sail.) The author, a sometime temperance lecturer, actor, and drunk who lived by his wits, followed up his success with *Buffalo Bill's Last Victory; or Dove Eye, the Lodge Queen*, and *Hazel Eye, The Girl Trapper*. Another Street and Smith writer, Prentiss Ingraham, eventually turned out two hundred Buffalo Bill dime novels. The first, *The Pony Express Rider; or Buffalo Bill's Frontier Feats*, accounted for many of the popular legends which finally surrounded the western figure.

The other major western image maker was Edward L. Wheeler, who wrote *Deadwood Dick*, based on an actual express guard for Black Hills gold shipments (and an Indian fighter). Wheeler finally drank himself to death, according to Gilbert Patten, the author of the Frank Merriwell stories. It was said that a Beadle's editor would lock Wheeler in a room for three-day periods, time enough to finish a thirty-three thousand-word "piece."

In the last quarter of the century cowboy heroes gave way to detectives. (An early one was *Old Sleuth, the Detective*, published by *Fireside Companion*.) Sometimes the genres were mixed, as in Civil War romances, romantic Westerns, and cowboy detectives (for example, *Injun Dick Detective; or Tracked from the Rockies to New York*, published in August, 1900).

The early orange-beige covers of Beadle novels were replaced by chromolithographs, almost always depicting action scenes, usually from the first chapter (the artists did not have time to read further). Often these cuts were reused, slightly altered to adapt to a new story if supplied with a changed caption. Illustrators included Edwin Penfield, John R. Chapin, and H. Fenn. It has been said that at the turn of the century dime-novel publishers did more four-color printing in a month than all other publishers could maintain in a year.

By 1895 the pulp magazines, so called because of the wood pulp consistency of their paper, had taken to the field, sharing it with "juveniles," then suffering seriously in competition with the nickelodeons. Many collectors feel that the dime novel was destroyed by the movies. Pulps, however, retained some vitality until the paper shortages of World War II, and then resurged with the popularity of science fiction.

The definitive history of dime novel publishing is Albert Johann-sen, *The House of Beadle and Adams and Its Dime and Nickel Novels; the Story of a Vanished Literature*. Mary Noel recorded the history of the popular story weekly in *Villains Galore . . . the Heyday of the Popular Story Weekly*. The history of Street and Smith was compiled by Quentin Reynolds, *The Fiction Factory, or From Pulp Row to Quality Street*. Other studies include Ed-mund Pearson, *Dime Novels* (Boston: Little, Brown, 1929); Gil-bert Patten, *Frank Merriwell's "Father"* (Norman: University of Oklahoma Press, 1964); Louis James, *Fiction for the Working Man, a Study of the Literature Produced for the Working Classes in Early Victorian England, 1830–1850*; and Jay Monaghan, *The Great Rascal, the Exploits of the Amazing Ned Buntline* (Boston: Little, Brown, 1952).

Studies of this literature appeared as early as William Everett, "Beadle's Dime Books," *North American Review* (July, 1864). Charles M. Harvey wrote "The Dime Novel in American Life" for the *Atlantic* (July, 1907). A chronological listing of news-paper and magazine articles appears in Johannsen (II, 328–38).

Students of American culture and history have considered such material a tool to their research. See:

Merle Curti. "Dime Novels and the American Tradition," *The Yale Review* (June, 1937), 761–78.
Don Russell. *The Lives and Legends of Buffalo Bill* (Norman: University of Oklahoma Press, 1960).
William A. Settle, Jr. *Jesse James Was His Name* (Columbia: University of Missouri Press, 1966).
Henry Nash Smith. *Virgin Land: The American West as Symbol and Myth* (Cambridge: Harvard University Press, 1950).
Kent Steckmesser. *The Western Hero in History and Legend* (Norman: University of Oklahoma Press, 1965).

Dickens' pervasive influence is noted in Gerald J. McIntosh, "The Influence of Charles Dickens on Gilbert Patten," *Dime Novel Roundup*, No. 35 (October 25, 1966). Dickens was one of the few authors who could compete with the hacks and his ef-fects are everywhere.

240

For general interest and much entertainment the reader is referred to *Dime Novel Roundup*, a publication for collectors which has been produced since 1931, first under the editorship of Ralph F. Cummings and more recently by Edward T. LeBlanc. *Dime Novel Roundup*, published monthly at 821 Vermont Street, Lawrence, Kansas 66044. Subscription $3.00 per year.

IV

LENSES

About 1812 a so-called Landscape lens was developed, fixed focus and covering a field of forty degrees. In 1859, Sutton perfected a water-filled sixty-to-eighty degree Panorama lens. A refinement by van Höegh at the turn of the century called Hypergon flat widened the field up to 150 degrees.

The earliest telephoto lenses in photography were themselves small Galilean telescopes with the eyepiece racked out far enough to project a real image on the photographic plate. In 1891 an achromatic negative lens was manufactured in adapters to be mounted behind ordinary photographic lenses: 2 to $8\times$ magnification but stopped only to $f/11$. The $f/$stop, of course, figured heavily in determining what could be photographed on orthochromatic film stocks. Zeiss produced a lens of 2 to $3\times$ at $f/6$ in 1898. Most manufacturers have made telephoto lenses since 1900, and they are common enough to be discussed as Tele-Photo systems in C. Francis Jenkins and Oscar B. Depue, *Handbook for Motion Picture and Stereopticon Operators* (Knega, Washington, 1908).

A 1902 catalogue describes 8, 10, and $12\times$ Prism Binoculars. It notes that Binocular Field Glasses, based on a prism system invented in 1850 by Porro (an Italian) were adapted practically by Carl Zeiss in 1895. The prism design diminished the overall length by one-third. There are testimonials on the military prowess of field glasses which date back to 1885. Telescopes at powers of 15, 20, 40, 50, 60, and 70 are advertised. Opera glasses cost two to nine pounds (a pound was worth $4.87). Seaside and tourist telescopes are displayed. (*Catalogue of Military, Naval, Field and Opera Glasses Manufactured by Ross, Ltd.*, London, 1902.)

Requiring fewer components, the portrait lens appeared earlier. J. Petzval of Vienna designed one with a field of twenty-five degrees at f/3.4 in 1841. (Most projection objectives descend from the concave element of this design.) It admitted sixteen times more light than Daguerre's lens. When used with a new hypersensitized plate invented by Goddard, it became possible to take portraits in less than a minute. A Convertible Protar (Rudolph, 1894) could adapt its focal length by adding or subtracting from among its components (it is still used in photoengraving). Rudolph also made a Planar lens for copying at unit magnification in 1895–96.

V

THE PHASMATROPE

A CONTRIBUTION TO THE HISTORY OF THE ART OF PHOTOGRAPHING LIVING SUBJECTS IN MOTION, AND REPRODUCING THE NATURAL MOVEMENTS BY THE LANTERN.

To the Editor of the Journal of the Franklin Institute:

SIR:—Among the earliest public exhibitions of photographs taken from living subjects in motion projected by the lantern upon a screen, was that given at an entertainment held in the Academy of Music, in Philadelphia, on the evening of February 5, 1870,[1] and a repetition of this exhibition was made before the Franklin Institute at its next following monthly meeting on March 16th, by the writer.

The objects exhibited embraced waltzing figures and acrobats, shown upon the screen in life-size, while the photographic images

---

[1] The printed program of this event contains the following allusion to this feature of the entertainment: "THE PHASMATROPE. This is a recent scientific invention, designed to give various objects and figures upon the screen the most . . . life-like movements. The effects are similar to those produced in the familiar toy called the Zoëtrope, where men are seen walking, running and performing various feats in the most perfect imitation of real life. This instrument is destined to become a most invaluable auxiliary to the appliances for illustration, and we have the pleasure of having the first opportunity of presenting its merits to our audience."

were only ¾ inch in height. At that day flexible films were not known in photography, nor had the art of rapid succession picture-making been developed; therefore, it was necessary to limit the views of subjects to those that could be taken by time exposures upon wet plates, which photos were afterwards reproduced as positives on very thin glass plates, in order that they might be light in weight. The waltzing figures, taken in six positions, corresponding to the six steps to complete a turn, were duplicated as often as necessary to fill the eighteen picture-spaces of the instrument which was used in connection with the lantern to project the images upon the screen.

The piece of mechanism, then named the "Phasmatrope," shown by the illustration, consisted in a skeleton wheel having nine radial divisions, into which could be inserted the picture-holders, each of which consisted of a card upon which was mounted two of the photopositives, in such relative position that, as the wheel was intermittently revolved, each picture would register exactly with the position just left by the preceding one. The intermittent movement of the wheel was controlled by a ratchet and pawl mechanism operated by a reciprocating bar moved up and down by the hand. It will be apparent that the figures could be moved in rapid succession or quite slowly, or the wheel could be stopped at any point to complete an evolution.

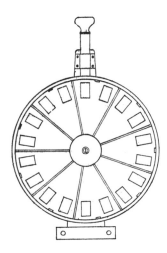

In the exhibitions at the Academy of Music, above alluded to, the movement of the figures was made to correspond to the time of the waltz played by an orchestra, and when the acrobat performers were shown a more rapid motion was given, and a full stop made when a somersault was completed. A shutter was then a necessary part of the apparatus to cut off the light rays during the time the pictures were changing places. This was accomplished by a vibrating shutter placed back of the picture wheel, that was operated by the same draw-bar that moved the wheel, only the shutter movement was so timed that it moved first and covered the picture before the latter moved, and completed the movement after the next picture was in place. This movement reduced to a great extent the flickering, and gave very natural and life-like representation of the moving figures.

HENRY R. HEYL

PHILADELPHIA, February 1, 1898.

From *The Franklin Institute*, Philadelphia, CXV (April, 1898).

VI

NINETEENTH-CENTURY DEVELOPMENTS IN PRINTING

By the end of the nineteenth century the products of commercial printing were contributing to the same mainstream of narrative structure that found expression in prose, theater, parlor toys, and public visual entertainments.

New freedoms for artists, as well as the penetration of still photography deep into the public consciousness, arose out of radical changes in techniques of graphic reproduction. Every area of printing underwent drastic innovation, particularly lithography and the intaglio processes, which settled finally into photoengraving and the later gravure impressions.

Ivins distinguishes between the translation of photographs into a printing process which gave infinite duplications and the nonrepeatable daguerreotypes.[1] Yet as early as 1841 daguerreotypes were etched in galvanic baths for printing on gravure presses, yielding decent results. There were many early experiments with photoengraving, dating back to the 1824 efforts of Niepce that preceded his association with Daguerre.

However, successful reproduction required the intermediary of a halftone process so that the middle definitions could be obtained. William Henry Talbot recommended, in 1852, that a gauze netting be used for such a purpose. In 1869, William A. Leggo tried a crossline screen and accomplished successful reproduction of a photograph in the *Canadian Illustrated News* in Montreal; Couperie[2] says that the first photographs appeared in a newspaper in England in 1880.

Depending on the amount of definition required of a print, the common practice was to supplement photos with the engraver's tool. For years the relation of artist and photograph was a supportive one. (The *Illustrated London News* has an "engraving taken from a photograph" made in India about 1858, for example.) A single line screen was used to print a photo of a New York slum district in *The Daily Graphic* of March 4, 1880. The Declaration of Independence for photographers dates from 1886, when Frederic Ives, a Philadelphian, patented his idea for the modern ruled crossline halftone screen. Before the outbreak of World War I his process was in common use throughout the world.

Halftone differs from all earlier engraving in that no interpretive functionary intervenes between the "original" (drawing or photograph) and its publication. One consequence of the publishing of photographs was a new freedom for photographers who had, until that time, depended on exhibition in the salons both for money and reputation. It also furthered the separation between the cameramen, who considered themselves working in the painter's tradition (replacing the artist as portraitist or else preparing other "artful" photographs for exhibition and sale to individual buyers), and the "press photographer," whose function was essentially journalistic. By 1910, with the development of the German roto-

1 Ivins, *Prints and Visual Communication.*
2 Couperie and Horn, *A History of the Comic Strip,* 9.

gravure process (which soon printed, at high speeds and by means of engraved press cylinders, both sides of a sheet: picture and text, delivered dried and cut), the vocabulary of pictures was available on a mass scale to a mass audience.

Until photoengraving, printed illustration consisted of wood-cuts and copper engraving. The presence of pictures helped to define audiences. For example, in 1861, George Augustos Sola, editor of *Temple Bar*, a British journal, said that he preferred to give readers sixteen extra pages of print rather than an illustration or two. But the *Illustrated London News* had been founded twenty years before. By 1891, *Strand* magazine boasted 110 woodcuts in a single issue.

The American magazines, less select in their clientele, had featured illustrations almost from birth. *Leslie's Weekly* (1855) and *Harper's Weekly* (1857) used many, especially during the Civil War. (*Harper's* began its life by bootlegging British authors.) Later the mass-circulation magazines of the nineties (like *Ladies' Home Journal, Cosmopolitan,* and the revitalized *Saturday Evening Post*) seized on modern reproduction methods to capitalize on pictures both for their editorial copy and for the increasingly dominant national advertising.

Halftone and line engravers began to advertise their services in periodicals.[3] In Frank Norris' *The Octopus* (1901), a California newspaper editor has a scheme to

". . . extend the *Mercury's* sphere of influence as far up and down the valley as I can. I want to illustrate the paper. You see, if I had a photo-engraving plant of my own, I could do a good deal of outside jobbing as well, and the investment would pay ten percent. But it takes money to make money. I wouldn't want to put in any dinky, one-horse affair. I want a good plant. I've been figuring out the business. Besides the plant, there would be the expense of a high grade paper, and that costs. Well, what with this and with that and running expenses till the thing began to pay, it would cost me about ten thousand dollars."

The other elements which shaped modern printing were new

[3] See, for example, *The Opera Glass*, February 17, 1894. It contains an ad from the New England Photo Art Engraving Co.

kinds of paper and modern presses: ". . . in 1798, Robert in France, invented and shortly afterwards in England, Fourdrinier perfected, a paper-making machine, operated by power, either water or steam, which produced paper by a continuous process. It also made possible the production of paper with a wove surface that was smoother than any that had previously been made in Europe."[4] Shortly afterward a power press was designed for the London *Times*. Later improvements both in press and paper grew from demands made on the machinery for the degree of definition necessary to service the halftones. By the end of the century high-speed presses using lithography could print two to five colors from one feeding.

Invented in 1798, lithography as an art process enjoyed cycles of popularity, first with the success of such artists as Daumier and Goya, followed by a midcentury slump consequent to the rise of photography. The nineties saw a revival with artists like Toulouse-Lautrec, Henri Bonnard, Steinlen, and Jules Chéret, who had been inspired by American circus posters. As a printing process, lithography was introduced to mass-production methods by its involvement with printed color. Chromolithography was patented in 1837, employed in England in the 1840's, and applied to surfaces other than paper in the 1860's. The garish chromolithograph became a staple of posters and figured also in the production of fashion designs and commercial labels.

New techniques of reproduction were not without their pitfalls. Before the metal sheets which eventually serve as lithographic plates can be treated, for example, an artificial "graining" is applied to them so that they will be porous to grease or water. This abrasive treatment varies in quality and size of grain. At worst it may result in an image reproduction which looks, as Robert Benchley once said, as though the pictures had been engraved on pieces of bread. As late as 1908 the famous (and waspish) lithographic artist Joseph Pennell thought that, "Still, illustration as an art is virtually dead . . . how long we shall have to endure the 'picture' made in German or Polish or Yiddish by a camera or a

---

4 Ivins, *op. cit.*, 18.

fluke I don't know—but I am surprised that *The Century* has been caught."[5]

Although Pennell would never compare photoengraving to etching, he did feel its use led to a greater command of line.[6] In fact, the invention of line photoengraving had freed the artist by introducing photography to reproduce the drawing and apply it directly to a medium like zinc for printing. This step encouraged pen drawings, replacing the lithographic crayons with their attendant problems of preserving neatness and making corrections. The freedom of line among the illustrators of the nineties is evidenced in Charles Dana Gibson. Artists began to study the effect of the photograph processes on the outcome of their drawings in print. In 1883, writing to Theo, Vincent Van Gogh describes experiments to adapt his sketches to the photolithographic process for maximum effect. "I saw at once that the black was of a very deep tone, and I can understand that this is a real necessity for the reproduction where photography and galvanography are used. . . . What is called black and white is in fact painting in black, meaning that one gives the same depth of effect, the same richness of tone value in a drawing that ought to be in a painting."[7]

VII

WINSOR McCAY

Winsor McCay was born in Spring Lake, Michigan, on September 26, 1869. When seventeen he was hired by a traveling circus to paint its attractions on billboards. A Cincinnati *Times-Star* editor sought out McCay as a staff artist in 1888. There he learned to sketch news events quickly. The next year he was hired by the competing Cincinnati *Enquirer*. In 1903, McCay joined the New York *Herald*, where he commenced *Little Nemo in Slumberland*, a weekly comic page. For the New York *Telegram,* also operated by James Gordon Bennett, McCay created *Dreams of A Rarebit*

[5] Pennell, *The Life and Letters of Joseph Pennell* II, 46. Letter dated February 13, 1908.

[6] *Ibid.*, I, 220.

[7] Auden, ed., *Van Gogh: a Self Portrait*, 128–29.

Fiend, a daily comic page done under the name of "Silas." Thus McCay did *seven full comic pages a week,* plus newspaper illustrations, editorial cartooning, and later three more strips (as Silas): *Sammy Sneeze, Hungry Henrietta,* and *The Pilgrim's Progress.*

By 1905, *Little Nemo* appeared internationally, translated into seven languages. Highly successful, it ran for ten years, until Arthur Brisbane, editorial director and writer for the Sunday Hearst papers, required the cartoonist to specialize his talents in illustrating the editor's words. *Little Nemo* reappeared in 1924, running until 1927. R. Winsor McCay, the cartoonist's son, briefly revived the strip.

Little Nemo was, in fact, McCay's son. "Nemo" is Latin for no name, chosen to expand his significance to all small children. In 1906 it appeared at the New Amsterdam Theatre in New York as a juvenile musical, commissioned by Klaw and Erlanger, starring Marie Tempest and Joseph Cawthorne (both of whom later entered films), with the music of Victor Herbert.

One resourceful element of the cartoon was McCay's sly criticism of society, cloaked in the dream adventures of Nemo, Flip (whose face was printed green), Impy, the dog Slivers, Professor, and Doctor Pill. In 1910, Nemo journeyed to Mars, where McCay observed the consequences of large monopolies. Elsewhere his panels witnessed poverty and slums.

As a graphic artist McCay enjoyed the highest reputation. Charles Dana Gibson termed him "the exemplar of pen and ink draftsmanship." The precision, care, and imagination which McCay brought to Nemo, his first love, has been rivaled perhaps only by Hal Foster (*Tarzan, Prince Valiant*) and Lionel Feininger, whose German *Kin-Der-Kids* were reproduced in color in the Chicago *Tribune* in 1906.

Relations between newspaper comics and the motion picture were many. As early as 1897, Frederick Burr Opper's *Happy Hooligan* was adapted into a (live) movie series in which J. Stuart Blackton played the tramp. In 1906, Blackton made *Humorous Phases of Funny Faces* on film. This has been sometimes termed the first animated cartoon, although Emile Cohl's work appears equally early, and Méliès did animated sequences, albeit not with individual drawings.

McCay's own statements, then, must be viewed in the light of rival claims. He said that he thought of *Dream of the Rarebit Fiend* in Engel's Cafe, off Herald Square, but the Edwin S. Porter–Edison film dates from the same year.

Some confusion surrounds dates of McCay's animated work. An early biographical sketch (prepared by J. P. Gleason, 1573 East 15th Street, Brooklyn, New York) places *Little Nemo* in 1909, an experimental work. However, according to Eileen Bowser (Associate Curator of the Department of Film at the Museum of Modern Art), this film corresponds to one called *Winsor McKay* (*sic*) which is reviewed in the *Moving Picture World* of April 22, 1911 (p. 900). It was produced and distributed by Vitagraph, and has Vitagraph players and executives seen in the film. Perhaps the live sequences were added later to facilitate public release independent of McCay's vaudeville tours with his films.

The same explanation might reconcile different dates given to *Gertie the Dinosaur*. It is variously located in 1909 and 1910, but (again from Eileen Bowser's notes) the *Moving Picture World* of December 26, 1914 (p. 1863) describes this film as *Gertie*, distributed by Box Office Attraction Co., William Fox, President; copyrighted at the end of 1914. The film does record McCay "talking with" his dinosaur in the manner he apparently used on stage.

McCay himself described his work in *Cartoons and Movies Magazine* of April, 1927:

> The part of my life of which I am proudest is the fact that I was the first man in the world to make animated cartoons. . . . My point is this: Winsor, Jr., as a small boy, picked up several flippers of "Magic Pictures" (the ancestor of the movies) from the street and brought them home to me. . . . From this germ I evolved the modern cartoon movies . . . in 1909, . . . I made 4,000 drawings of Little Nemo move . . . they were flashed on the screen of Hammerstein's Theatre in old New York. . . . Then I drew "How a Mosquito Operates." . . . While these made a big hit, the theatre patrons sus-

pected some trick with wires. . . . Not until I drew "Gertie" the dinosaurus, did the audiences understand that I was really making the drawings move. . . . I lectured in connection with the screen presentation, inviting "Gertie" to eat an apple (which I held up to her) in my hand. . . . "Gertie" would lower her long neck and swallow the fruit, much to the delight of the audience. Artists haven't taken animation seriously enough yet. . . . When they do they will make some marvelous pictures. . . . I went into the business and spent thousands of dollars developing the new art. . . . It required considerable time, patience, and careful thought—timing and drawing the pictures. . . . I animated even the "stills" figures, which some movie cartoonists don't do. . . . Unless all the live figures vibrate, the picture really isn't animated. . . . This is the most fascinating work I have ever done—and I hope to do it again—this business of making cartoons live on the screen.

According to Bowser, Universal-Jewel released one of McCay's cartoons, *The Sinking of the Lusitania*, in 1918. This would have been the next-to-last animated work of the cartoonist, who died on July 25, 1934. Following his death a theatrical fabrics dealer named Irving A. Mendelsohn located many of the early films in the family garage. With the help of Robert Bretherton, a CBS television film editor, Mendelsohn classified and preserved the material. When Expo '67 was planning an animation retrospective in Montreal, researchers located this source and underwrote transfers from the deteriorating cellulose nitrate stock. Le Cinematheque Canadienne dates the McCay material as follows:

Little Nemo (1909)
Gertie the Trained Dinosaur (1910)
How a Mosquito Operates (1910)
Bug Vaudeville (c. 1916)
The Pet (c. 1916)
The Adventures of a Rarebit Eater series (1916–17)
Gertie on Tour (1917) fragment
The Sinking of the Lusitania (1918)
The Flying House (1920)

Additional references to McCay can be located in the following periodicals.

William Rose Benet, *The Saturday Review of Literature* (September 9, 1944), 25.

Claude Bragdon. "Mickey Mouse and What He Means," *Scribner's Magazine* (June, 1934), 40–43.

Barnet G. Braver-Mann. "Mickey Mouse and His Playmates," *Theatre Guild Magazine* (March, 1931).

John Canaday. "Little Nemo at the Met," *The New York Times* (February 13, 1966), Section X, 21.

Freeman H. Hubbard. "Movie-Cartooning Secrets," *Saint Nicholas* (March, 1929).

Winsor McCay, *Cartoons and Movie Magazine* (April, 1927).

"Winsor McCay Illustrates How His Cartoons are Born," Chicago *Examiner* (January 30, 1928).

VIII

MUSICAL MACHINES

Parlor toys were not the only public-private media of the era. An entire generation of coin-operated instruments evolved from the actions of Louis Glass, general manager of the Pacific Phonograph Company, who installed nickel-in-the-slot devices and electric motors on the Edison phonographs at the Palais Royal Saloon in San Francisco in 1899. The phonographs were adapted with four listening tubes, a nickel slot for each. (Before that time coin machines dispensed only gum and weight.) Soon the phonograph and, shortly after, the kinetoscope provided private entertainment in the public centers.

Business quickly recognized the potential of these little mechanisms. The next year Felix Gottschalk, secretary of the Metropolitan Phonograph Company, organized the million dollar-capitalized Automatic Phonograph Exhibition Company of New York to make coin phonographs and to lease them on a profit-sharing basis.

A trade letter from the company indicated that "receipts increase or decrease in various machines as the records, which are changed daily, are good or mediocre, and the different localities require different attractions." Preferred fare included comic songs, monologues, whistling, and band records. In some saloon locations hymns were quite popular. It might be noted that reproduction through the tubes was superior to what was available by way of the accoustic horns in family machines.

Louis Glass had invented a moneymaker. The Louisiana Phonograph Company announced that one coin phonograph took in one thousand dollars during an April. In 1891 the Missouri Phonograph Company had fifty machines on location which were doing at least hundred-dollar-a-week business. Twenty-eight Edison phonographs were placed in the Vitascope Hall in Buffalo, New York, in company with the Kinetoscopes.

The coin machines probably inspired coin music boxes and the coin player piano, which soon came to dominate the field. Coin phonographs tried to counter the new competition with accompanying cards to illustrate the songs. Another entry, by 1906, was the Wurlitzer Harp, covered by plate glass, actuated by perforated rolls and a nickel. The harps sold for $750, a large enough investment that their popularity must have been guaranteed.

The period of high coin-phonograph popularity ran from 1890 until about 1908, to be replaced by the home phonograph and the player piano. The latter grew out of an 1880 invention by R. W. Pain, who constructed a thirty-nine note pneumatic self-playing instrument. The eighties and nineties saw patents of cams and motors, invented to work the keys and the piano rolls.

The popularity of the player piano was accelerated by efforts of the Aeolian Company when it was taken over by W. B. Tremaine in 1899. By 1909, 45,414 instruments were being produced, most of them uprights. "Even pop can play it"; the parlor piano ran popularly into the days of radio.

Edison's cylinder phonographs soon suffered in competition with the disc machines, which were selling early in the 1900's for as little as $5.00 and $7.50. The 1905 Zonophone Talking Machine ranged in price from $27.50 to $55.00. In order to invade the home successfully, the phonograph followed the designs of early sewing machines. In 1906, Victor marketed a machine with an internal horn and record storage space, which contributed enormously toward marketing the product to middle-class families as furniture.

Sales and bourgeois interest were also spurred by Caruso's 1902 recordings, a kind of *Birth of a Nation* for the home phonograph. The preservation of operatic performance was an early enthusiasm of Edison's. He hoped that the motion picture would contribute to it, and did make an early sound-film excerpt from *La Bohême*.

Before the phonograph could penetrate a mass market, however, records themselves had to transcend the limitations of individually recorded production. Photoengraving was responsible for this accomplishment. Emile Berliner adapted an earlier theory of Gros by making a lateral-cut, photoengraved matrix, prepared by submitting a waxed recording to an acid bath and then electrotyping the matrix, which was then used to stamp out a plastic record. With increased production and competition, the price of records dropped. In 1903 the cost of a seven-inch disc was fifty cents; ten-inch, one dollar; twelve-inch, a dollar fifty. In 1905, Victor reduced its prices and the other companies followed. Seven-inch recordings were thirty-five cents; ten-inch, fifty cents. The Sterling quarter record appeared in 1906. By 1912 the phonographs were big business, and Victor had $1 million budgeted for advertising—a testimonial, too, to the increased circulation and effectiveness of national magazines. Recording also permeated business and daily life, enough so that in *Dracula*, the ardant diary keeper, Dr. Seward, can note on 25 October, "How I miss my phonograph! To write diary with a pen is irksome to me; but Van Helsing says I must."

For further information on musical machineries, the reader might consult:
Read and Welch, *From Tin Foil to Stereo.*
Gelatt, *The Fabulous Phonograph.*
Mosoriak, *The Curious History of Music Boxes.*
Boston and Langwill, *Church and Chamber Barrel-Organs.*
Bescoby-Chambers, *The Archives of Sound.*
Batten, *Joe Batten's Book: the Story of Sound Recording.*
Blesh and Janis, *They All Played Ragtime.*

IX

CHRONOLOGICAL LISTING OF FILM TITLES[1]

Title	Producer	Copyright date
Elopement on Horseback	Edison	November 26, 1898
Strange Adventure of N.Y. Drummer	Edison	June 17, 1899
Love and War	James H. White	November 28, 1899
Uncle Josh's Nightmare	Edison	March 21, 1900
Terrible Teddy, the Grizzly King	Edison	February 23, 1901
Love by the Light of the Moon	Edison	March 16, 1901
Circular Panorama of Electric Tower	Edison	August 14, 1901
Martyred Presidents	Edison	October 7, 1901
Panorama of Esplanade by Night	Edison	November 11, 1901
Uncle Josh At the Moving Picture Show	Edison	January 27, 1902
The Twentieth Century Tramp	Edison	January 27, 1902
Fun in A Bakery Shop	Edison	April 3, 1902
Jack and the Beanstalk	Edison	June 20, 1902
Grandpa's Reading Glass	AM&B	October 3, 1902
Life of An American Fireman	Edison	January 21, 1903
The Inn Where No Man Rests	Méliès	June 25, 1903
A Spiritualist Photographer	Méliès	July 6, 1903
Uncle Tom's Cabin	Edison	July 30, 1903
A Search For Evidence	AM&B	August 3, 1903
Gay Shoe Clerk	Edison	August 12, 1903
The Dude and the Burglars	AM&B	August 13, 1903
The Kingdom of the Fairies	Méliès	September 3, 1903
A Romance of the Rail	Edison	October 3, 1903
The Magic Lantern	Méliès	December 9, 1903
The Pickpocket	Gaumont	December 10, 1903

1 From Kemp Niver, *In the Beginning: Program Notes to Accompany One Hundred Early Motion Pictures.* Used by permission of the author. The same Library of Congress material is examined in even greater detail in Niver's handsomely illustrated volume, *The First Twenty Years.*

255

Title	Producer	Copyright date
How the Old Woman Caught the Omnibus	Hepworth	December 19, 1903
The Story (of) the Biograph Told	AM&B	January 8, 1904
The Clock Maker's Dream	Méliès	February 23, 1904
The Cook in Trouble	Méliès	May 9, 1904
The Mermaid	Méliès	May 18, 1904
The Child Stealers	Gaumont	June 9, 1904
Raid on a Coiner's Den	Gaumont	June 23, 1904
The Eviction	Gaumont	June 23, 1904
Personal	AM&B	June 29, 1904
Bold Bank Robbery	Lubin	July 25, 1904
The Bewitched Traveller	Hepworth	August 12, 1904
The Moonshiner	AM&B	August 19, 1904
European Rest Cure	Edison	September 1, 1904
The Widow and the Only Man	AM&B	September 8, 1904
Rounding Up of the "Yeggmen"	Edison	September 16, 1904
The Hero of Liao Yang	AM&B	September 22, 1904
Revenge!	Gaumont	October 1, 1904
A Railway Tragedy	Gaumont	October 10, 1904
The Lost Child	AM&B	October 15, 1904
An Englishman's Trip to Paris from London	Clarendon, Gaumont or Hepworth	October 28, 1904
Decoyed	ditto	October 28, 1904
The Suburbanite	AM&B	November 11, 1904
The Ex-Convict	Edison	November 19, 1904
The Other Side of the Hedge	Clarendon, Gaumont or Hepworth	November 28, 1904
A Race for a Kiss	ditto	November 28, 1904
The Lover's Ruse	ditto	November 28, 1904
The Kleptomaniac	Edison	February 4, 1905
The Seven Ages	Edison	February 27, 1905
Tom, Tom, the Piper's Son	AM&B	March 9, 1905
How Jones Lost His Roll	Edison	March 27, 1905
The Nihilists	AM&B	March 28, 1905
The Whole Dam Family and the Dam Dog	Edison	May 31, 1905
Rescued by Rover	Hepworth	August 19, 1905
Fine Feathers Make Fine Birds	unknown	August 25, 1905
The Great Jewel Mystery	AM&B	October 23, 1905

Title	Producer	Copyright date
A Kentucky Feud	AM&B	November 7, 1905
The Silver Wedding	AM&B	March 8, 1906
The Black Hand	AM&B	March 24, 1906
The Paymaster	AM&B	June 23, 1906
The Tunnel Workers	AM&B	November 10, 1906
The Skyscrapers	AM&B	December 11, 1906
Mr. Hurry-Up of New York	AM&B	January 31, 1907
The Girl From Montana	Selig	March 14, 1907
His First Ride	Selig	March 29, 1907
The Bandit King	Selig	April 11, 1907
The Tired Tailor's Dream	AM&B	August 27, 1907
An Acadian Elopement	AM&B	September 16, 1907
The Boy Detective	AM&B	March 7, 1908
Her First Adventure	AM&B	March 13, 1908
Caught By Wireless	AM&B	March 18, 1908
The Sculptor's Nightmare	AM&B	May 4, 1908
At the French Ball	AM&B	June 20, 1908
A Calamitous Elopement	AM&B	July 28, 1908
Balked at the Altar	AM&B	August 15, 1908
Where Breakers Roar	AM&B	September 15, 1908
An Awful Moment	AM&B	December 10, 1908
The Bank Robbery	Oklahoma Natural Mutoscene	December 28, 1908
The Cord of Life	AM&B	January 22, 1909
The Girls and Daddy	AM&B	February 3, 1909
Golden Louis	AM&B	February 17, 1909
At The Altar	AM&B	February 26, 1909
She Would Be an Actress	Lubin	August 5, 1909
Drunkard's Child	Lubin	August 9, 1909
An Unexpected Guest	Lubin	August 12, 1909
Fools of Fate	Biograph	October 7, 1909
Faithful	Biograph	March 28, 1910
His Trust	Biograph	January 19, 1911
His Trust Fulfilled	Biograph	January 24, 1911
Enoch Arden	Biograph	June 13 & 17, 1911
The Girl and Her Trust	Biograph	March 28, 1912
The Aviator's Generosity	Nordisk (Oes)	April 10, 1912
Love and Friendship	Nordisk (Oes)	April 24, 1912
A Temporary Truce	Biograph	June 10, 1912
A Dash Through the Clouds	Biograph	June 28, 1912

Bibliography

For well-known works which have appeared in several editions, the publisher and place of publication have been omitted and only the first date of publication listed. In the text, references to these works are by chapter rather than by page, so that the reader can refer to any one of the several editions available.

Adams, John Paul, ed. *The Funnies Annual No. 1*. New York, Avon, 1959.

Allen, Captain Quincy. *The Outdoor Chums in the Forest; or Laying the Ghost of Oak Ridge*. Cleveland, Goldsmith, 1911.

Anonymous. *Frank James on the Trail*. New York, Morrison's Sensational Series, I, No. 46, 1882. Reprinted by Pioneer Historical Society, Harriman, Tennessee, n.d.

———— (An Old Scout). *Young Wild West, the Prince of the Saddle*. No publisher, n.d. Reprinted by Pioneer Historical Society, Harriman, Tennessee, n.d.

Antonioni, Michelangelo. *L'Avventura*. New York, Grove, 1969.

Arnheim, Rudolf. *Film as Art*. Berkeley, University of California Press, 1958.

————. *Visual Thinking*. Berkeley, University of California Press, 1969.

————. "What Do the Eyes Contribute?" *Audio-Visual Communications Review*, X, No. 5.

Arvidson, Linda (Mrs. D. W. Griffith). *When the Movies Were Young*. New York, Dutton, 1925.

Bailey, J. O., ed. *British Plays of the Nineteenth Century*. New York, Odyssey, 1966.

Barnouw, Eric. *Mass Communication*. New York, Reinhardt, 1956.

————. *A History of Broadcasting in the United States. A Tower in Babel*, Vol. I. New York, Oxford, 1966.

258

Barry, Iris and Eileen Bowser. *D. W. Griffith: American Film Master.* New York, Museum of Modern Art, 1965.

Barthes, Roland. *Writing Degree Zero; Elements of Semiology.* Boston, Beacon, 1970.

Barzun, Jacques. *The Energies of Art.* New York, Harper, 1956.

Batten, Joe. *Joe Batten's Book; the Story of Sound Recording.* London, Rockliff, 1956.

Beach, Joseph Warren. *The Technique of Thomas Hardy.* New York, Russell and Russell, 1962.

———. *The Twentieth Century Novel.* New York, Century, 1932.

Becker, Stephen. *Comic Art in America.* New York, Simon and Schuster, 1959.

Beerbohm, Max. *The Happy Hypocrite.* New York, J. Lane, 1906.

Belasco, David. *The Girl of the Golden West.* New York, A. L. Burt, 1911.

———. *Six Plays.* Boston, Little, Brown, 1929.

Bennett, Arnold. *The Glimpse.* New York, D. Appleton, 1909.

Bergson, Henri. *Creative Evolution.* New York, H. Holt, 1911.

———. *Matter and Memory.* London, G. Allen, 1911.

Bescoby-Chambers, John. *The Archives of Sound.* Aylesbury, Buckshire, Oakwood Press, 1964.

Bessy, Maurice. "Méliès." Paris, *Anthologie du Cinéma.* 1966.

Biggs, John R. *Illustration and Reproduction in Printing.* New York, Pellagrini and Cudahy, 1952.

The Bioscope, February 6, 1929.

Blesh, Rudi, and Harriet Janis. *They All Played Ragtime.* New York, Knopf, 1950.

Bluestone, George. *Novels Into Film.* Baltimore, Johns Hopkins, 1957.

Bond, Kirk. "Eastman House Journal." *Film Culture*, No. 47, Summer, 1969.

Booth, Michael. *English Melodrama.* London, Herbert Jenkins, 1965.

———, ed. *Hiss the Villain.* London, Eyre and Spottiswoode, 1964.

Boothby, Guy. *A Bid for Fortune.* New York, D. Appleton, 1895.

Boston, Canon Noel, and Lyndesay G. Langwill. *Church and Chamber Barrel-Organs.* Edinburgh, Lyndesay G. Langwill, 1967.

Brannan, Robert Louis. *Under the Management of Mr. Charles Dickens.* Ithaca, Cornell University Press, 1966.

Breitenbach, Edgar. "The Poster Craze." *American Heritage*, XIII, No. 2, February, 1962.

Brown, John Mason, ed. *The Ladies' Home Journal Treasury*. New York, Simon and Schuster, 1956.

Brownlow, Kevin. *The Parade's Gone By.* . . . New York, Knopf, 1969.

Buntline, Ned (Edward Zane Carroll Judson). *Wild Bill's Last Trail*. New York, Diamond Dick Library, No. 192, 1896. Reprinted by Pioneer Historical Society, Harriman, Tennessee, n.d.

Butterfield, Roger. "Pictures in the Papers." *American Heritage,* XIII, No. 4, June, 1962 (adapted from paper presented at American Antiquarian Society, Worcester, Massachusetts, 1961).

———, ed. *The Saturday Evening Post Treasury*. New York, Simon and Schuster, 1954.

Cable, George Washington. *The Grandissimes*. New York, Scribner, 1880.

Carroll, Lewis (Charles L. Dodgson). *Through the Looking Glass*. 1872.

Carson, Gerald. "The Piano in the Parlor." *American Heritage,* XVII, No. 1, December, 1965.

Cassedy, Ralph. "Monopoly in Motion Picture Production and Distribution: 1908–15." *Southern California Law Review,* XXXII, No. 4, 1959.

Casty, Alan. *The Dramatic Art of the Film*. New York, Harper and Row, 1971.

Catalogue of Military, Naval, Field and Opera Glasses Manufactured by Ross, Ltd. London, 1902.

Ceram, C. W. (Kurt Wilhelm Marek). *Archaeology of the Cinema*. London, Thames and Hudson, 1965.

Charvat, William. "Literature as a Business." In Robert Spiller, Willard Thorp, Thomas H. Johnson, Henry Seidel Canby, Richard M. Ludwig, eds. *Literary History of the United States*, 3rd. ed. rev. 2 vols. New York, Macmillan, 1963.

Chesterton, G. K. *The Man Who Was Thursday*. New York, Boni and Liveright, 1908.

Churchill, Winston. *The Crisis*. New York, Grosset and Dunlap, 1901.

Coke, Van Deren. *The Painter and the Photograph*. Albuquerque, University of New Mexico Press, 1964.

Conrad, Joseph. *Lord Jim*. Published serially 1899–1900, *Blackwood's*.

———. *The Nigger of the Narcissus*. London, Heinemann, 1897.

Corelli, Marie. *The Soul of Lilith*. London, Metheun, 1897.

Cook, Olive. *Movement in Two Dimensions*. London, Hitchinson, 1963.

Cook, William Wallace. *Jim Dexter, Cattleman*. New York, Frank A. Munsey, 1905.

Cooper, James Fenimore. *The Prairie*. 1827.

Couperie, Pierre, and Maurice C. Horn. *A History of the Comic Strip*. New York, Crown, 1968.

Crane, Stephen. *Maggie: a Girl of the Streets*. Introduction by Joseph Katz. Gainesville, Florida, Scholars' Facsimiles and Reprints, 1966.

Crawford, F. Marion. *Children of the King*. New York, Macmillan, 1893.

Crosby, Sumner McK. *Helen Gardner's Art Through the Ages*. 4th ed. New York, Harcourt, Brace, 1959.

Crowther, J. O. *Famous American Men of Science*. New York, Norton, 1937.

Croy, Homer. *The Story of D. W. Griffith: Star Maker*. New York, Duell, Sloan and Pearce, 1959.

Curwen, Harold. *Processes of Graphic Reproduction in Printing*. London, Faber and Faber, 1963.

Darrah, William Culp. *Stereo Views: A History of Stereographs in America and Their Collection*. Gettysburg, Time and News, 1964.

Davies, Richard Harding. *Soldiers of Fortune*. New York, Scribner's, 1897.

De Vries, Leonard. *Panorama 1842-1865*. Boston, Houghton Mifflin, 1969.

Dickens, Charles. *Bleak House*. 1853.

――――. *A Christmas Carol*. 1843.

――――. *Oliver Twist*. 1838.

――――. *A Tale of Two Cities*. 1859.

Dickinson, Thorold. *A Discovery of Cinema*. London, Oxford, 1971.

Dime Novel Roundup. December, 1965. 821 Vermont St., Lawrence, Kansas.

――――. May, 1969.

Disher, Maurice Willson. *Blood and Thunder*. London, Frederick Muller, 1949.

――――. *Melodrama: Plots That Thrilled*. London, Rockliff, 1954.

Dixon, Thomas. *The Klansman*. New York, Doubleday and Page, 1905.

Dreiser, Theodore. *Sister Carrie*. New York, Doubleday and Page, 1900.

Drinkwater, John. *The Life and Adventures of Carl Laemmle*. New York, Putnam, 1931.

Dujardin, Édouard. *Les Lauriers sont Coupés*. 1888 (Published serially

1887). Trans. Stuart Gilbert, *We'll To the Woods No More.* Intro. by Leon Edel. New York, New Directions, 1957.

Dulles, Foster Rhea. *The United States Since 1865.* Ann Arbor, University of Michigan Press, 1959.

Du Maurier, George. *Peter Ibbetson.* New York, Harper, 1891.

Durgnat, Raymond. "Fake, Fiddle and the Photographic Arts." *The British Journal of Aesthetics,* V, No. 3, July, 1965.

Durham, Victor G. *The Submarine Boys and the Middies.* Philadelphia, Henry Altemus, 1909.

Edel, Leon. *The Psychological Novel, 1900–1950.* New York, Lippencott, 1955.

Eisenstein, Sergei M. *Film Essays and a Lecture.* New York, Praeger, 1970.

————. *Film Form.* New York, Harcourt, Brace, 1949.

————. *The Film Sense.* New York, Harcourt, Brace, 1942.

Elliot, Alexander. *Three Hundred Years of American Painting.* New York, Time, Inc., 1957.

Ellis, Edward S. *Seth Jones; or, The Captives of the Frontier.* Beadle's Half-Dime Library, Nov. 9, 1877. Reprinted New York, Odyssey, 1966.

Ewen, David. *The Life and Death of Tin Pan Alley.* New York, Funk and Wagnalls, 1964.

Farber, Manny. "Underground Films," *Commentary,* November, 1947.

Feiffer, Jules. *The Great Comic Book Heroes.* New York, Dial, 1965.

Fiedler, Leslie. *Love and Death in the American Novel.* New York, Criterion, 1960.

Flaubert, Gustave. *Madame Bovary.* 1857.

Ford, Ford Madox. *Joseph Conrad: a Personal Remembrance.* Boston, Little, Brown, 1925.

Forster, E. M. *Aspects of the Novel.* New York, Harcourt, Brace, 1927.

Freud, Sigmund. *The Interpretation of Dreams.* New York, Macmillan, 1922.

Friedenberg, Edgar Z. *The Vanishing Adolescent. Boston,* Beacon, 1959.

Frost, A. B. *Frost's Stuff and Nonsense.* New York, Scribner's, 1884.

Fuchs, Theodore. *Stage Lighting.* Boston, Little, Brown, 1929.

Fuller, Buckminster. "Change as the Fundamental Norm." *Class.* Spring, 1970.

Furnas, J. C. *The Americans: A Social History of the United States 1587–1914.* New York, Putnam's, 1969.

Galsworthy, John. *The Man of Property.* New York, Scribner's, 1906.

Garis, Roger. *My Father Was Uncle Wiggley.* New York, McGraw-Hill, 1966.

Geduld, Harry M., ed. *Focus on D. W. Griffith.* Englewood Cliffs, N.J., Prentice-Hall, 1971.

Gelatt, Roland. *The Fabulous Phonograph.* Philadelphia, Lippencott, 1955.

Gernsheim, Helmut and Alison. *A Concise History of Photography.* New York, Grosset and Dunlap, 1965.

Gessner, Robert. "The Moving Image." *American Heritage,* XI, No. 3, April, 1960.

Gillon, Edmund Vincent, ed. *The Gibson Girl and Her America.* New York, Dover, 1969.

Gish, Lillian. *The Movies, Mr. Griffith, and Me.* Englewood Cliffs, N.J., Prentice-Hall, 1969.

Glasgow, Ellen. *The Deliverance.* New York, Doubleday, Page, 1905.

Godard, Jean-Luc. *Masculine-Feminine.* New York, Grove, 1969.

Gombrich, E. H. *Art and Illusion,* 2nd ed. rev. New York, Pantheon, 1961.

———. *The Story of Art.* New York, Phaidon, 1952.

Gorelik, Mordecai. *New Theatres for Old.* New York, Samuel French, 1957.

Grau, Robert. *The Business Man in the Amusement World.* New York, Broadway, 1910.

Green, Anna Katherine. *The Filagree Ball; Being a Full and True Account of the Solution of the Mystery Concerning the Jeffrey-Moore Affair.* New York, Bobbs Merrill, 1903.

Grey, Zane. *The Spirit of the Border.* New York, A. L. Burt, 1905.

Griffith, David Wark. *A Fool and a Girl: a Dramatic Composition of Five Acts.* Manuscript, Library of Congress, 1906.

Grimsted, David. *Melodrama Unveiled.* Chicago, University of Chicago Press, 1968.

Haggard, H. Rider. *She.* London, Longman's, 1887.

———. *Ayesha.* London, Ward, 1905.

Hall, Ben M. *The Best Remaining Seats.* New York, Potter, 1961.

Hammett, Dashiell. *The Maltese Falcon.* New York, Knopf, 1930.

Hampton, Benjamin B. *History of the American Film Industry from Its Beginnings to 1931.* New York, Dover, 1970.

Hancock, H. Irving. *Chiggins, the Youngest Hero of the Army; a Tale of the Capture of Santiago.* Philadelphia, Altemus, 1904.

Hardy, Thomas. *The Mayor of Casterbridge*. London, Smith, Elder, 1886.

Hartnell, Phyllis, ed. *Oxford Companion to the Theatre*. 3rd. ed. London, Oxford University Press, 1967.

Harvey, Charles M. "The Dime Novel in American Life." *Atlantic Monthly*, C, July, 1907.

Hauser, Arnold. *The Philosophy of Art History*. New York, Knopf, 1958.

Head, J. A. and D. F. *Journey to the Gold Diggins by Jeremiah Saddlebags*. Cincinnatti, H. P. James, 1849.

Heilman, Robert. *Tragedy and Melodrama*. Seattle, University of Washington Press, 1968.

Henderson, Robert. *D. W. Griffith: the Years at Biograph*. New York, Farrar, Straus and Giroux, 1970.

Henney, Keith, and Beverly Dudley. *Handbook of Photography*. New York, Whittlesey House, 1939.

Heym, George. *The Autopsy*. Trans. by Michael Hamburger. Stephen Spender, ed. *Great German Short Stories*. New York, Dell, 1960.

Heymann, Mme. Alfred. *Lunettes et Lorgnettes de Jadis*. Paris, J. Leroy, 1911.

Holbrook, Stewart H. "Frank Merriwell at Yale Again—and Again and Again." *American Heritage*, XII, No. 4, June, 1961.

Hope, Anthony (Sir Anthony Hope Hawkins). *Rupert of Hentzau*. Bristol, Arrowsmith, 1908.

Hopkins, Albert A. *Stage Illusions and Scientific Diversions*. New York, 1897. Reprinted New York, Benjamin Blom, 1967.

Hopwood, Henry V. *Living Pictures: Their History, Photo-Production and Practical Working*. London, Optician and Photographic Trades Review, 1899.

Hughes, Glenn. *A History of the American Theatre: 1700–1950*. New York, Samuel French, 1951.

Hughes, Robert. *Heaven and Hell in Western Art*. New York, Stein and Day, 1968.

Humphrey, Robert. *Stream of Consciousness in the Modern Novel*. Berkeley, University of California Press, 1954.

Hyman, Stanley Edgar. *The Tangled Bank*. New York, Atheneum, 1962.

Ingraham, Col. Prentiss. *California Joe, the Mysterious Plainsman: the Strange Adventures of an Unknown Man, whose real identity (like that of the "Man of the Iron Mask") is still unsolved.* Beadle's

Boys' Library, II, No. 54, Dec. 20, 1882. Reprinted by Pioneer Historical Society, Harriman, Tennessee, n.d.

Irwin, Will. *The House that Shadows Built.* Garden City, Doubleday Doran, 1928.

Israel, Fred L., ed. *1897 Sears Roebuck Catalogue.* New York, Chelsea House, 1968.

Ivins, William M., Jr. *Notes on Prints.* New York, Metropolitan Museum of Art, 1930.

————. *Prints and Visual Communication.* Cambridge, Harvard University Press, 1953.

Jackson, Mason. *The Pictorial Press.* London, Hurst and Blackett, 1885. Reprinted Detroit, Gale Research, 1968.

Jacobs, Donald H. *Fundamentals of Optical Engineering.* New York, McGraw-Hill, 1943.

Jacobs, Lewis. *The Rise of the American Film.* New York, Harcourt, Brace, 1939.

Jacobs, W. W. *Many Cargoes with thirty-two black and white illustrations by E. W. Kemble.* New York, Stokes, 1903.

James, Henry. *The Lesson of the Master.* New York, Macmillan, 1892.

James, William. *Principles of Psychology.* New York, H. Holt, 1890.

Jenkins, C. Francis, and Oscar B. Depue. *Handbook for Motion Picture and Stereopticon Operators.* Washington, Knega, 1908.

Jobes, Gertrude. *Motion Picture Empire.* Hamden, Conn., Archon, 1966.

Johannsen, Albert. *The House of Beadle and Adams and Its Dime and Nickel Novels.* Norman, University of Oklahoma Press, 1950, 1962.

Johnson, Edgar and Eleanor. *The Dickens Theatrical Reader.* Boston, Little, Brown, 1964.

Johnston, Annie Fellows. *The Little Colonel's Knight Comes Riding.* Boston, Page, 1907.

Karr, Jean. *Zane Grey, Man of the West.* New York, Greenberg, 1949.

Kepes, Gyorgy. *The New Landscape in Art and Science.* Chicago, Paul Theobold, 1956.

Kracauer, Siegfried. *Theory of Film: the Redemption of Physical Reality.* New York, Oxford University Press, 1960.

Kyrou, Ado. *L'Age d'Or de la Carte Postale.* Paris, A. Balland, 1966.

Lauterback, C., and A. Jakovsky. *Postkarten Album . . . auch eine Kulturgeschichte.* Cologne, M. Du Mont Schauberg, 1961.

Lennig, Arthur. *The Silent Voice: A Text.* Troy, N.Y., Walter Snyder, 1969.

Leroux, Gaston. *The Phantom of the Opera.* First American edition New York, Bobbs Merrill, 1911.

Leverton, Garrett H. *Plays for the College Theatre.* New York, Samuel French, 1948.

———. *The Production of Late Nineteenth Century American Drama.* New York, Teachers College, Columbia University, 1936.

Levin, Harry. *The Gates of Horn.* New York, Oxford, 1963.

Lichten, Frances. *Decorative Art of Victoria's Era.* New York, Scribner's, 1950.

Lindsay, Nicholas Vachel. *The Art of the Moving Picture.* New York, Macmillan, 1915.

London, Jack. *Brown Wolf and Other Jack London Stories.* New York, Macmillan, 1920.

———. *White Fang.* New York, Macmillan, 1905.

Loos, Anita. *A Girl Like I.* New York, Viking, 1966.

Lord, Walter. *The Good Years.* New York, Harper, 1960.

Maltin, Leonard. *Behind the Camera.* New York, Signet, 1971.

Mann, Thomas. *Buddenbrooks.* 1901.

———. *Death in Venice.* 1911.

———. *Tonio Krüger.* 1903.

Marcus, Stephen. *The Other Victorians.* New York, Basic, 1956.

Mason, A. E. W. *The Four Feathers.* New York, Macmillan, 1905.

McCay, Winsor. *Little Nemo in Slumberland.* New York, McCay Features Syndicate, 1945.

McCarthy, Mary. "Reflections: One Touch of Nature." *The New Yorker,* January 24, 1970.

McLuhan, Marshall, and Harley Parker. *Through the Vanishing Point: Space in Poetry and Painting.* New York, Harper and Row, 1968.

McLuhan, Marshall. *The Gutenberg Galaxy: the Making of Typographic Man.* Toronto, University of Toronto Press, 1962.

———. *Understanding Media.* New York, McGraw-Hill, 1964.

Mendelowitz, Daniel M. *A History of American Art.* New York, Holt, Rinehart and Winston, 1960.

Merleau-Ponty, Maurice. *Sense and Non-Sense.* Trans. Hubert L. Dreyfus and Patricia Allen Dreyfus. Evanston, Ill., Northwestern University Press, 1964.

Mitchel, F. A. *Sweet Revenge.* New York, Harper's, 1897.

Moses, Montrose J., ed. *Representative British Dramas, Victorian and Modern*. Boston, Little, Brown, 1927.

Mosoriak, Roy. *The Curious History of Music Boxes*. Chicago, Lightner, 1943.

Muybridge, Edweard. *Animals in Motion*. London, Chapman, 1907.

Newhall, Beaumont. *The Daguerreotype in America*. New York, Duell, Sloan and Pearce, 1961.

Nick Carter, Detective. New York, Macmillan, 1963.

Nicoll, Allardyce. *A History of English Drama 1600–1900*, Vol. 5, New York, Cambridge University Press, 2nd ed., 1959.

The Nineties. New York, American Heritage, 1967.

Niver, Kemp. *In the Beginning: Program Notes to Accompany One Hundred Early Motion Pictures*. New York, Brandon Books, n.d.

—————. *Motion Pictures from the Library of Congress Paper Print Collection 1894–1912*. Berkeley, University of California Press, 1967.

—————. *The First Twenty Years: A Segment of Film History*. Los Angeles, Locare Research Group, 1968.

Nizhny, Vladimir. *Lessons with Eisenstein*. Trans. and ed. Ivor Montagu and Jay Leyda. New York, Hill and Wang, 1969.

Noel, Mary. *Villains Galore . . . the Heyday of the Popular Story Weekly*. New York, Macmillan, 1954.

Norris, Frank. *The Octopus*. New York, Doubleday, Page, 1901.

Noxon, Gerald. "The Anatomy of the Closeup." *Journal of the Society of Cinematologists*, I, 1961.

—————. "Cinema and Cubism." *Journal of the Society of Cinematologists*, II, 1962.

Nye, Russel. *The Unembarrassed Muse*. New York, Dial, 1970.

O'Connor, Frank. *The Mirror in the Roadway*. London, Hamish Hamilton, 1957.

The Opera Glass (weekly newspaper). Galveston, Texas. Vol. 29, August 27, 1887.

The Opera Glass: a Musical and Dramatic Magazine. I, No. 1 Boston, February 17, 1894.

Orczy, Baroness. *The Scarlet Pimpernel*. London, Greening, 1905.

Ormond, Leonee. *George Du Maurier*. London, Routeledge and Kegan Paul, 1969.

Paine, Albert Bigelow. *Life and Lillian Gish*. New York, Macmillan, 1932.

Patten, Gilbert (Burt L. Standish). *Frank Merriwell Down South.* Philadelphia, D. McKay, 1903.

Pennell, Elizabeth Robins, ed. *The Life and Letters of Joseph Pennell.* 2 vols. Boston, Little, Brown, 1929.

Perry, George, and Alan Aldridge. *The Penguin Book of Comics.* Baltimore, Penguin, 1967.

Peterson, Theodore. *Magazines in the Twentieth Century.* Urbana, University of Illinois Press, 1964.

Phillips, Henry Albert. *The Photodrama.* Larchmont, N.Y., Stanhope-Dodge, 1914.

Pitt, George Dibdin. *Sweeney Todd the Demon Barber of Fleet Street.* Montagu Slater, ed. London, John Lane, 2nd ed. 1934.

Poe, Edgar Allen. *The Spectacles.* 1844.

Porta, John Babtista. *Natural Magick.* London, 1958. Facsimile edition New York, Basic, 1957.

Porter, William Sydney (O. Henry). *A Municipal Report.* 1910.

Proust, Marcel. *Swann's Way.* 1913. Trans. C. K. Scott Moncrieff. London, Chatto and Windus, 1922.

Pudovkin, Vselvolod I. *Film Technique.* London, Lear, 1954.

Ramsaye, Terry. *A Million and One Nights.* 2 vols. New York, Simon and Schuster, 1926.

Rahill, Frank. *The World of Melodrama.* University Park, Pa., Pennsylvania State University Press, 1967.

Raynall, Maurice. *Cézanne.* Switzerland, Skira, 1954.

Read, Oliver, and Walter L. Welch. *From Tin Foil to Stereo.* Indianapolis, H. W. Sams, 1959.

Reed, Walt. *The Illustrator in America 1900–1960.* New York, Reinhold, 1966.

Renoir, Alain. "Point of View and Design for Terror in Beowolf." Donald K. Fry, ed., *The Beowolf Poet.* Englewood Cliffs, N.J., Prentice-Hall, 1968.

Reynolds, Quentin. *The Fiction Factory; or, From Pulp Row to Quality Street.* New York, Random House, 1955.

Richardson, F. H. *Motion Picture Handbook: a Guide for Managers and Operators of Motion Picture Theatres.* New York, Moving Picture World, 1910.

Richardson, Robert. *Literature and Film.* Bloomington, Indiana University Press, 1969.

Ripley, John W. "All Join in the Chorus." *American Heritage*, X, No. 4, June, 1959.

Rockwood, Roy (Edward Stratemeyer syndicate name). *Five Thousand Miles Underground; or, the Mystery of the Centre of the Earth.* New York, Cupples and Leon, 1908.

Rowell, George, ed. *Nineteenth Century Plays.* London, Oxford, University Press, 1936.

Sansom, B. W. *Lithography: Principles and Practice.* London, Pitman, 1960.

Scull, Penrose. *From Peddlers to Merchant Princes.* Chicago, Follett, 1967.

Sell, Henry Blackman, and Victor Weybright. *Buffalo Bill and the Wild West.* New York, Oxford University Press, 1965.

Sharp, Dennis. *The Picture Palace.* London, Hugh Evelyn, 1969.

Sitney, P. Adams. "Ideas Within the Avant-Garde." *Film Library Quarterly*, III, No. 1, Winter, 1969–70.

Slade, Mark. "The Amber Light and Patterns of Ambiguity." *Art Journal*, VI, 1967.

Staff, Frank. *The Picture Postcard and Its Origins.* New York, Praeger, 1966.

———. *The Valentine and Its Origins.* New York, Praeger, 1969.

Stern, Seymour. "Griffith: 1—The Birth of a Nation." *Film Culture*, No. 36, Spring–Summer, 1965.

Stevens, D. W. *The James Boys in Minnesota.* New York, The Five Cent Wide Awake Library, Frank Tousey, I, No. 479, March 8, 1882. Reprinted by Pioneer Historical Society, Harriman, Tennessee, n.d.

Stevenson, Robert Louis. *Dr. Jeckyl and Mr. Hyde.* 1886.

———. *Kidnapped.* 1886.

Stoker, Bram (Abraham). *Dracula.* New York, Doubleday, 1897.

———. *The Jewel of Seven Stars.* London, Heinemann, 1903.

———. *The Mystery of the Sea.* London, Heinemann, 1902.

———. *The Snake's Pass.* New York, Harper, 1890.

———. *The Watter's Mou'.* London, T. L. DeVinne, 1894.

Taylor, Edward C. *Ted Strong's Manful Task; or Work and Win.* New York, Street and Smith, 1906.

Thackeray, William Makepeace. *Vanity Fair.* 1848.

Travers, Col. J. M. *Custer's Last Shot; or, the Boy Trailer of the Little Horn.* New York, Wide Awake Library, II, No. 1196, March 31, 1894. Reprinted by Pioneer Historical Society, Harriman, Tennessee, n.d.

Trutat, Eugene. *La Photographie Appliquée à l'Archaéologie.* Paris, 1879.

——. *La Photographie Appliquée à l'Histoire Natureelle.* Paris, Gauthiers-Villars, n.d.

——. *La Photographie Animeé, avec un Préface de J. Marey.* Paris, 1899.

——. *La Photographie en Montagne.* Paris, 1894.

Tyler, Parker. *Sex, Psyche, and Etcetera in the Film.* New York, Horizon, 1969.

——. *Underground Film: a Critical History.* New York, Grove, 1969.

Van Gogh, Vincent. *Van Gogh: a Self Portrait,* letters selected by W. H. Auden. Greenwich, Connecticut, New York Graphic Society, 1961.

Vardac, A. Nicholas. *Stage to Screen: Theatrical Method From Garrick to Griffith.* Cambridge, Harvard University Press, 1949.

Wallis, F. G., and H. Howitt. *Photo-Litho in Monochrome and Colour.* London, Pitman, 1963.

Webster, Frank V. *Bob Chester's Grit; or, From Ranch to Riches.* Akron, Saalfield, 1911.

Wechter, Dixon. *The Hero in America.* New York, Scribner's, 1941.

Wells, H. G. *The First Men on the Moon.* London, G. Newnes, 1901.

——. *The Invisible Man.* New York, E. Arnold, 1897.

——. *The Island of Dr. Moreau.* New York, Stone and Kimbell, 1896.

——. *The Time Machine.* New York, H. Holt, 1895.

——. *The War in the Air.* London, G. Bell, 1908.

——. *The War of the Worlds.* New York, Harper, 1898.

Weyman, Stanley J. *A Gentleman of France.* New York, Longman's, Green, 1918.

Wharton, Edith. *The House of Mirth.* New York, Macmillan, 1905.

Wheeler, Edward L. *Deadwood Dick on Deck; or, Calamity Jane, the Heroine of Whoop-Up.* New York, Beadle's Pocket Library, V, No. 57, Feb. 11, 1885. Reprinted New York, Odyssey, 1966.

White, David Manning, and Robert H. Abel, ed. *The Funnies: an American Idiom.* Glencoe, Ill., Free Press, 1963.

Wilde, Oscar. *The Picture of Dorian Gray.* 1891.

Winfield, Arthur M. (Edward Stratemeyer). *The Rover Boys Out West.* New York, Grosset and Dunlap, 1900.

Wister, Owen, *The Virginian.* 1902.

Wolf, Glenn Joseph. *Vachel Lindsay: the Poet as Film Theorist.* State University of Iowa, Ph.D. Dissertation, 1964.

Wollen, Peter. *Signs and Meaning in the Cinema.* London, Secker and Warburg, 1969.

Wood, Franklin. *Photogravure.* London, Pitman, 1949.

Woodberry, George Edward. *A History of Wood-Engraving.* New York, Harper, 1883.

Woolcott, Alexander. *Mr. Dickens Goes to the Play.* c. 1922. Reprinted Port Washington, N.Y., Kennicat Press, 1967.

Woolf, Leonard. *Downhill All the Way.* London, Hogarth, 1967.

Index of Names

Abbe, Ernest: 9
Alberti, Leon Battista: 196
Anderson, Bronco Billy: 233
Appleton, Victor (pseud.): 41
Arnheim, Rudolf: 164
Astor, John Jacob: 3
Autant-Lara, Claude: 190

Balzac, Honore de: 24
Barbaro, Daniel: 133
Barker, Robert: 137, 227
Barnum, Phineas Taylor: 205
Barrymore, Lionel: 31
Bayliss, Blanche: 161
Beadle, Erastus P.: 5, 40, 46, 53, 238
Beadle, Irwin: 238
Belasco, David: 13, 18, 21, 25, 30, 173, 210, 216
Bell, Alexander Graham: 4
Bellows, George: 11, 167
Benchley, Robert: 247
Bennett, Arnold: 66
Bennett, James Gordon: 248
Bergson, Henri: 10, 64, 233–34
Berlin, Irving: xi, 11
Berliner, Emile: 231, 254
Berman, Shelly: 106
Bertholdi, Mme.: 212
Bewick, Thomas: 210
Black, Alexander: 10, 161, 161 n.
Blackton, J. Stuart: 212, 249
Blake, William: xiii
Bleriot, Louis: 4, 11
Blink, George: 16
Bonnard, Henri: 247
Bonner, Robert: 238
Boothby, Guy: 41, 48
Boucicault, Dion: 12–13, 16, 18, 22–24, 25n., 50, 223
Bouton, Charles Marie: 137

Bowen, James L.: 47
Brady, Matthew: 170
Bragaglia, Antonio Giulio: 164n.
Bracque, Georges: 192, 196, 229
Brakhage, Stanley: 69
Bray, John Randolph: 93
Brewster, Sir William: 128
Briggs, Clare: 106
Brisbane, Arthur: 258
Brotherton, Robert: 251
Browning, Robert: xiv
Bruce, E. L.: 30 n.
Buntline, Ned (E. Z. C. Judson): xi, 50, 232, 238
Bunuel, Luis: 109

Cable, George Washington: 73
Caniff, Milton: 89
Cantor, Eddie: 144
Caracci, Agostino: 185
Carnegie, Andrew: 5
Carroll, Lewis (Charles L. Dodgson): 67
Caruso, Enrico: 254
Case, Anna: 233
Cawthorne, Joseph: 249
Cezanne, Paul: 192–93, 196
Chapin, John R.: 239
Chaplin, Charles: 210
Cheret, Jules: 247
Chesterton, Gilbert K.: 71
Chirico, Georgio di: 229
Churchill, Winston: 80
Clarke, Arthur C.: 39
Cody, William: xi, xv, 9, 50, 124, 205, 212, 232
Cocteau, Jean: 53
Cohl, Emile: 81, 249
Cohn, Harry: 144
Collins, Wilkie: 31
Conrad, Joseph: 10, 63, 77, 196, 198

273

276

General Index